BREAKING
THE CHAINS

Bruno M. Cormier
and the McGill University Clinic
in Forensic Psychiatry

In Two Volumes

Volume One: TRIBUTES
Bruno M. Cormier, M.D.
(1919-1991)

Volume Two: PAPERS
The McGill University Clinic
in Forensic Psychiatry
(1955-1997)

BREAKING
THE CHAINS

Bruno M. Cormier
*and the McGill University Clinic
in Forensic Psychiatry*

In Two Volumes

Volume One: TRIBUTES
Bruno M. Cormier, M.D.
(1919-1991)

*Edited by Renée Fugère, M.D.,
and Ingrid Thompson-Cooper, Ph.D.
Foreword by Cyril Greenland
Portraits by Irma Coucill*

Robert Davies Multimedia Publishing

ISBN Volume 1:1-55207-019-0
ISBN Volume 2:1-55207-021-2

Ordering information:

USA/Canada
General Distribution Services,
1-800-387-0141/387-0172 (Canada)
1-800-805-1083 (USA)
FREE FAX 1-800-481-6207
PUBNET 6307949

or from the publisher:

Robert Davies Multimedia Publishing Inc.
330-4999 St. Catherine St. West,
Westmount, QC H3Z 1T3 Canada
514-481-2440 Fax 514-481-9973
e-mail: rdppub@netcom.ca

Manufactured in Canada

The publisher wishes to thank
The Canada Council for the Arts and the Sodec
for their support for its publishing programs

To Ruby

Contents

Cyril Greenland

Foreword

 It was my privilege to be invited by Ruby Cormier and by the editors, professors Ingrid Thompson-Cooper and Renée Fugère, to contribute a Foreword to this collection of tributes to Dr. Bruno M. Cormier. Almost all the contributors, men and women distinguished in professions, had the pleasure of working directly with Dr. Cormier over many years. They have good stories to tell and they do so with enviable enthusiasm.

I never worked with Dr. Cormier and was only an infrequent visitor to his clinic. But I was aware of his work and reputation before we met. Long before our first meeting, over thirty years ago, I recognized in Dr. Cormier a visionary, humanitarian, and passionate advocate of the victims of Canada's criminal justice system and penal institutions. Years later, I learned that he was also a poet and by inclination a connoisseur of fine art.

In the 1960s, as Social Work Adviser to the Mental Health Branch of the Ontario Department of Health, I had a long-standing interest in criminology and in the treatment of mentally ill offenders. At that time, I discovered that Dr. Cormier's idealism was not universally admired. Very few forensic psychiatrists in those days shared his vision and commitment to reforming Canada's beleaguered penitentiaries.

In order to set the scene for what follows, readers may welcome a little more information about the circumstances of my first contact with Dr. Cormier.

From 1965 to 1970, I worked alongside Professor Hans Mohr as a

[?][?][?][?][?]

Research Scientist in the Social Pathology Section of the Clarke Institute of Psychiatry in Toronto. One of my first projects was a long-term study of violence associated with mental disorder. Part of this work involved the survey of Dangerous Sexual Offenders (DSOs) in Canada and their treatment in the penitentiary system. Unlike inmates committing similar offences, DSOs were subject to indeterminate sentences. This usually involved many years of incarceration—often under the most degrading conditions.

The results of my research[1] showed that about one-third of the hundred or so DSOs had indeed engaged in serious, life-threatening sexual assaults. The criminal behaviour of the middle third was extremely offensive but not physically violent. The remaining third, mostly homosexual men interacting with consenting partners in public or semi-public places, were neither violent nor offensive. Even when the law concerning homosexuality was amended in 1969, many of these inmates were retained in prisons. My concern about their plight led me to seek Dr. Cormier's help.

Having served for about ten years as psychiatrist at the notorious St. Vincent de Paul Penitentiary, Dr. Cormier was familiar with the problem. However, while sympathizing with my concerns, he declined to be associated with my half-baked scheme to secure the release of the small group of DSOs. Instead, he argued that society would be much safer if all sex offenders were released from prison and were provided with intensive treatment.

In the years that followed, I had many hectic discussions with Dr. Cormier on these and related topics, but it was not until I read *The Watcher and the Watched*,[2] published in 1975, that I began to understand him. Now, thanks to Pierre Gauvreau's contribution to this volume, I realize that the impulse that impelled the young Cormier to sign the revolutionary manifesto *Refus global* in 1948 also explains the older Dr. Cormier's hatred of prisons and imprisonment, as well as his life-long passion for liberty and liberation.

Yes! even in Canada, an outspoken psychiatrist who ruffles the feathers of politicians and opposes government bureaucrats risks losing credibility and the support of professional colleagues. In this context, it is appropriate to recall Dr. Cormier's passionate denunciation of the Federal Government's decision to build the Archambault maximum security penitentiary. (In doing so, I express my debt to Dr. Guy Mersereau who includes, as part of his contribution to this volume, the letter Dr. Cormier wrote to the Hon. Guy Favreau, Minister of Justice.) When deputations from the Canadian Corrections Association failed to convince the Minister to abandon the plan to build super-maximum security institutions, Dr. Cormier refused to be silenced.

Here is the gist of his letter:

- "Since I have been employed as a part-time psychiatrist at St. Vincent de Paul, I cannot refrain from protesting the construction on the new maximum security facility."
- "The proposed institution ignores the psychology of the deprivation of liberty and its effects on the individual prisoner—most particularly the 'hardened, rebellious' individuals who need very special care."
- "This inhumane institution will cause deterioration of inmates who are already socially and psychologically ill."
- "As professor in charge of Forensic Psychiatry at the McGill University, I have the right to address you directly. A career devoted entirely to research and criminology imposes its responsibility."

Dr. Cormier's prophetic warning about the potentially explosive situation at Archambault was tragically fulfilled with the riot[3,4,5] in July 1982 which resulted in the deaths of three prison guards and the suicides by cyanide of two inmates who were attempting to escape. This was neither the first nor the last tragedy to occur at Archambault. In 1976, there was a four-month strike by inmates who refused to work until they were promised better living conditions and more humane treatment. Since then there have been fairly regular reports of suicides by inmates, many of them patients in the psychiatric unit.

Dr. Cormier's observation[6] on the Archambault riot may be found in his review of Claire Culhane's book *Still Barred from Prison: Social Justice in Canada* (1985), which appeared in Montreal's *The Gazette*, July 13, 1985. After expressing sympathy with Culhane's abolitionist principles, Dr. Cormier stated that a prison-less society remains a dream. But he stated that we should ask ourselves why we continue to punish so severely those for whom creative alternatives to prisons may be found.

"In future," wrote Dr. Cormier, "prison riots will consist of hostage taking or desperate action by a few willing to risk all to escape or seek revenge." He concluded, "We hope that the correctional services will learn from Archambault that one cannot compress life indefinitely, and that the best security does not lie in steel gadgets and oppressive architecture."

The validity of this view was well supported by the MacGuigan Report of 1976-77[7] on the Millhaven maximum security institution in Ontario. Millhaven shares an identical architectural design with Archambault. MacGuigan stated:

> Its early history was marked by the use of clubs, shackles, gas and dogs often in combination. Dogs were let loose on inmates in the yard and in the cells. Gas was used to punish the inmates frequently—March 1973, as often as three or four times a week. Inmates were first shackled, sometimes hands and feet together, were then beaten with clubs, made to crawl on the floor and finally gassed.

The latest disturbances at Millhaven, which occurred between January 21 and March 23, 1997, suggest that Correctional Service Canada (CSC) has not yet found a solution to the baleful effects of "oppressive architecture" on inmate populations. On this occasion, the entirely predictable riot resulted in the murder of an inmate and $1-million worth of damage. However, the Board of Investigation[8] concluded that "...no single event or issue precipitated the two months of disruption...Rather, an accumulation and combination of conditions and grievances acted as a trigger." The difficulties indentified by the Board included the following:

- A shortage of meaningful employment opportunities for inmates;
- Inadequacy and inefficiency of kitchen facilities;
- Food quality and quantity;
- Limited interaction between inmates and staff and little contacts with outside groups and volunteers.

Responding to the report of the Board of Investigation on January 13, 1998, the CSC announced[9] that "...more than $4.5 million will be spent on renovations and improvements to Millhaven maximum security institution, near Kingston, Ontario."

Even if the CSC officials were familiar with Dr. Cormier's views on the negative effects of incarceration, they chose not to mention it. This is regrettable because they could have learned a great deal from reading or rereading *The Watcher and the Watched*. Central to Dr. Cormier's philosophy is the conviction that the "deprivation of liberty, as a form of punishment, is usually accompanied by depression and regression, the extent to which is pre-determined by the offender's personality." In accepting that incarceration is required for the most persistent offenders, Dr. Cormier said that we must accept the consequences that it will aggravate existing conflicts. In summary, he stated that the penal system gives rise to many problems:

1. Though intended as a means of reform as well as punishment, prison eventually becomes a way of life.
2. Imprisonment is accompanied by a great loss of responsibility which the persistent offender most lacks.
3. Prison itself is a means of establishing and reinforcing ties between the inmate and criminal society.
4. Men become not so much habitual offenders as habitual prisoners.
5. In any setting where freedom is cut off or severely limited, paranoid thinking becomes a specific response. This paranoid thinking affects both the guards and the inmates.

Readers unfamiliar with this book should know that *The Watcher and the Watched* provides a detailed account of the operation by the McGill Clinic of a therapeutic community at the Dannemora State Hospital in Clinton, N.Y. Starting with an analysis of the barriers to forming therapeutic relationships, Dr. Cormier had no illusions about the complexity of the task. He concluded: "To understand the psychology and psycho-pathology of deprivation of liberty is to break down the barrier. But even when this has been overcome it is only the beginning of a long journey."

The many trips taken by Dr. Cormier and his colleagues from Montreal, Que., to N.Y., and back again between 1966 and 1972, had a profound effect on everyone concerned. This is apparent from the accounts of these journeys that appear in a number of the contributions to this volume. Sadly, the experiences and insights of Dr. Cormier and his colleagues had little impact on the subsequent development of penal policy in Canada. This may be deduced from the Chalke Report.[10]

Chaired by Dr. F.C.R. Chalke, Associate Dean of Medicine, University of Ottawa, the Advisory Board, consisting for the most part of representatives of the Canadian psychiatric establishment, was not guided by any discernible philosophy of corrections. Unlike Dr. Cormier, they saw no value in involving psychiatrists in the development of therapeutic communities within the existing penitentiaries. Instead, the Board recommended the establishment of five, university-affiliated Psychiatric Centres (RPCs) "to be located in as close proximity as possible to a large urban and university centre, for penitentiary patients requiring acute short-term care, and with associated appropriate ambulatory care facilities." This is, of course, the antithesis of the role of forensic psychiatry as envisioned by Dr. Cormier and his colleagues.

This foreword is not the place to dwell on the troubled history of the Centres. But it is safe to conclude that whatever their merits, the RPCs have not improved the quality of life of the inmates or of the staffs of Canada's overcrowded and chaotic penitentiaries. Exhausted by an almost constant state of crisis, CSC and others who are professionally concerned with the plight of prisoners have little cause for optimism.

But the publication in 1991 of the CSC Report of the Task Force on Mental Health[11] prompts me to conclude on a positive note. Chaired by Jacques H. Roy, M.D., Director General, Health Care Services, Correctional Service Canada, the Task Force made no overt reference to Dr. Cormier or his work. Despite this, the influence of his teaching may be gleaned from many of the recommendations and to some extent from the Task Force's "statement of purpose."

> Mental Health Care contributes to the Mission and Strategic Objectives of the C.S.C.—to reduce recidivism, assist the offender to become law-abiding, and facilitate reintegration into the community—by developing, implementing and evaluating an integrated continuum of mental health promotion, assessments, treatment and relapse-prevention services from reception to sentence expiry, aimed at reducing the incidence and impact of psychological dysfunction, through social and cognitive skills development and the promotion of healthy positive interactions between the offender, the Service and the community.

Because of its bureaucratic language, some cynics may read this "statement of purpose" as pompous and pious. But reading between the lines, one can discern a major change in correctional policy and direction. I think that Dr. Cormier, a very practical idealist, would have welcomed this glimmer of hope as an indication of belated understanding.

As with many great teachers and reformers, in Canada and abroad, official recognition and honours came late in Dr. Cormier's distinguished career. Here is a partial list of distinctions and honours achieved or bestowed upon him:

- President, Société de Criminologie du Québec, 1968
- President, American Society of Criminology, 1969
- Isaac Ray Award of the American Psychiatric Association, 1977
- Prix Philippe Pinel de l'Institute Philippe Pinel, à Montreal, à l'occasion du XIIè Congrès International de Droit et de Psychiatrie, 1986
- The Golden Apple Award of the American Academy of Psychiatry and Law, awarded posthumously, 1991

Another memorial to this remarkable man is *Breaking the Chains*. A celebration of his life and work, *Breaking the Chains* is the title of two volumes, the general subtitle being "Bruno M. Cormier and the McGill University Clinic in Forensic Psychiatry." Volume One is headed "Tributes: Bruno M. Cormier, M.D. (1919-1991)." Volume Two is headed "Papers: The McGill University Clinic in Forensic Psychiatry (1955-1997)."

This work would never have been produced but for the determination, unfailing humour, diligence, and generosity of Ruby Cormier. Working with her has given me the greatest pleasure. I also acknowledge the invaluable contributions of other contributors who willingly and indeed joyfully recalled their treasured memories of Dr. Cormier. Sharing various tasks with these talented and dedicated people has been an adventure and a labour of love.

Toronto, May 1, 1998

Cyril Greenland, *M.Sc., Ph.D., Professor Emeritus, School of Social Work, Associate, Department of Psychiatry, Faculty of Medicine, McMaster University, Hamilton, Ont., 1970-1985.*

Research Scientist, Clarke Institute of Psychiatry; Associate, Department of Psychiatry, Faculty of Medicine, University of Toronto, 1965-1970; Social Work Adviser, Mental Health Branch, Ontario Department of Health and, part-time, Director of Social Work, Toronto Psychiatric Hospital, 1960-1965; Director of Social Work, Ontario Hospital, Whitby, Ont., 1958-1960; Director of Psychiatric Social Work, Crichton Royal, Dumfries, Scotland, 1948-1958.

Notes

1. Greenland C., "Dangerous Sexual Offender Legislation in Canada, 1948-1977: An Experiment that Failed." *Canadian J. Criminology,* 26.1. 1-12, Jan. 1984.

2. Cormier, Bruno M., *The Watcher and the Watched,* Tundra Books of Montreal, 1975.

3. Correctional Service of Canada, Report of the Inspector General'sSpecial Inquiry into Riot, Archambault Institution, July, 1982. Ottawa, undated.

4. Amnesty International Report on Allegations of Ill-treatment of Prisoners at Archambault Institution, Quebec, Canada, 10 to 15 April, 1983.

5. Stewart, R.L., Correctional Investigator, Report on Allegations of Mistreatment of Inmates at Archambault Institution Following the Events which Occurred on July, 25th, 1982. Ottawa, June 21, 1984

6. Cormier, Bruno, M., "Seeking solutions to the misery in jail: A long time social reformer catalogues prison violence in her plea for abolition." Book review of "Still Barred from Prison: Social Injustice in Canada" by Claire Culhane, Black Rose Books, inThe Gazette (Montreal), July 13, 1985.

7. MacGuigan, Mark, Chair, Sub-Committee on the PenitentiarySystem in Canada, Report to Parliament, Ottawa, 1976-77. (Quoted from the Amnesty International Report, 1983.)

8. Correctional Service of Canada, Board of Investigation into a major disturbance at Millhaven Institution and the murder of inmate Sereno Guiseppe, Ottawa, 1997.

9. Correctional Service of Canada, "News release, inquiry report into murder of an inmate and a series of disturbances at Millhaven Institution, Jan. 21, 1997." Ottawa, Jan. 13, 1998.

10. Chalke, F.C.R., Chair, Advisory Board of Psychiatric Consultants. Report of

The General Program for the Development of Psychiatric Services in Federal Correctional Services in Canada.Solicitor General of Canada, Ottawa, 1972.

11. Correctional Service of Canada, Report of the Task Force on Mental Health, Ottawa, June, 1991.

Acknowledgements

After the closing of the McGill University Clinic in Forensic Psychiatry, in January 1997, we met with a small group of colleagues and friends to discuss the possibility of putting together a book about Dr. Bruno Cormier and about the clinic, which he founded and directed until his retirement in 1987.

We wish now to thank the many people without whose generous co-operation this book would never have been published. In particular, we acknowledge the unique contribution of Pierre Gauvreau, artist and life-long friend of Cormier, who recalls their school-age friendship and some of the highlights of growing up in Montreal in the 1940s, as well as the pervading atmosphere that led to the Refus global. Those friends and associates whose contributions appear in Volume One readily agreed to write about their association with Dr. Cormier. Cyril Greenland and Baila Markus assisted us with the selection of papers for Volume Two; Karine Gore researched and prepared the bibliography of unpublished papers.

At the outset, we sought the assistance of John Robert Colombo, the editor who is known as Canada's Master Gatherer. Assisted by Cyril Greenland, he oversaw the production process before text was despatched to Robert Davies of Robert Davies Multimedia Publishing Inc.

We are grateful to Irma Coucill for her pencil portraits; to Tom Coucill for his drawing of the "Man Breaking Chains" motif (based on the Philippe Pinel Award, presented to Dr. Cormier in 1986); and to David Shaw for his overall design of the two volumes. A special mention is given to Chantal Carstens, who agreed to proof-read the entire work.

We express our thanks also to Maurice Perron and Serge Jongué for their photographs; to Ray Ellenwood and Lesley Benderavage for their translations; to Jonathan G. Colombo for legal advice; to Alan Hustak for his contribution on the history of the clinic; to Cyril Greenland for the Foreword to Volume One and Gilbert Pinard for the Foreword to Volume Two.

In expressing our great debt to Ruby Cormier, we recognize that the successful completion of this work was ensured by her generosity, determination and selfless commitment to the memory of Dr. Bruno Cormier.

Renée Fugère, M.D
Ingrid Thompson-Cooper, Ph.D.

BREAKING
THE CHAINS

TRIBUTES

Pierre Gauvreau

"C'était un temps déraisonnable
On avait mis les morts à table."
Aragon

 C'était le temps des idéologies; tentatives nouvelles de combler le vide laissé par l'affaiblissement des mythes religieux comme porteurs de solutions. Le conservatisme des Eglises les rendaient insensibles à la légitimité des revendications des nouvelles classes sociales créées par l'activitié industrielle. Des produits inconnus jusqu' alors bouleversaient à tout instant les modes de vie traditionnels.

Londres, par ses banques, contrôlait une large part de l'économie mondiale. Paris, largement endetté par la guerre de 1914, et les conflits sociaux qui agitaient sa classe ouvrière, devait tenir compte des intérêts de Londres jusque dans sa politique étrangère.

En Italie, Mussolini trônait à son balcon; en Allemagne, Adolf Hitler faisait ses premières sorties en tant que Fuehrer et metteur-en-scène d'une idéologie à grand spectacle: le nazisme.

Les rois du balcon eurent bientôt leurs imitateurs: Sir Oswald Mosley en Grande Bretagne; les Silver Shirts *(sic)* aux Etats-Unis; au Canada des cellules naquirent un peu partout et se regroupèrent dans la Canadian Union of Fascists. A Montréal, Adrien Arcand dirigeait le *Parti national socialiste chrétien.* Lors du congrès tenu à Toronto, le 4 juillet 1939, *The Globe and Mail* écrit: "Arcand, the brilliant young French Canadian..." *Life* lui consacre un reportage ainsi qu'à sa famille. Et Adrien Arcand devient grand fuehrer pancanadien aux applaudissements de la foule réunie au Massey-Hall.[1]

Et la France? La douce France, pays de nos aieux? Avec un gouvernement socialiste et un Juif, Léon Blum, socialiste en plus,
comme premier ministre, elle subissait le juste châtiment pour
avoir banni Dieu de ses écoles, et avoir coupé le cou à ce brave
Louis XVI et à sa charmante épouse, comme on dit aujourd'hui à
la télévision, Marie-Antoinette. En oubliant, bien sûr, les millions
de culs-terreux qui, dans un semi-esclavage fournissaient le labeur
nécessaire au maintien de Versailles et autres similitudes.

Que vient faire tout cela dans la vie de Bruno Cormier? Plus
qu'on ne pourrait le soupçonner. C'était la soupe médiatique
dont nous étions nourris. Comme nos enfants se forment, en ce
moment, en écoutant le récit des aventures de Jean Chrétien, Jean
Charest et Lucien Bouchard.

"C'était un temps déraisonnable
On avait mis les morts à table."

J'ai fait la connaissance de Bruno Cormier en 1934. Il venait
d'être accepté au Collège Sainte-Marie, tout comme moi, pour y
faire des études classiques. Celles-ci menaient au droit, à la
médecine et à la prêtrise. Au choix ou selon ses propres relations!
Les Jésuites avaient le mandat de diriger nos âmes et forger nos
caractères.

Ma mère, ma tante Adrienne, mon frère Claude habitions rue
Saint-Denis, sur la Montée du Zouave, aujourd'hui la Terrasse
Saint-Denis.

Le zouave en question était Louvigny de Montigny qui avait
recruté et commandé ces braves soldats, les menant en Italie
défendre le Pape assiégé par les troupes révolutionnaires de
Garibaldi. Quand les Zouaves arrivèrent en Italie, la guerre était finie.
Mais ils en rapportèrent un grand prestige au pays, et figurèrent doré-
navant dans tous les défilés de la Saint-Jean-Baptiste. Le mot "zouave"
acquit par la suite le sens d'un gars un peu naïf, pas très déluré.
Bruno m'apprit à faire le zouave ni dans un sens ni dans l'autre.

Tous les matins, Bruno qui habitait non loin de chez moi, rue Laval, m'attendait et nous faisions route ensemble jusqu'au collège. Même manège pour le repas de midi car nous remontions chez nous pour manger. Nous retournions au collège pour les cours de l'après-midi et l'étude obligatoire, avant de pouvoir rentrer chez nous. Ce temps consacré aux déplacements n'était pas perdu. Nous refaisions le monde de mille façons plutôt qu'une ...

Bruno avait 15 ans, j'en avais 12. Cette différence d'âge n'était pas exceptionnelle. Les élèves de la Commission des Ecoles catholiques de Montréal mettaient huit ans à atteindre le niveau pour être admis au collège classique. Ceux du cours préparatoire donné par les Soeurs de la Providence en mettaient cinq ... Ce qui avait comme résultat qu'en Eléments latins, une partie des élèves étaient des "tit-culs" de 12 ans tandis que l'autre partie était composée de "grands frais-chiés" de 15.

On comprend facilement que les rapports aux filles étaient différents. Les "tit-culs" ouvraient grandes leurs oreilles lorsque les "grands frais-chiés" racontaient leurs exploits de la fin de semaine. Sans doute une ruse de Satan, mais collège Saint-Marie acceptait des externes. Quel plaisir que d'être exposés aux dangers de la grande ville! Qui sont nombreux, chacun sait!

Dans le quadrilatère compris entre les rues Craig et Sherbrooke, Saint-Denis et Saint-Laurent, s'étendait le "Red Light" qui donnait à Montréal son surnom de "Gay Paree" nord américain. Montréal, la ville aux cent clochers et aux mille bordels!

Avec nos bérets et nos sacs d'écolier, nous devions sans doute paraître sympathiques aux filles masquées par les persiennes des fenêtres ... "Hé, les p'tits gars, avez-vous bien appris votre leçon de catéchisme pour aujourd'hui?" Puis un rire éclatait qui, sans que nous sachions pourquoi, nous humiliait ... Maudits bérets! Maudits sacs-d'école!

La guerre venue, le Red Light fut fermé à la suite de pressions venant du haut commandement militaire. La chaude-pisse allait-elle compromettre la victoire encore incertaine de nos forces militaires? Plus tard, comme partie du plan Dozois, le quartier fut rasé pour y recevoir des logements à prix modiques. La morale y gagna, mais pas notre prestige international. Un jour, un homme, visiblement un touriste américain, nous aborde Bruno et moi, sur la rue. Agité, l'air désemparé, il ne cesse de répéter les mêmes mots: "They're closed! What will I do? Where will I go?" Dans les années subséquentes, Montréal perdit beaucoup du prestige que son effort de guerre lui avait valu auprès des Américains.

Bruno avaient plusieurs frères et soeurs; il était le sixième d'une famille de sept enfants. Les garçons se prénommaient: Bernardin, Hector, Charles et Bruno, le sixième, avant Marcelle qui avec ses deux soeurs aînées, Georgette et Jacqueline, complétaient la tablée familiale. Le père de Bruno gérait un magasin de chaussures. J'ai gardé un souvenir de lui, le soir, à la cuisine, souriant et silencieux. Madame Cormier gérait avec douceur et humour cette grouillante nichée de jeunes grossie par la présence des copains, des "chums," des visiteurs imprévus. Car, dans cette ère pré-écran cathodique et ses plaisirs solitaires, les jeunes, adoptaient des familles plus accueillantes que d'autres comme lieu de rencontre et d'échange.

Les frères ainés de Bruno étaient très actifs, militant dans le milieu syndical si mon souvenir est exact. Ils avaient également un goût et un talent pour la mécanique. Une année, ils avaient "patenté" un véhicule à pédales, pour deux personnes. Monté sur quatre roues, le "pédalo" permettait de faire des randonnées assez longues. Un jour, Bruno m'invita à l'accompagner dans les Cantons de l'Est visiter un oncle qu'il avait à Lister. C'est chez cet oncle qui possédait un magasin général que Bruno allait gagner les sous nécessaires au soutien de ses études. Inutile de dire que Bruno a fait sensation et recueilli un prestige qui rejaillissait jusque sur moi, son co-équipier.

Ma mère et ma tante avaient hérité de la bibliothèque de mon grand-père maternel. Bruno et moi en fouillions les rayons qui contenaient un bon nombre de livres défendus par l'Index, dont la tyrannie sévissait au collège.

Un jour, Bruno et moi, nous avions acheté, chez Eaton, au rayon des livres français, un exemplaire de *Les Fleurs du Mal,* de Baudelaire, et un autre de *Les Illuminations* de Rimbaud. Nous avons été dénoncé par un anonyme bien-pensant, et vu nos livres confisqués disparaître derrière les portes de l'Enfer. C'était un lieu fermée à clef où se trouvaient réléguées les oeuvres inspirées par Satan ... Qu'advenait-il de ces livres maudits une fois l'infernale porte refermée? Je l'ignore encore à ce jour! ...

Le maire de Montréal, Camillien Houde, fut interné pendant la guerre pour avoir pris position contre la conscription. Il est vrai qu'à cause de son allure personnelle, il s'amusait du surnom qu'on lui donnait: le Mussolini canadien. Tribun efficace, il était l'idole des quartiers populaires. Bruno et moi devons à "Camillien" notre premier contact avec la dure réalité politique et les rêves qu'on doit lui sacrifier.

Nous nous étions rendus écouter Camillien Houde faire un discours. Il y annonça son intention de doter Montréal d'un Orphéon ...

"C'est quoi un Orphéon?"

"Une chorale de voix d'hommes" me répondit Bruno. Une chorale, je savais ce que c'était.

"On va aller féliciter Camillien!" annonce Bruno. Aussitôt dit, aussitôt fait!

La bedaine en avant plan, Camillien se met à rire, imité par les admirateurs qui l'entourent.

"Je vous ai ben eus, hein, les p'tits gars?" Et tout le monde de s'esclaffer ...

C'est là que Bruno et moi avons compris qu'entre la parole et l'acte, en politique, il n'y a pas nécessairement de relation. C'est dans de pareilles circonstances qu'un certain cynisme se développe comme bouclier de la sensibilité.

Un jour, Bruno me propose de nous rendre à Orford, "sur le pouce," et d'y escalader le mont qui domine le village. A cette époque le mont, à toutes fins pratiques, est un lieu sauvage. Une route pour accéder au sommet a été commencée puis abandonnée à cause de la World War II. Mais ce n'est pas par ce versant que Bruno propose l'escalade, mais par l'opposé, abrupte et dépourvu de sentiers praticables.

Une fois rendus au sommet, triomphants mais épuisés, nous avons dressé notre petite tente, et nous avons dormi la tête appuyée sur nos sacs-à-dos.

Au matin, les pains que nous avions apportés avaient été vidés de leur mie par les mulots.

En prenant le versant plus practicable pour la descente, nous arrivons devant un camp de bûcherons abandonné, vestige des travaux entrepris avant la guerre. Bruno propose d'y passer le reste de la journée, d'y dormir et de reprendre notre chemin le lendemain matin. Excellente idée!

Au réveil une surprise nous attend. Une famille d'ours prend ses ébats dans le ruisseau qui longe notre campement. Il faudra plusieurs heures avant de reprendre la route abandonnée qui nous conduira finalement vers un hot-dog et la civilisation urbaine ... Mais nous étions fiers, dans notre inconsciente jeunesse d'avoir triomphé du redoutable mont Orford et ses périls ...

Bruno avait pris connaissance des oeuvres de Paul Claudel, écrivain catholique et diplomate de carrière. Une oeuvre, en particulier, allait le marquer, ainsi que moi-même: "Le soulier de satin."

Homme d'une grande érudition et admirateur de Shakespeare, Paul Claudel avait développé une écriture empreinte à la fois de mysticisme et de sensualité, loin des angoisses puritaines qui pervertissaient nos jeunes consciences canadiennes-françaises. Que fallait-il de plus pour séduire deux adolescents en rupture de ban avec l'Eglise et ses supercheries trop visibles. Notre fréquentation de Claudel nous mit à l'abri des remords malsains quant à nos relations avec les jeunes filles; Claudel avait haussé la sensualité au rang des vertus cardinales.

C'est ainsi que Bruno écrivit plusieurs pièces de théâtre

d'influence claudélienne, en plus de poèmes. Une des pièces—
plus exactement un jeu dramatique—fut montée au Théâtre du
Gésu, dans le cadre d'exercices pédagogiques comme on dirait de
nos jours. Un sympathique jésuite, le R.P. Dauteuil était responsable de la salle. Grand amoureux du Théâtre, il était affligé d'une
voix si gutturale qu'un crapaud même en aurait rougi. Mais il avait
le coeur d'un ange. Les décors et les chorégraphies étaient de
moi. Raymond David, plus tard vice-président au réseau français
de Radio-Canada, tenait le rôle principal.

Je viens de mentionner la chorégraphie du spectacle ...
Françoise Sullivan, dont la contribution à l'art de la scène et à
celui de la peinture est immense, m'avait enseigné la danse car
elle était à la recherche d'un partenaire masculin. Bruno se joignit
à nous. A un moment donné Françoise fit une chorégraphie
inspiré de celle de Petrouchka, sur la musique de Stravinsky.
Bruno, le clown triste et moi, Arlequin, nous disputions le coeur
de la belle Françoise-Colombine.

Est-il besoin de rappeler qu'à cette époque la musique de
Stravinsky avait comme effect de vider une salle de ses oreilles raf-
finées ... Que de plus, de voir des jeunes hommes porter des collants
faisant injure au bon goût et, possiblement, aux bonnes moeurs ...

En juin 1944, je m'enrôlai dans l'armée canadienne active et je
servis avec le rang de lieutenant jusqu'en 1946. De son côté, mon
ami Bruno avait entrepris des études en médecine.

Pendant cette période de grands bouleversements à l'échelle
planétaire, un groupe de jeunes artistes et intellectuels s'était
formé autour du peintre Paul-Emile Borduas. Parmi eux: Jean-Paul
Riopelle, Marcel Barbeau, Marcelle Ferron, Jean-Paul Mousseau,
Fernand Leduc. Auxquels il faut ajouter le photographe Maurice
Perron qui allait fonder, un peu plus tard: Mithra–Mythe, une maison d'édition pour la publication du manifeste *"Refus global,"* et
d'autres oeuvres.

En 1948, Borduas et plusieurs personnes de son entourage
éprouvèrent le besoin de définir leur position face à l'art, mais

surtout face à la société contemporaine de même qu'aux porteurs des différentes idéologies qui se proposaient pour en forger le futur.

Dans le cas de Borduas, de moi-même, de mon frère Claude, de Riopelle, Barbeau, Mousseau qui étions à Montréal, alors que d'autres avaient émigré à Paris ou à New-York fuyant l'obscurantisme pratiqué par Maurice Duplessis et le clergé, nous avions formé le projet d'une vaste exposition aux tableaux fracassants, accompagné d'un manifeste. Finalement, seul le manifeste, *"Refus global,"* accompagné d'autres textes et de reproductions de tableaux, parut le 9 août 1948. [2]

Bruno Cormier fut l'un des 16 signataires et le seul à ne pas être un artiste, bien que le manifeste circula dans de nombreux milieux, y compris parmi les amis de Borduas lui-même.

De plus, Bruno Cormier contribua un article qui parut en même temps que *Refus global,* intitulé: "L'oeuvre d'art est une expérience."

Le rôle de Bruno Cormier et celui de Ruby, sa femme, ont été déterminants dans la conservation des oeuvres de cette époque. Beaucoup de musées canadiens doivent à Ruby et Bruno Cormier de pouvoir aujourd'hui montrer les oeuvres acquises par eux, alors qu'elles étaient rejetées par les "connaisseurs" et ridiculisées, et que les institutions les ignoraient carrément. Dans le cas de Ruby et Bruno Cormier, des années quarante à aujourd'hui, leur goût, leur curiosité et leur audace n'ont jamais fait défaut.

Ils furent un point de rencontre, de convergence susceptible de rassembler les signataires du manifeste et de maintenir entre eux une solidarité vive et lumineuse, en dépit des années nombreuses à s'accumuler depuis le 9 août 1948.

Pour beaucoup, cet aspect de la vie du docteur Cormier sera une révélation. Très présent aux autres, cet ami a toujours été d'une discrétion exemplaire quant à lui-même. Animé d'une foi dans l'humanité et dans la capacité de celle-ci de se tirer des ornières de l'ignorance, de se frayer un chemin vers un futur

ouvert à toutes les aventures du coeur et de l'esprit, Bruno
Cormier demeure un phare lumineux pour quiconque veut se
frayer un chemin vers les demains à bâtir.

Je terminerai ce récit des souvenirs de ma jeunesse mon-
tréalaise et de mon amitié si enrichissante pour Bruno Cormier
avec ces deux paragraphes qui terminent l'article écrit par cet
homme à la générosité illimitée—je répète: illimitée—et faisait
partie intégrante du manifeste: *Refus global.*

"Il n'y a pas de doute. L'art est plus que jamais une 'voie
royale' vers la conscience, voie qui part des zones les plus
éloignées du rêve en s'élargissant vers la pleine lumière. Le spectateur n'a plus qu'à lire l'expérience.

Encore faut-il que le spectateur soit aux aguets à son tour:
jamais le chasseur ne pourra immobiliser l'oiseau entre nuage et
terre, il y aura toujours un coup d'aile imprévisible."[3]

Notes

1. *The Swastika and the Maple Leaf: Fascist Movements in Canada in the Thirties.*
   Lita-Rose Betcherman. Fitzhenry & Whiteside. 1975
2. Les signataires de *Refus global* furent: Paul-Emile Borduas, Magdeleine
   Arbour, Marcel Barbeau, Bruno Cormier, Claude Gauvreau, Pierre
   Gauvreau, Muriel Guilbault, Marcelle Ferron-Hamelin, Fernand Leduc,
   Thérèse Leduc, Jean-Paul Mousseau, Maurice Perron, Louise Renaud,
   Françoise Riopelle, Jean-Paul Riopelle, Françoise Sullivan. Mithra–Mythe.
   Montréal. 1948.
3. L'oeuvre d'art est une expérience. Bruno Cormier dans *Refus global.*
   Mithra–Mythe. Montréal. 1948.

Pierre Gauvreau

Adventures of the Heart and Mind

"It was a time for going nuts
We asked the dead to spill their guts."
Aragon

 It was a time of ideologies, of fresh attempts to fill the void left as religious myths (and the solutions they offered) grew ever weaker. The churches were too conservative to show any sympathy for the legitimate demands of social classes newly created by industrialization. Products never seen before were constantly upsetting traditional ways of life.

Through its banks, London controlled a major part of the world economy. Paris, hugely indebted by the 1914 war and by social upheavals within its working class, had to follow London's lead, even in foreign policy.

In Italy, Mussolini sat enthroned on his balcony; in Germany, Adolf Hitler made his first sorties as Fuehrer and Director of an ideology in the grand theatrical style: Nazism.

The Kings of the Balcony soon had imitators: Sir Oswald Mosley in Britain; the Silver Shirts *(sic)* in the United States; and in Canada, cells springing up almost everywhere to come together in the Canadian Union of Fascists. In Montreal, Adrien Arcand directed the *Parti national socialiste chrétien.* Reporting on one of their congresses held in Toronto on the fourth of July, 1939, *The Globe and Mail* wrote of "Arcand, the brilliant young French Canadian..." *Life* published an article not only on him, but his family. So Adrien Arcand became the great pan-Canadian *fuehrer* to the applause of crowds gathered at Massey Hall[1].

And France, dear France, land of our ancestors? With a socialist government and a Jew, Léon Blum, as Prime Minister, she was being justly punished for banishing God from the schools and for chopping off the head of that gallant King Louis XVI and his charming wife (as they say nowadays on television) Marie Antoinette. Never mind the millions of sod-busters working in semi-slavery to provide the labour necessary for maintaining Versailles and other excesses.

What has all this got to do with Bruno Cormier's life? More than you might think. It was the media soup that we grew up on, just as our children are nourished today by watching the adventures of Jean Chrétien, Jean Charest, and Lucien Bouchard.

"It was a time for going nuts
We asked the dead to spill their guts."

I met Bruno Cormier in 1934. We'd just been accepted at the Collège Sainte-Marie in the *"études classiques"* stream, the one leading to Law, Medicine or the Church, according to what you or your relatives chose. Directing our souls and forging our characters would be the responsibility of the Jesuits.

My mother, my aunt Adrienne and my brother Claude and I lived on rue Saint-Denis on the Montée du Zouave, now called Terrasse Saint-Denis. The Zouave in question was Louvigny de Montigny, who had recruited and commanded a band of brave soldiers destined to save the Pope from the siege of Garibaldi and his revolutionary troops. By the time the Zouaves got to Italy the war was over, but their great prestige reflected on the whole nation, which explains why they've marched in the Saint-Jean-Baptiste day parade, ever since. As time went on, the word "Zouave" came to mean a naive kid, not too swift. Bruno taught me how not to be a Zouave, in the old or new sense of the word.

He lived nearby, on rue Laval, and every morning he waited for me so we could walk to school together; same routine at noon because we both went home for lunch. We'd go back for afternoon classes and the obligatory study period, before we were free to go home. It was not wasted time, all this walking back and forth; in our talk we remade the world in a thousand ways.

Bruno was fifteen years old; I was twelve. Such a difference in age was not unusual. Pupils in the Montreal School System took eight years after elementary school before they were ready to go on to the Collège Classique, but the ones who came from the enriched classes of the Soeurs de la Providence only took five. The result was that in *Eléments latins* some of the class was made up of *tit-culs* twelve years old, while the rest were *grands frais-chiés* of fifteen.[2]

Not surprisingly, there were considerable differences in sophistication with girls. The *tit-culs* were all ears when the *grands frais-chiés* talked about their weekend exploits. Somehow, Satan had convinced the Collège Sainte-Marie to accept external students. What greater pleasure than being exposed to the dangers of the big city? And God knows there were lots of them! In the quadrilateral enclosed by Craig, Sherbrooke, Saint-Denis, and Saint-Laurent lay the red-light district that gave Montreal its reputation as North America's Gay Paree. Montreal, the city of a hundred steeples and a thousand brothels!

With our berets and school bags we must have looked cute to the girls hidden behind the shutters ... "Hey boys, how'd it go with catechism today? Did you learn your lesson?" Then a scream of laughter that made us feel humiliated, without knowing why ... Goddamn berets! Goddamn school bags!

When the war came, the red-light district was closed in response to pressure from the military high command. Were they afraid the clap might compromise the still uncertain glory of our armed forces? Later on, as part of the Dozois plan, the whole neighbourhood was razed to make way for low-cost housing. Morality won, but our international prestige suffered. One day a man stopped Bruno and me in the street. He was obviously an American tourist, very agitated, looking distraught, repeating the same words over and over: "They're closed! What will I do? Where will I go?" In the years that followed, Montreal lost much of the honour it had gained with the Americans as a result of its war effort.

Bruno came from a large family. The boys were Bernardin, Hector, Charles and Bruno, the sixth before Marcelle who, with her two older sisters, Georgette and Jacqueline, made up the family slate. Bruno's father managed a shoe store. I remember him sitting in the kitchen, in the evenings, silent and smiling. This teeming pack of young people, enlarged by friends, "steadies," and uninvited guests, was overseen by the gentle and humorous authority of Madame Cormier. In that time before the cathode screen and its solitary pleasures, young people gravitated to the most welcoming homes where they could get together and talk.

Bruno's older brothers were strong union activists, if I remember correctly. They also had a taste and talent for things mechanical. One summer they patched together a four-wheeled pedal car built for two, suitable for quite long trips, and Bruno invited me to ride with him into the Eastern Townships, to visit an uncle living in Lister. In that same uncle's general store Bruno eventually made the money that put him through school. Needless to say, Bruno and his machine were a sensation and some of the prestige even rubbed off on me, his co-pilot.

My mother and aunt were heirs to the library of my maternal grandfather. Bruno and I read ferociously in it, naturally, because it had books that were on the forbidden list of the Index, still in total force at the Collège. He and I once bought, off the French Literature shelves at Eaton's, a copy of Baudelaire's *Les fleurs du mal* and Rimbaud's *Illuminations* only to be denounced by an anonymous guardian of public virtue and to see our confiscated books disappear behind the doors of the *Enfer*, that hellish place in which were kept under lock and key all works inspired by Satan. What became of those condemned books once the infernal gates had closed? To this day I don't know!

The Mayor of Montreal, Camillien Houde, was jailed during the war for having spoken out against conscription. The truth is, he had a lot of charisma and he was amused by what people called him: the Canadian Mussolini. The working class loved him because he was an effective spokesman. It was to "Camillien" that Bruno and I owed our first taste of the hard realities of politics and their way of breaking dreams. We'd gone to hear Camillien Houde make a speech in which he announced he was going to endow Montreal with an "Orphéon."

"What's an Orphéon?"

"A male voice choir," replied Bruno. I knew what a choir was.

"We'll go up and congratulate Camillien!" Bruno announced.

No sooner said than done! And Camillien's pot belly shook with mirth, echoed by an admiring crowd around him.

"I guess I really put one over on you, eh boys?"

Everybody snorted with laughter.

So Bruno and I learned how, in politics, there's not necessarily any relationship between word and act. At times like that, a kind of shield of cynicism develops to protect our sensitivities.

Another time, Bruno suggested we hitch-hike to Orford and climb the mountain that looks down on the village. At that time, for all practical purposes, it was an untamed wilderness. They'd started building a road to the top, but the construction was halted because of World War II. Anyway, Bruno wasn't thinking of going up that side, but the opposite one, which was steep and devoid of cleared walkways.

Having reached the top, triumphant and exhausted, we pitched our little tent and slept with our heads on our backpacks. In the morning, the soft centre of our bread had been mined by field mice. Taking the easier side to go back down, we came upon a logging camp, abandoned when work stopped for the war. Bruno suggested we stay for the rest of the day, sleep there, and set off again next morning. Good idea! But there's a surprise waiting when we wake up: a family of bears is frolicking in the stream running past our camp. So it's a few hours before we can take the abandoned road that leads eventually to a hot-dog stand and civilization ... But our young innocence was proud of conquering the great Mount Orford and its perils.

Bruno had come to know the writing of Paul Claudel, the Catholic author and career diplomat. One work in particular would influence him, and me as well: *Le Soulier de satin*. A very erudite man and an admirer of Shakespeare, Claudel had developed a style marked at one and the same time by mysticism and sensuality; worlds away from the puritan angst that was perverting our French-Canadian consciences. Is it any wonder Claudel seduced two adolescents rebelling against the Church and its patently ridiculous tricks? By frequenting him, we were safe from unhealthy guilt about our relations with girls, Claudel having raised sensuality to the level of a cardinal virtue.

That was how Bruno came to write several plays influenced by Claudel, and some poems as well. One of those plays—more accurately a dramatic interlude—was performed at the Gésu Theatre, under the rubric of what they used to call pedagogical exercises. A good-natured Jesuit called Father Dauteuil ran the theatre. Great lover of the stage, he was afflicted with a voice guttural enough to make a toad blush, but he had the heart of an angel. I did the sets and choreography. Raymond David, later vice-president of Radio-Canada, played the lead.

Having mentioned the choreography in this show, I should point out that Françoise Sullivan, whose contributions to both the performing and visual arts have been immense, had taught me to dance because she needed a male partner. Bruno made up a third. Françoise even did a piece of choreography inspired by Petrouchka, based on Stravinsky's music. Bruno the sad clown, and I the Harlequin, vied for the heart of the beautiful Françoise-Columbine. Need I recall how Stravinsky's music, back then, was guaranteed to empty any hall of its refined ears? And young men in tights—surely they were an affront to good taste, possibly even to public decency.

In June of 1944, I enrolled in the Canadian Army and served at the rank of lieutenant until 1946. At the same time, Bruno Cormier began his medical studies.

During this period of great upheaval on a planetary scale, a group of young artists and intellectuals was forming around the painter Paul-Emile Borduas. Among them were Jean-Paul Riopelle, Marcel Barbeau, Marcelle Ferron, Jean-Paul Mousseau, and Fernand Leduc, and also the photographer Maurice Perron who, a little later on, would found Mithra–Mythe, the publishing house of *Refus global* and other works.

In 1948, Borduas and other people in the group felt the need to define their position as artists, but especially with regard to contemporary society and to promoters of various ideologies who considered themselves shapers of the future. As for Borduas, myself, my brother Claude, Riopelle, Barbeau, and Mousseau (who were in Montreal while others had left for Paris or New York, fleeing the obscurantism of Maurice Duplessis and the Church) we had decided to mount a huge exhibition of revolutionary paintings, accompanied by a manifesto. In the end, only the manifesto, *Refus global*, accompanied by other texts and reproductions of paintings, appeared on August 9, 1948.[3]

Bruno Cormier was one of the sixteen signatories and the only one who was not an artist, though the manifesto circulated in a number of milieux, including among Borduas' friends. Bruno also contributed an article that appeared in the *Refus global* pamphlet, a text entitled "A Pictorial Work is an Experiment and an Experience."

Bruno and his wife, Ruby, have played a crucial role in the preservation of artworks from that period. Many Canadian museums can show these works today only because Ruby and Bruno Cormier had the foresight to collect them when they were being rejected by connoisseurs intimidated by public ridicule, and while the art institutions refused to hear anything about them. From the Forties to the present, the good taste, curiosity and daring of Ruby and Bruno never faltered. They were also a catalyst that could bring together the signatories of the manifesto and maintain a lively and warm solidarity among them, despite the accumulation of many years since August 9, 1948.

For many people, this aspect of the life of Dr. Cormier will be a revelation. Always ready with a friendly and supportive gesture for other people, he was impeccably discreet about his own life. Inspired by a faith in humanity and in humanity's ability to get out of the rut of ignorance, to clear a path to the future, open to all possible adventures of the heart and mind, Bruno Cormier remains a shining light for those wanting to discover tomorrows not yet built.

I will end my little memoir of youth in Montreal, and of my so enriching friendship with Bruno Cormier, by citing the last two paragraphs of the article written by this man of limitless generosity (and I repeat, limitless) as his contribution to the manifesto *Refus global*:

> There is no doubt about it: art is more than ever a "royal road" leading to consciousness, a road that starts in the most distant areas of dream and sets off in the direction of broad daylight. All the spectator has to do is read the experiment and the experience.
>
> And so the spectator must also wait and watch. No hunter can immobilize a bird between earth and cloud; there will always be an unforeseen wing-beat.[4]

Translation: Ray Ellenwood

Pierre Gauvreau, *artist, one of the first people to associate with Paul-Emile Borduas; signatory of* Refus global.

Mr. Gauvreau participated in close to 150 exhibitions and remains very active as a painter. TV producer (1955-1968; 1973-1979). Chief of French Production at the National Film Board (1971-1972). Author of the drama trilogy: Le temps d'une paix, Cormoran, Le volcan tranquille *(Radio Canada, 1990-2000).*

Notes

1. *The Swastika and the Maple Leaf: Fascist Movements in Canada in the Thirties.* Lita-Rose Betcherman. Fitzhenry & Whiteside. 1975.

2 Translator's note: *Eléments latins* was the first year; the nicknames might be translated "little assholes" and "big fresh turds."

3 The signatories of *Refus global* were: Paul-Emile Borduas, Magdeleine Arbour, Marcel Barbeau, Bruno Cormier, Claude Gauvreau, Pierre Gauvreau, Muriel Guilbault, Marcelle Ferron-Hamelin, Fernand Leduc, Thérèse Leduc, Jean-Paul Mousseau, Maurice Perron, Louise Renaud, Françoise Riopelle, Jean-Paul Riopelle, Françoise Sullivan. Mithra–Mythe. Montreal. 1948.

4. L'oeuvre d'art est une expérience. Bruno Cormier in *Refus global.* Mithra–Mythe. Montreal. 1948

Colin Angliker

Serendipity: The faculty of making happy discoveries by accident.
Oxford English Dictionary, 1983

 It is the spring of 1968 and I am the Chief of Service at Stearns Pavilion, Douglas Hospital, in Verdun. My plans to go to the United States have fallen through, and I am at a loss as to where I want to go and work as, heretofore, all my energies had been directed towards "south of the border." For weeks I had been mulling over where to go and what to do, and everything I had contemplated was not very enticing.

Grand Rounds at the Douglas were a regular occurrence, and I tried to attend them; interesting "firemen" often came to spread the word about various and sundry topics. On this certain spring day, Dr. Bruno Cormier was the invited guest speaker; so along I went as I had fond memories of him when he had taught us as residents at McGill University. I have long since forgotten his topic, but I do very well remember what I was thinking about while he talked. I said to myself, "I wonder what it is like to work behind bars. I wonder if Dr. Cormier has an opening at the Forensic Clinic."

After Rounds were over, I asked him if he had any openings at the Clinic, to which he said he thought he might, as he was in the process of negotiating a new contract with the State of New York. He asked me to call him and he would let me know. I did. He said that there would be an opening and that I could start as soon as I had completed my obligations to the hospital and the Province of Quebec.

Unlike nowadays, there were no formal interviews, no application forms to fill out, no tours of the place—nothing! My interview consisted of the few minutes I had spent with him after his talk at Douglas, *et voilà!* I had a job! Such was the informality by which Dr. Cormier lived and worked.

I started at "509" on the first of July 1968. The Clinic in those days was a hive of activity. Everyone was assigned to one or more research projects. As well, everyone was seeing patients both on an out-patient basis and in the nearby penitentiaries and jails. Every facet of crime was explored and every age group investigated. For the first time in my life I was to come face to face with all types of criminals: from petty thieves to murderers, with sex offenders in between. We literally studied crime and criminals from the cradle to the grave.

As to the cast of "characters" who worked at or visited the Clinic, these were as varied as the United Nations. Practically all the provinces were represented at one time or another. We had *émigrés* from Hungary, France, the Netherlands and other European countries, Ireland, the British Isles, Israel, and Mexico, and as far away as Australia, to name but a few. We were a mosaic-like crew if ever there were one! We came there for one purpose: to be with and learn from Bruno Cormier, the Father of Canadian Forensic Psychiatry.

One of the collective highlights for those of us who worked at the Clinic in those early days was travelling each week to Clinton Prison in Dannemora, New York. It was at the Dannemora Project where I first gained experience working with prisoners and their custodians in very close proximity. The therapeutic community approach to treating offenders taught me a lot, and with the passage of time I learned how to confront the so-called hardened criminals without fear of retaliation. One of the most fascinating aspects of working with delinquents is how well they respond to a direct and straightforward approach *vis-à-vis* therapy. The convoluted verbal or non-directive approaches expounded in various therapies were and are poorly received amongst this group of individuals. To them "a spade is a spade" and not an entrenching tool! These men and women are unable to tolerate ambiguity, for it is very likely to lead to much anxiety and, not infrequently, verbal as well as physical violence. Although the direct approach is better suited to *my* temperament, it, needless to say, provoked much personal anxiety when first I broached this technique with such a captive audience.

The weekly community meeting with all staff and inmates present was an experience to behold especially when Bruno was present. Confrontation was second nature to him, and he seemed to revel in raising the ire of one or all. Bruno told it the way it was and took no hostages! To the novice, such as myself, this mode of confrontation or "reality therapy" was a new approach, for I had been used to stuffy mentors, particularly psychoanalysts, who would barely note the existence of their patients let alone remark that their behaviour was unacceptable and/or inappropriate. Surprisingly, the inmates accepted Bruno's observations and criticisms and even went as far as to thank him for being straight with them. It was a most valuable lesson, one of which I had to put into practice over and over again in subsequent years when dealing with criminals.

The Dannemora Project had a remarkable effect upon the guards at the institution, something I had never seen before and have rarely seen since then. The usual barrier of "we," the custodians, versus "they," the inmates, was less marked than what is typically seen in all prisons. Many of the obstacles and taboos encountered in prison were broken down, and over time a genuine concern to help an inmate deal with some of his problems, both real and imagined, was accomplished without any repercussions from the administration or their peers. It was quite an experience for the guards. Most of them were "lifers" themselves, having spent many years working behind bars since leaving high school or returning from military service. Dr. Cormier frequently noted that the officers spent a much longer time in prison than many of their charges. For a few officers who were unable to tolerate this approach, they requested and were granted transfers elsewhere in the New York prison system. Most of the officers who remained were a delight to work with, for many were able to share first-hand experiences with us neophytes, none of which could have been gleaned from a textbook.

As for us "professionals," who had recently finished training, the kind of information provided by the guards had an invaluable effect upon the inmates. We were often criticized by them for talking "out of a textbook," that is, giving them the party line according to the gospel of Freud *et alia*, rather than "telling them how it is"! The camaraderie that developed between the officers and the McGill clinicians resulted in several life-long friendships. It was an environment in which we all learned from each other and readily, too. It was the best classroom I had ever experienced, and I got paid for it to boot!

The two hours' journey to and from Montreal to Dannemora, two to three times each week in all kinds of weather, was a venture in itself. We would travel as a group, and our topic of conversation would be a detailed review of all that had transpired that day. Even the customs officers at the Canadian/U.S. border came to know us as the "shrinks" who worked in the state prison, and rarely did we meet with a problem crossing the border. Most of them would give us that all-knowing look, as if to say, "Those nuts ...!" and nod us onward on our journey. Although physically tired by the time we reached home, our thoughts were abuzz. It was an emotional "high" that we underwent weekly for as long as the programme lasted. For many of us, the memories of those days have remained unchanged. Such was the influence Bruno had upon all of us.

Back at the Clinic, between our trips south of the border, our work was no less stimulating. We still had our research projects to complete, testify in court, attend to our out-patients, present cases before the master, write and correct papers, *ad infinitum*. There were never enough hours in the day; yet Bruno would continue long after we left, and on the next day he would confront us with several fresh ideas that he had thought about the night before. His ability to free-associate was remarkable, and he was unafraid to commit his thoughts to writing. The man never stopped thinking! Yet rarely did he thrust his ideas upon us, demanding that one accept what he said as being the last word on the subject. He was, however, a determined and stubborn man when it involved the provision of good clinical care to inmates. Rarely did he suffer fools gladly, no matter whence they came. It mattered not if they were politicians, lawyers, judges, students, colleagues, or inmates. He was an equal-opportunity critic, and it was a special treat to watch him "lecture" to a judge on certain forensic issues right in the midst of testifying; the expression on the judge's face was priceless as, I am sure, were his thoughts.

Unlike so many "experts" in forensic psychiatry, who spend most of their professional lives only examining defendants and then testifying in court for one side or the other, Cormier refused to be molded into that category. He was most critical of them, for they were specialists only in examining and testifying and in nothing else. Rarely did they ever treat such offenders over the long term, observe them in any depth, or even work in a correctional facility or a mental hospital where these men and women are sent following their pontifications in court. Very few have any idea—let alone first-hand experience—about the life cycle of crime.

Not so in Bruno Cormier's case. He insisted upon not only thorough evaluations of the offender we had to examine, but also, if possible, on interviews with the family of origin so that an accurate picture could be developed as to the course of criminality through the generations. He cared little how much we had to write or how much the court had to read. He demanded a complete and accurate picture of each case. His agenda had multiple facets: a thorough evaluation for the court, thoughtful and realistic recommendation or recommendations as to disposition, and provisions for the report to be used for research purposes at some point in the future. Nothing was ever to be carried out in isolation. Thus, over the years, he and his staff built up a veritable archive of accounts of criminal behaviour, much of which made their way into the many articles, chapters, theses and books that were written by us.

One of the most amusing and sometimes frustrating aspects of Bruno was his difficulty in expressing himself clearly, either in French or in English. His verbal expression lagged far behind his thoughts, and he would often stop talking, mid-sentence, literally, then go on to complete the sentence by waving his hands to signify what he meant. Those of us who got to know him well were able to complete the sentence, so to speak, and we would often be required to act as "translators" for those present who did not know him well. I was often approached after a meeting with a request to explain what Dr. Cormier had just said. I would then provide the listeners with the gist of what had been said, much to their relief and appreciation. All had felt that they should have understood what he said but were so fearful to ask him to repeat or explain himself. They behaved as if they were His Majesty's loyal subjects, and were fearful of interrupting or asking lest they would lose their proverbial heads! There was no question he had a magisterial aura about him, but what many people failed to grasp was not so much how Bruno expressed himself but the content of the ideas and thoughts he was presenting.

His topics for research were uniquely his. Rarely have I ever seen other researchers pursue their topics in the same vein, either then or since then. One of the research subjects he worked on was about homicide: a subject that fascinated me then and now. Not only did he study the offence itself, he added a new dimension: that of the perpetrator's relationship with the victim. Thus, he developed a classification of homicide based upon how well the victim was known to the murderer. It was a novel approach and one that I employ in my research and clinical practice to this day. Since I left the Clinic, hardly a month has gone by without my having thoughts and or making references to Bruno and various aspects of his work.

Two of Bruno's closest colleagues at the Clinic were Miriam Kennedy and Raymond Boyer. Miriam came from a social-work background, while Raymond had been a Professor of Chemistry at McGill University. Both had been working with Bruno since the Clinic first opened. Those three were the backbone of the Clinic and together they worked harmoniously on many projects over the years. Miriam was involved not only in research but also in the treatment of offenders and their families. She, too, adhered to Bruno's dictum that one should not enmesh oneself solely in research to the exclusion of clinical observations and the treatment of offenders and their families. Similarly, one cannot just provide expertise in court without having clinical experience with those who have transgressed the law. To be knowledgeable in forensic psychiatry, one must approach it from many different avenues: medicine, law, psychology, sociology, and even literature, to name only some. Bruno was forever referring to great literary works, both historical and fictional, and it was from these that he acquired many of his ideas for his research topics. All three members of the Clinic were avid readers, and when they theorized about various topics, one was then provided with a broad perspective which was not limited to scientific issues. For, after all is said and done, what we practise is still very much an art rather than a science.

Miriam's forte was the study of incestuous behaviour, and over the years she worked with and studied many hundreds of subjects and their families. Despite the subject matter and the pathological aspect of incest, Miriam always approached the individuals and their families with the utmost of decorum, and never was she judgmental of her clients. Neither was she a "bleeding heart." She was firm but non-confronting; she was kind but not effusive; and, most importantly, she cared about what she did and nothing was approached in a frivolous manner. It was as a result of her work and interest in incest that several clinicians at the Clinic continued on with her studies. One clinician was successful in acquiring a

Doctorate from Cambridge on that very subject.

Raymond Boyer was different from both Miriam and Bruno. He was a "behind-the-scenes" kind of man, who went quietly about his work with very little fanfare. He "lived" on the top floor of the Clinic, spending most of his day gathering and collating data from all sources. Those were the days before computers, when everything was done by hand. I often wonder what we would have done then had we access to personal and laptop computers. Rarely did Raymond venture out of his office. However, his door was never closed to us, and he was always available for advice and assistance. Although he was not a clinician in the strictest sense, he was very knowledgeable about clinical matters and had vast personal experience with legal and penal topics despite his background in chemistry. His basic training and experience in the pure sciences was of great assistance to all of us when it came to organizing our work in a methodical way. As with Miriam, his approach and demeanour was a quiet one, and never did I see him angry or hear him raise his voice despite the many frustrations with which he had to contend. He was a gentleman in every sense of the word.

In practically all work situations there are always several unsung heroes and heroines, and the McGill Clinic in Forensic Psychiatry was no exception. Such men and women work behind the scenes, get very little recognition for the vast amount of work they perform, and their names are not included on papers or in books. They do not go to conferences; in fact, they remain *in situ* most of their working days, only to return home each evening by bus. One such person was Lorna Graham.

Lorna worked at the Clinic long before I arrived and for several years after I left. Among her many talents was the one for which she was hired, namely, her talent as an editorial secretary. Not only was she required to provide us with perfect typewritten documents, but she was also expected to correct our English into proper English, by no means an easy task! Lorna was widely travelled and read; she loved art and spent many hours in museums during her travels. The walls of her tiny office were covered with repro-ductions of all the masters and little *objets d'art*: a veritable mini-museum. She loved collecting calendars, too, and we would vie for all sorts—art subjects, travel calendars and those from pharma-ceutical companies, just about anything that was colourful or pleasing to the eye. Lorna was always busy and would have several projects on her desk at any one time. When she was not typing and editing for Bruno, she was editing our work, doing transla-tions, or reviewing newspaper articles about crimes or related subjects. She was always on the go and after work her activities increased! If she was not working towards the completion of her Bachelor's degree, she was going to a concert, a museum, or an art gallery or, best of all, she would be preparing a meal for a "few" invited friends. Lorna's ability to cook was second to none, and to be invited for a meal was indeed a pleasure. She loved to experi-ment and would practise until she acquired perfection. For exam-ple, you could literally read a newspaper through one of her crêpes! Yes, Lorna added another dimension to the Clinic, especial-ly for those who were privileged to be considered friends, for it was a friendship for keeps. Her letters, her observations, and her comments were priceless, and she would always include newspa-per clippings on topics about which she knew we were interested. Very little escaped her eyes and ears.

Such was the composition of the Forensic Clinic during the years I was there. We learned, we worked hard, and we had fun. It is a rare experience in one's professional life to be able to work in such an atmosphere where it is both a pleasure and a privilege to be each day. To Bruno Cormier a great debt of gratitude is owed for providing such leadership and guidance.

One last comment about Bruno: Bruno after work and at his farm. He loved his tree farm and would go there as often as he could. In the summertime he would invite us there to spend the day and picnic with him and Ruby. Having no children of his own, he loved to be with our children—young or old—and would take them for endless rides in his battered old red jeep, going in and out through the trees all afternoon, cheerfully chattering and singing all the way. Bruno was grandfather to all of them, and my four daughters still recall those days when we used to go out to the farm and ride in the jeep. All his cares and worries seemed to dissipate when he was at his farm.

The year 1977 was the time for me to make another decision: to stay in Montreal or to leave. The children were of a school age, so that if one was to move, now was the time to do it because later would be too disruptive. The decision to move was made, and so in December of that year we headed south of the border, first to Connecticut, then to Louisiana, and finally to Virginia, where I have been for the past ten years. All the while I have continued to practise forensic psychiatry. For the past ten years I have worked in a prison psychiatric hospital for the Virginia Department of Corrections as its medical director. Working full-time in the prison system has given me new insights into clinical criminology, and I very much prefer this milieu to the milieux of some of the other systems in which I have worked.

One of Bruno's ambitions was to develop a prison hospital that was university-affiliated. He felt that mental-health services should be provided to inmates by clinicians who worked *in* prison, and that upon release it would be the responsibility of those staff to continue monitoring their care in the community, rather than involving several other mental-health agencies, as most of those do not care one whit about such clientele. We who have worked with Bruno continue to strive to reach this uphill goal and to provide the inmate with the best possible medical care, both while incarcerated and once paroled.

Meeting Bruno in the spring of 1968 was indeed serendipity, and to him I owe a deep debt of gratitude. May he rest in the knowledge that we are continuing his work on several continents.

Colin C.J. Angliker, *M.B. and B.Ch., B.A.O. (Belf.)*, Dip. Psych. *(McGill), FRCP(C), FAPA, Medical Director and Chief Psychiatrist, Marion Correctional Treatment Centre, Marion, VA; Associate Clinical Professor, Department of Psychiatric Medicine, University of Virginia, 1988-present.*

Clinical Director, Feliciana Forensic Facility, Jackson, Louisiana, 1986-1988; Director, Whiting Forensic Institute, Associate Clinical Professor, School of Medicine, Yale University, 1977-1986; Psychiatrist, McGill Clinic in Forensic Psychiatry, 1968-1977; Chief of Service, Adolescent Unit, Douglas Hospital, Verdun, Quebec, 1967-1968.

Yann Bogopolsky

Une brêche ouverte dans l'opacité
de l'acte ... le trait de l'inconscient

 Ce qui se clôt appelle l'ouverture. La fermeture de la "Forensic Clinic" comme elle était couramment appellée, n'a pu que raviver le désir déjà émis lors de la disparition du Dr. Bruno Cormier de laisser des traces ... Comme autant d'échos de ses propres écrits, révélant la vie de sa pensée toujours en mouvement. Ce lieu était un véritable vivier où chacun d'entre nous qui a eu la chance ou le bonheur d'y travailler, c'est à dire d'apprendre, de découvrir, de réfléchir et de mettre à l'oeuvre sa propre expérience—était poussé par l'énergie créatrice de son directeur à mettre une question au travail: l'humain, l'autre était constamment à intérroger, à découvrir.

Si la nostalgie tentait de nous envelopper ou la tristesse de nous envahir de cette période où Bruno M. Cormier dirigeait les destinées de la clinique de Psychiatrie Légale de l'Université McGill, ou de celle qui suivit où Renée Fugère mit toute son énergie à laisser vivant cet héritage, il n'est que de penser à quel point cet enseignement, tant de criminologie clinique que d'éthique, reste présent aujourd'hui dans ma pratique d'analyste ou dans mon travail de transmission de ce savoir.

Tenter d'évoquer avec vous la richesse de l'oeuvre du Dr. Cormier c'est déjà tourner la tête au-dessus de mon épaule, et me replonger quelques vingt-cinq ans en arrière à l'époque où étudiante en psychologie à la Faculté de Nanterre, je décidais de m'inscrire à l'Institut de Criminologie de Paris.

Je me souviens de l'étonnement qui me saisit lorsque je réalisais que nous n'étions que quatre à intégrer la Faculté de Droit en venant du domaine de la psychologie; de plus parmis tous ces étudiants en droit nous faisions figure d'intrus, pour ne pas dire d'égarés. L'enseignement se composait de deux certificats l'un en sciences criminelles l'autre en sciences criminologiques.

Il n'est pas dans mon intention de passer en revue cet enseignement mais de vous transmettre les impressions du moment qui me sont encore vivaces aujourd'hui. Bien sûr nous faisions notre entrée dans le vaste domaine des institutions pénales et de leurs applications, mais je me souviens du plaisir (fort peu partagé d'ailleurs) que j'avais eu à remonter à la source de ces lois qui constituaient le droit avec les cours de philosophie pénale du Professeur Michel Villey.

Je me souviens avec grand intérêt du souci humaniste qui traversait l'enseignement de Jacques Vérin relatif au traitement pénal des délinquants adultes et qui mettait un point d'honneur à nous exposer les perspectives les plus récentes de pénologie, tentant des alternatives là où l'incarcération apparaîssait encore en France comme l'outil incontournable.

Les cours de psychiatrie, où nous était assénée sans aucune explicitation une pensée anti-psychanalytique, me laissaient perplexe quant à la formation de la pensée que l'on pouvait espérer acquérir en parcourant un cursus universitaire.

J'étais impatiente de connaître ce que pouvait dévoiler un cours de psychiatrie criminelle: j'y ai découvert les éléments de la nosogaphie psychiatrique qui pouvaient être présents ou révélés lors de la commission d'un acte criminel. Comme étudiante en psychologie, j'entendais dans les présentations du Dr. Roumajon, le soucis d'une lecture dynamique qui ne réduisait pas le sujet à son acte.

Et puis, dans l'histoire des idées et des grandes doctrines de la criminologie qui nous était enseignée par Jean Pinatel lequel dans les années 70 tenait lieu de référence officielle en France (au moins dans ce qu'en retransmettaient les médias) une correspondance m'avait marquée:

- D'un côté, l'importance de l'oeuvre de Lombroso qui voua sa vie et son labeur à trouver dans le corps de l'humain la marque de sa criminalité, "l'homme criminel" était en quelque sorte comme l'esclave marqué au fer rouge, sinon que cette inscription n'était pas faite sur son corps par un tiers, mais qu'elle était sensée exister dans son corps dès sa naissance.

- De l'autre, la propre théorie du Professeur Pinatel qui s'articulait autour de ce qu'il nommait "le noyau central de la personnalité criminelle" en quatre traits irréductibles, me semblait être une transcription au niveau psychique de la théorie lombrosienne; pour l'étudiante que j'étais déjà interrogée par la question de l'inconscient chez le sujet humain, ce parraléllisme me laissait perplexe.

  La surprise vient, comme de bien entendu, là où on ne l'attend pas et pour moi ce fut du côté de la sociologie; j'ai encore aujourd'hui en mémoire le poids que Jacques Selosse attribuait à la parole, à ce qu'elle laisse surgir de nous comme colère et comme agressivité, à ce qu'elle permet dans l'expression et la résolution d'un conflit, et au contraire lorsqu'elle venait à manquer si l'on n'avait pas les mots pour le dire, ni même la connaissance de la langue comme expatriés, à quel point la solution restait le corps et les gestes qui l'agitent—où ajouterais-je ces gestes qui expriment ce qui s'agite en nous.

Toutefois je terminais ces certificats avec un certain malaise, espérant un enseignement clinique que bien sûr je n'avais pas à attendre d'une faculté de Droit, mais avec un désir évident de ne pas en rester au niveau de cette première approche théorique, et le souhait de conjuguer ces éléments à un autre regard sur l'humain . . . mais où et comment? En dépit de ces questions à l'époque sans réponse, j'avais néanmoins décidé pour clôre ce diplôme de m'atteler à un mémoire qui envisageait une question clinique.

J'avais entendu parler de l'équipe lyonnaise de Colin et Hochmann qui travaillaient en milieu carcéral, mais à cette époque je ne connaissais pas la teneur de leurs écrits. Lyon me semblait loin de Paris ... mais la distance vécue comme empêchement existe d'abord dans sa tête ... puisque l'année suivante je décidais d'émigrer au Québec!

La distance curieusement laisse un autre accès au savoir; et ce n'est donc que dans l'après coup que je découvris leurs ouvrages,[1] ainsi que la poursuite des réflexions de Jacques Selosse et les textes des Dr. Ellenberger et Dongier dans les tomes de *l'Evolution Psychiatrique.* Voici la lunette au travers de laquelle je tentais de prendre connaissance des théories criminologiques qui avaient cours en France dans les années soixante-dix; en France cela m'avait paru un chemin rude, malaisé et marginal.

Ayant traversé un océan, je découvrais une autre envergure au domaine de la criminologie:

- D'abord au niveau universitaire, je constatais l'existence d'un cursus allant jusqu'au doctorat de 3e cycle, ainsi qu'un centre international de criminologie comparée qui était facilement accessible.
- Et au niveau professionel, un vaste champ qui faisait de ce domaine une profession à part entière dont l'éventail s'ouvrait de gardien de prison à policiers, en passant par les services de libération conditionnelle ou encore les lieux thérapeutiques, sans compter l'existence d'une association professionnelle à laquelle j'avais à coeur de redonner de l'élan à travers de congrès et colloques et d'un nouveau code de déontologie.

Nouvellement immigrée je fis donc mon entrée dans la vie professionnelle comme criminologue à Institut Philippe Pinel de Montréal où j'apprenais un nouveau contexte législatif, juridique et pénal. Au décours de ce travail j'éprouvais la nécessité d'éclaircir les différentes acceptions que recouvrait le terme de "clinique."

Tout travail qui sortait du domaine de la recherche purement théorique et qui amenait le professionnel à entrer en contact avec le délinquant comme personne, était appelé travail "clinique," que sa visée soit sociale (réinsertion) ou thérapeutique—quelque soit par ailleurs la référence théorique à partir de laquelle ce travail s'élaborait.

Somme toute, cela n'était pas très éloigné du modèle dit "médical" présent dans les théories criminologiques circulant en Europe où l'on parlait de diagnostic, traitement et pronostic du délinquant; mais bien sûr cela pouvait tout aussi bien être entendu comme traitement judiciaire que pénal ou psychiatrique.

Quant à moi, sans savoir encore comment l'argumenter, j'éprouvais le besoin de faire la distinction entre pratique et clinique; une pratique criminologique nous mettant en lien de personne à personne, étant entendu que divers niveaux d'intervention pouvaient soutenir ce lien, et, la "clinique" étant du côté du malaise ou du mal-être qui se fait entendre dans les mots du sujet ou le brouhaha social que ses actes engendrent et qui font retour pour lui par le truchement ou non de la loi.

Participant en tant qu'auditrice libre au cours du Dr. Bruno M. Cormier, j'appréciais la possibilité qui nous était offerte d'être présents aux entretiens avec les délinquants en milieu carcéral, lesquels acceptaient ainsi de partager l'histoire de leur vie devant un auditoire, certes limité, mais tout de même pas aussi restreint que dans l'entretien individuel classiquement conçu.

J'y découvrais combien la visée qui soustend la démarche, l'ecoute du thérapeute, le silence ou la liaison entre ses dires permettait au sujet d'entendre autrement son histoire qu'il avait répétée bien des fois.

Dès la fin de ce cours, le Dr. Cormier me proposa de faire partie de l'équipe de la Forensic Clinic. J'étais déjà sensibilisée à la richesse, ne serait-ce qu'au niveau de ma formation professionnelle, que représentait une telle offre, et j'avais également l'assurance de trouver dans ce cadre une question clinique à traiter pour mon mémoire de l'Institut de Criminologie de Paris—travail qui put se concrétiser grâce à la présence de la directrice des études Pierrette Poncela, qui connaîssait déjà le travail clinique du Dr. Cormier, et accepta à un océan de distance de parrainer mon mémoire relatif à "l'âge délinquant et la crise de l'âge mûr" thème choisi parmi les moments charnières qui jalonnent la vie de l'être humain et dont le Dr. Cormier avait souligné l'importance dans la vaste recherche qu'il avait entreprise dans le milieu des années cinquante.

Mais avant de m'arrêter à l'originalité de l'oeuvre du Dr. Cormier, je souhaite m'attarder un moment sur la place occupée par la théorie psychanalytique des années soixante.

Fort rares furent les psychanalystes qui ont travaillé avec des criminels, mais bon nombre après Freud tentèrent des explications théoriques à partir d'un concept. Ces tentatives d'appréhension des mécanismes inconscients qui avaient pu être présents dans la commission d'un acte furent instrumentalisées par la criminologie "clinique."

En effet, cette dernière qui cherchant à accéder au statut de science, était en quête d'un objet: le crime ou le criminel, ou ce qui chez le criminel venait signer le crime, à savoir la notion si présente de "passage à l'acte" autour de laquelle s'est organisée la criminologie clinique avec comme prolongement celle de "dangerosité." Mais ces éléments essentiels d'une science: objet et méthode, ne sont pas sans lien avec la visée qu'ils poursuivent et dans les débats houleux qui la confrontèrent aux autres sciences humaines comme le droit et la sociologie, la criminologie clinique cherchait à asseoir son savoir, empruntant tout autant aux notions psychologique que psychiatrique voire psychanalytique.

Les concepts psychanalytiques utilisés en criminologie semblent venir en lieu et place d'un principe organisateur entendu au sens de principe de causalité.

Il n'est que de relire les articles des Dr. Ellenberger et Dongier dans les numéros de *l'Evolution Psychiatrique* des années 1966 où retraçant les "conceptions actuelles de la criminogénèse" ils évoquent le rôle fondamental des vicissitudes du complexe d'oedipe à l'origine de la criminogénèse[2] ou encore "la complexité plus ou moins inconsciente entre le criminel d'une part et les autorités répressives et le public tout entier d'autre part" venant expliciter les "cercles vicieux entre le criminel et la société."[3]

On voit là combien les concepts retirés du contexte de la théorisation qui leur donnent sens sont en quelques sortes vidés de leur contenu.

Peut-on ainsi isoler des éléments des mythes fondateurs de la théorie psychanalytique freudienne—celui de la horde primitive ou du conflit oedipien—comme le meurtre et la culpabilité par lesquels Freud nous indique à quel point pour le sujet de l'inconscient, désir et interdit sont intimement unis, et les transposer ainsi dans le registre de l'activité consciente? Ce serait oublier ce que Freud lui-même nous dit dans Totem et Tabou,[4] à propos des désirs refoulés communs à tous les humains:

..."Lorsqu'un individu a réussi à satisfaire un désir refoulé, tous les autres membres de la collectivité doivent éprouver la tentation d'en faire autant; pour réprimer cette tentation il faut punir l'audace de celui dont on envie la satisfaction, et il arrive souvent que le châtiment fournit à ceux qui l'exécutent l'occasion de commettre à leur tour, sous le couvert de l'expiation, le même acte impur. C'est là un des principes fondamentaux du système pénal humain, et il découle naturellement de l'identité des désirs refoulés chez le criminel et chez ceux qui sont chargés de venger la société outragée" ...

D'autres notions, comme "une forte fixation orale"[5] ou "un idéal du moi pathologique"[6] ou encore "un surmoi terrifiant,"[7] censées dévoiler un mécanisme inconscient, accréditeraient le "passage à l'acte" comme notion clef de la criminologie clinique en lui garantissant une signification.

En effet cette notion qui a donné lieu à de nombreuses définitions tout au long de l'histoire de la criminologie en reste comme le pilier central qui viendrait enfermer l'humain dans une catégorie spécifique et reconnaissable, sécurisant par ce savoir le reste du corps social qui s'en différencierait. Mais contrairement à ce qui est trop souvent exprimé pour la psychanalyse, l'instance consciente du psychique humain n'a pas pour fonction première la socialisation, mais la constitution par le sujet d'une représentation, d'une image de lui-même et pour lui-même. Ce processus de subjectivation ne peut s'effectuer sans le double mouvement d'une identification à l'image de l'autre, pris dans un système culturel qui fixe les échanges obligés et interdits. Le sujet est lui-même aux prises avec une autre instance où il disposerait de plaisirs illimités, une instance imaginaire qui le mettra dans un tension nécessaire où, par l'acceptation de la perte, il trouvera sa position de sujet.

Aussi, si la théorie psychanalytique a pu proposer comme prévalente une instance de l'inconscient ou un mécanisme de défense du sujet, cette lecture ne peut qu'être replacée dans la dialectique du sujet entre pulsion de vie et pulsion de mort, et les avatars de sa propre agressivité et de l'aliénation à laquelle tout sujet est contraint.

Il ne s'agit pas pour elle d'établir les traits spécifiques d'une personnalité antisociale, voire dangereuse; peut-être, la confusion vient-elle du glissement souvent opéré de psychanalyse à psychiatrie, et de la demande faite aux psychiatres dans leur expertise au pénal, de manifester un savoir sur la présumée dangerosité d'un sujet. Par ailleurs la société ne cesse de revendiquer l'assurance de ce savoir afin de n'être pas confrontée à la blessure que leur renvoient ceux qui ont transgressé les interdits fondamentaux du meurtre et de l'inceste.

Les auteurs qui se tiennent en décalage de ce savoir sont souvent absents des manuels même lorsque ces derniers traitent de criminologie clinique.

Déjà au début des années soixante, Colin et Hochmann inauguraient avec leurs collaborateurs leurs "études de criminologie clinique" par un article intitulé "Diagnostic et traitement de l'état dangereux" dans lequel ils différencient état et acte dangereux; ils pointaient que "c'est l'intolérance au fou qui crée l'état dangereux. Il apparaît donc important dans une telle situation de séparer l'auteur de l'acte de sa victime. L'agressivité est une forme particulière du drame humain qui exige aux moins deux acteurs" ... et plus loin ils ajoutent: "l'acte dangereux est une expression de la personne, un engagement dans l'intersubjectivité, une création"—Question qui pourtant ne cessera d'occuper le devant de la scène criminologique de la décennie suivante.

Poussant la porte de la "Forensic Clinic" toute liberté était laissée à chacun pour y trouver sa place et découvrir la cohérence qui l'animait.

Dans un premier temps je passais de longues heures dans le bureau où étaient engrangés tous les dossiers de recherche et je tentais de saisir les lignes directrices de ce vaste projet. Pour ce faire je me plongeais (dictionnaire anglais-français à portée de mains) dans la lecture de multiples articles qui m'initièrent à cette pensée.

Le premier texte paru en 1957 intitulé "Presentation of a Basic Classification for Clinical Work and Research in Criminality" posait les jalons d'un travail d'appréhension de l'homme délinquant à l'entrecroisement du social et de l'individuel—L'acte est posé dans la réalité sociale, il engendre des conséquences pour celui qui l'a perpétré—Il implique une réaction sociale où toute société met en scène ses idéaux, le poids de ses interdits à travers ses lois et son système répressif sa propre conception de l'humain. Mais le sujet lui-méme ne sera pas appréhendé uniquement dans le donné à voir de son acte, mais dans toute la dimension de son historisité, remontant à l'enfance, moments où les conflits de la vie psychique permettent la structuration de son moi et son advenir comme sujet parlant.

Ainsi s'opérait pour moi dans le discours théorique un déplacement du regard qui tente d'objectiver le délinquant par le truchement de son acte vers une écoute de ce que ces hommes avaient à dire de leur histoire, d'eux-mêmes et de leurs actes. Ces dires, leurs dires, donnaient à entendre du clivage, de la projection, du triomphe, de la dévalorisation, de l'agressivité, et laissaient dans le silence la question de la perte, l'éprouvé de culpabilité, le souci pour l'autre et l'ambivalence.

Ces constuctions et reconstructions de leur histoire reccueillies auprés d'hommes détenus puis libres, âgés de vingt à plus de soixante ans, dessinaient le tracé d'un parcours où l'idéalisation (n'ayant d'égale que la force de l'agression extérieure qu'ils éprouvaient) perdait autour de la quarantaine de son intensité, avec l'envahissement d'un sentiment dépressif sous le poids de l'épreuve de réalité ... Non, le prochain délit ne serait pas la réalisation magique d'un acte les mettant à l'abri de la loi et comblant un désir toujours inassouvi, la perte s'insinuait venant faire barrage au déni de leur réalité et à l'effroi de l'autre vécu à l'aune de leur propre destructivité.

Autant d'éléments qui ne sont pas sans rappeler la théorie de Mélanie Klein, avec ce passage décisif pour l'advenir de l'humain de la position schizoparanoïde à la position dépressive; c'est pourquoi le Dr. Cormier postula l'hypothèse pour ces hommes qui avaient concrétisé leur vie dans une "carrière criminelle," que la répétition de leurs agirs illégaux venait projeter sur le théâtre de leur vie leur activité psychique inconsciente, clivant la figure de la mère—société comme leur moi était clivé, arborant les défenses maniaques comme autant de barrages les empêchant de s'effondrer sous les angoisses de morcellement.

Ainsi leur vie durant, ils répètent sur la scène sociale les avatars de ce passage longtemps vécu comme impossible, de la reconnaissance de leur réalité psychique différenciée de la réalité extérieure: d'une culpabilité qu'ils ne pouvaient reprendre à leur compte, car elle était trop terrifiante et d'une réparation symbolique qui ne pouvait advenir et donner prise, par l'épreuve de la dépression, à l'existence de l'autre.

Tout ce travail théorique mené pendant deux décennies et transmis au fur et à mesure de sa progression par de multiples écrits et communications, parut en français dans un article intitulé "Passage aux actes délictueux et états dépressifs."[8]

Ainsi le psychanalyste interrogeait-il les mécanismes inconscients qui poussaient ces humains non seulement à agir, mais à
avoir cette représentation psychique d'eux-mêmes et de l'autre.

C'est au travers de cette référence théorique que s'est bâtie
pierre après pierre ce qui est devenu l'oeuvre de toute une vie.

Ce sont les interdits fondamentaux du meurtre et de l'inceste
qu'il ne cessa d'interroger dans les répercussions psychique et
sociale de leur transgressivité.

C'est la mise en oeuvre du travail de l'inconscient qui l'amena
à poursuivre sa réflexion sur les effets de l'oeuvre de la plusion de
mort, de la répétition et de la transmission des avatars de la problématique de la castration d'une génération à une autre.

Ce sont les concepts de la métapsychologie freudienne et klein-
nienne qui servirent d'arc-boutants à l'étayage de cette pensée, telles
les problématiques de l'elaboration du moi, et de la relation d'objet
ainsi que la mise en oeuvre des mécanismes de défense. Une écoute
qui permettait à l'autre de se dévoiler à lui-même et qu'il a toujours
questionnée de la place de l'analyste en insistant sur la mise au travail incontournable de la question du contre-transfer.[9]

Chacun ou chacune d'entre nous s'arrimait à cette pensée toujours en ébullition et choisissait de creuser un sillon autour d'une
même problématique ou d'interroger tel au tel aspect de fontion-
nement psychique, selon les aléas de son propre cheminement.

Ainsi le Dr. Cormier s'intéressant à la transgression du tabou
de l'inceste[10] dès le début de sa pratique psychiatrique en mileu
carcéral, d'autres poursuivent avec lui le travail, et parmi les collègues que j'ai le mieux connus, Ingrid Cooper publia sur les
implications sociales et légales de cette question, tout comme sur
sa transmission de génération en génération.[11]

Quant aux agirs meurtriers c'est au travers de la relation objectale
que le délinquant noue avec sa victime que le Dr. Cormier les
appréhenda, dans ces moments critiques de la vie où d'aucuns ne
peuvent vivre la séparation que dans l'agir d'une rupture irréversible.

Pour ces adolescents comme pour les couples en crise, la
coupure agie dans la réalité sur le corps de l'autre, vient faire retour

sur le corps de l'autre et instaurer un remaniement psychique qui sera lié au moment où le travail de deuil pourra s'élaborer.

Ainsi Baila Markus concentra sa réflexion sur la problémattique des adolescents meurtriers, voire même parricides.[12]

Pour d'autres encore, telle Renée Fugère,[13] on découvrira sous la diversité de ses écrits traitant aussi bien des pulsions agressives que du choix d'objet d'amour pédophilique, ou encore des "attaques" contre les biens pour les femmes dans la quarantaine, une trame éclairée par divers aspects d'un travail de deuil pathologique.

Autant d'instantanés pour évoquer par delà le quotidien du travail composé d'entretien thérapeutique, d'expertise ou de supervision d'étudiant, la nécessité de penser, du travail du symbolique ... peut-être en contrepoint du reçu de ces agirs plus ou moins éprouvants dont nous devenions les dépositaires.

En tant que psychiatre, le Dr. Bruno Cormier était un praticien "engagé." Il n'hésitait pas à créer des projets qui allaient à l'encontre des peurs et des préjugés, tel le projet de Dannemora (mis sur pieds au moment où les rébellions explosaient dans les pénitenciers américains) qui s'adressait aux délinquants jugés les plus dangereux par l'administration pénitentiaire, à savoir les détenus qui avaent commis plusieurs meurtres.

Ce projet visait à prendre en compte les pathologies inhérentes à l'enfermement, les problématiques surgissant du milieu carcéral et de ce qu'il induit pour l'humain quant à la place donnée au regard et soustraite à la parole.[14]

Il tentait de mettre la société en mouvement tant au niveau social que juridique. On peut dire que la nouvelle loi de la protection de la jeunesse édictée en 1977 prenait en compte les points de vue nombreux qui découlaient de ses élaborations théoriques des processus psychiques à l'oeuvre chez ceux pour qui l'agir faisait symptôme.

La richesse qui émane de cette expérience professionelle n'aurait pas pris forme sans la personne même du Dr. Cormier. Son engagement comme signataire du *Refus global* est resté vivant en lui tout au long de sa vie, signifiant par là son désir d'être à la marge des idées reçues, d'être en bordure dans le décentrement qui peut laisser surgir la création artistique... ou le travail de l'inconscient.

Notes

1.   "Etudes de criminologie clinique," M. Colin, *et al.* (1963), Masson, ed. "La relation clinique en milieu pénitentiaire," J. Hochmann (1964), Masson, ed.

2.   *Evolution Psychiatrique* (1966) 37760, A. 30, p. 7, Alexander (1930).

3.   *Idem* (p. 5), Freud et Alexander, et Staub.

4.   Freud, *Totem et Tabou* (1913), Payot, 1972, p. 86.

5.   Ellenberger et Dongier, *Evolution Psychiatrique* (1966), 37760, A.30, p. 7.

6.   Aichhorn, *La Jeunesse à l'abandon* (1925).

7.   M. Klein, "Les Premiers stades du complexe oedipien,"*PuF* (1975), p. 15, "La Psychanalyse des enfants."

8.   *Acta Psychiatrica Belgica* (1970), pp. 103-153.

9.   Entre autres dans son article, "Expertise on dangerosity—a multidisciplinary approach," *Annales Int de criminologie* (1981), 19. 1. 2, pp. 167-183.

10.   "Psycho-dynamics of father-daughter incest," Cormier, B.M., M. Kennedy, J.M. Sangowicz in Proceedings of 12th Int. Course of Criminology, Jéruselem, September 1962, Vol. II, part 1, pp.14-54.

11.   "Inter-generational transmission of incest," Ingrid Cooper and Bruno M. Cormier, *Canadian J. Psychiatry*, Vol. 27, April 1982.

12.   "Longitudinal study of adolescent murderers," B.M. Cormier et Baila Markus, *Bulletin of the American Academy of Psychistry and the Law*, 8, (1980), pp. 240-260.

13.   "Rétaliation: épousailles de la haine ou écueil de l'amour," Renée Fugère, Yann Bogopolsky, Bruno M. Cormier, Communication présentée au Congrès de l'Association des Psychiatres du Canada, Montréal, P.Q., September 1982, "Considerations of the dynamics of Freud and shoplifting in adult female offenders," *Canadian J. of Psychiatry*, Vol. 40, April 1995.

14.   *The Watcher and the Watched* (1975), Bruno M. Cormier, Montréal, Tundra Books.

Yann Bogopolsky

As one door closes, another opens. So it was with the closing of the Forensic Clinic, for those of us privileged to have worked there. We all felt a need to carry on the work of Dr. Bruno Cormier, a man whose creative energy inspired us to learn and to develop. What I learned during that period, and later under Renée Fugère's tenure, remains with me in my work as an analyst and teacher.

It was in Nanterre that I began my university studies. I later enrolled at the Institut de Criminologie de Paris, where I was one of just four psychology students taking law courses. These included penal philosophy under Professor Michel Villey and newer, more humane approaches to treatment under Jacques Verin, at a time when incarceration was still considered an inevitable outcome for adult offenders in France.

I recall being puzzled by the extent to which our psychiatry courses discounted psychoanalysis. What they did cover was the range of conditions that could be present or come to light during the commission of an offence. Dr. Roumajon's psychology courses stressed the need to see offenders as individuals and not just as adjuncts to their crimes. Professor Jean Pinatel taught the history and doctrines of criminology. I remember being struck by, on the one hand, the work of Lombroso, who believed that certain individuals are born with criminal tendencies, and, on the other, that of Pinatel himself, who described a central core of the criminal personality. My studies in sociology were influenced by Jacques Selosse, whose work highlighted the degree to which behaviour is affected by the ability, or inability, to express oneself in words.

I completed these courses but found myself hungering for more than just theories and decided that my thesis subject would involve clinical work. I had heard of the Colin and Hochmann team, which was working in a prison setting in Lyon. At the time, Lyon seemed a long way from Paris. Little did I know that just a year later I would emigrate to Quebec, where I found many more opportunities for professional development.

I began my Canadian work experience as a criminologist at the Institut Philippe Pinel in Montreal. While employed there, I began auditing a course taught by Dr. Bruno Cormier and was allowed to sit in on interviews with prison inmates. Towards the end of the course, Dr. Cormier invited me to join the Forensic Clinic team. I realized at once what a great opportunity this was, not only in terms of my professional development but also as possible subject matter for a thesis. I chose, as my thesis subject, offender age and mid-life crisis, inspired by Dr. Cormier's extensive research during the 1950s and his focus on critical turning points in life. Pierrette Poncela, then an academic director at the Institut de Criminologie de Paris, kindly agreed to serve as my thesis adviser, even from across the ocean, as she was very familiar with Dr. Cormier's clinical work.

In the Sixties, there were very few psychoanalysts who had worked with offenders, although many since Freud had developed theories about the influence of the unconscious mind on criminal actions. Clinical criminology was struggling for recognition as a discipline distinct from psychology, psychiatry and psychoanalysis. Each field cast its own particular light on the origins of criminality and dangerousness. Early in the 1960s, Colin and Hochmann's team had launched their "studies in clinical criminology" with an article on diagnosing and treating dangerousness.

We were given free rein to find our own paths at the Forensic Clinic. When I started there I spent long hours in the office reading files and research papers, trying to get a sense of this ambitious project. The earliest of these papers was an article published in 1957 titled "Presentation of a Basic Classification for Clinical Work and Research in Criminality." What came to interest me particularly was hearing what offenders had to say about themselves, their backgrounds and their offences. Many of the elements involved took me back to the theories of Melanie Klein and Dr.

Cormier in this area, some of which are reflected in a French-language article published in 1970 in *Acta Psychiatrica Belgica* titled "Passage aux actes délictueux et états dépressifs" (Criminal Offenses and Depression).

One of Dr. Cormier's interests, from the outset of his psychiatric practice with inmates, was cases involving incest. Others worked along with him in this field, and I particularly remember Ingrid Cooper's work on the social, legal and inter-generational aspects of father-daughter incest. Dr. Cormier's interest in murderers focused on the way offenders objectify their victims. Baila Markus worked with him on a study of adolescent murderers, including parricides.

As a psychiatrist, Bruno Cormier was deeply committed to his work. He was an innovator, venturing into areas that others would have considered too controversial. The Dannemora Project, which was set up at a time when American prisons were facing inmate riots, was designed for the offenders seen by prison officials as the most dangerous, those having committed several murders. The project aimed to take into account the effects of incarceration on inmates.

Dr. Cormier worked for social and judicial change. His research influenced the 1977 legislative amendments in the area of child protection. The commitment he demonstrated as a signatory to *Refus global* remained with him throughout his life and was one more instance of how he challenged mainstream thinking in his field.

English Summary: Lesley Benderavage

Yann Bogopolsky *began her studies in Philosophy and Psychology, subsequently studying Criminology at the Institute of Criminology, Paris.*

After emigrating to Quebec, she worked at the McGill Clinic in Forensic Psychiatry from 1976 to 1984. She now works in France as a psychoanalyst in private practice and in institutions for youth who suffer behaviour misconduct. She is the supervisor of half-way houses for women and is a member of the French Association of Criminology.

Justin Ciale

"Criminology will fail to be a human science if it concerns itself only with crime. Beyond the symptom, the doctor is required to know the patient; beyond the crime, the criminologist must know the patient."

Cormier et al., 1959

 The road to Bruno Cormier's dream of humanizing imprisonment was beset by many obstacles. He was neither interested in empire-building nor concerned with erecting a mausoleum to commemorate his memory. He accepted inmates unconditionally as human beings. He respected their dignity and tried to make them understand why they had committed their criminal acts, thus enabling them to exercise their autonomy and live free from criminal impulses. This attitude was misinterpreted by penal authorities as the desire to dominate the application of penal sanctions. It was erroneous thinking on their part.

Bruno Cormier was born in humble circumstances. His father was a store manager. Bruno grew up in mid-town Montreal in an area characterized by cold-water flats. Residents sweltered in summertime and chilled their feet on cold linoleum in wintertime. A child of the Depression, he was raised in a neighbourhood where people were treated roughly, at times brutally, by the police, an area where people vacated their flats on the First of May, a tradition in Montreal during the 1930s when everyone moved either to escape a belligerent landlord or perhaps to seek a flat with more conveniences or one with cheaper rent.

It was a neighbourhood that bred armed robbers as well as social reformers and artists. The inhabitants argued in city parks on ways and means of changing social conditions that afflicted relatives, friends, and neighbours. Unemployment, disease, and poor

53

nutrition were the norm. Bruno witnessed not only the victims of poverty but also the victims of injustice. It oriented him towards the tortuous road to forensic medicine.

He had the misfortune of growing up in the 1930s, a repressive era in the province. Maurice Duplessis was the Premier of the Province; as Attorney General, he arbitrarily invoked the Padlock Law to shut down any establishment owned by people who expressed undesirable ideologies or who worshipped in religions he did not like—Communists and Jehovah's Witnesses, as well as bawdy-house keepers who refused to pay protection money. In Montreal, Camillien Houde was the mayor with connections to organized crime (Caron Report); over two hundred police officers were on the take.[1] It was the social conditions of the day that drove Bruno's creative spirit. It was a character trait that he would manifest for the rest of his life.

He was a revolutionary in the world of esthetics and art, one of the fearless signatories of Paul-Emile Borduas' *"Le Refus global,"* the manifesto of the Automatistes, published August 9, 1948 (Bourassa and Lapointe, 1988). He was a poet as well as a counsellor to that small group of artists who fought for freedom of expression in all its forms. *"Le Refus global"* was the harbinger of Jean Lesage's 1960 Quiet Revolution which unfettered Quebec's intellectuals from the shackles of clerical control.

Returning from a period of study in England, where he trained in psychoanalysis, he sought to establish a graduate program in psychiatry at the University of Montreal. Quebec doctors who sought post-graduate training in psychiatry preferred to study in Boston or Europe to complete their studies.[2] Memories die hard. University of Montreal officials rejected his application: They remembered him as one of the signatories of *"Le Refus global."* Fortunately for him and clinical criminology, McGill University, on the other side of Mount Royal, recognizing his potential appointed him Professor of Psychiatry. Within a year of his appointment as psychiatrist at Saint Vincent de Paul, he established a graduate program in clinical criminology at McGill. It became known as the

McGill University Clinic in Forensic Psychiatry. It was situated at 509 Pine Avenue West. It became a world-renowned institute.

Cormier came to the attention of Dr. Léo Gendreau, Deputy Commissioner of Penitentiaries in 1955. He was responsible for establishing medical services in Canadian penitentiaries. Cormier assumed his duties as penitentiary psychiatrist on November 1, 1955, but only after lengthy negotiations over conditions of employment. Before accepting his appointment, he insisted on the following conditions:

1. Psychiatric services should be accessible to all inmates.
2. There should be complete in-patient and out-patient services entirely autonomous from the penal administration.
3. The Canadian Penitentiary Services would respect his academic freedom and his work should be accessible to the university. He left in 1970, when the last condition failed to be respected by the CPS (LeBeuf & Gauthier, 1986).

His first encounter with his new quarters at Saint Vincent de Paul penitentiary was a flashback akin to Philippe Pinel's experience when he entered Bicêtre in Paris in 1793; Pinel recoiled with horror when he saw the inmates chained to the walls. His immediate reaction was to remove their chains (Zilboorg, 1941, p. 188).

Cormier's hospital was located below the penitentiary infirmary; it was an Auburn cell-block with back-to-back inside cells: dark, dank, humid, and reeking with the smell of feces and urine. There were several inmates occupying some of the cells at the time. They stared blankly at him, stunned at the visit of a stranger. One inmate was covered with his own excrement; it was the only pastime which inmates could indulge in to while away the hours incarcerated in their cells. The walls in the adjoining empty cells were covered with dried-out excrement which previous inmate-occupants had plastered on them. Each cell was furnished with a metal slatted bed and a sanitary bucket (toilet) standing in front of the barred doors. Most of the light came from opaque windows directly in front of the barred doors. Aeration was poor. Inmates were usually kept in their cells twenty-four hours a day.

The penitentiary doctor told Cormier, "This is your psychiatric hospital!" It was rumoured that he dispensed large doses of "number nine" pills to inmates who dared appear for sick parade in the morning. "Shit pills!" was how they were described.

It took Cormier's small staff over two weeks of scraping the walls and washing the cells with hot water mixed with heavy doses of detergent and soap to get rid of the odour and make the cells fit for human occupancy. The facilities were still primitive and far from meeting the standards recommended by the American Correctional Association. This condition had been allowed to persist for seventeen years after the Archambault Commission (1938) had recommended that psychiatrists should be assigned to every penitentiary to manage mentally disturbed inmates as well as mental defectives, and eight years after General Ralph Gibson (1947) had inaugurated penal reform in Canada based upon the Archambault Report.

Psychiatric facilities for the criminally insane in the district of Montreal were equally primitive in 1955. D Wing of La Prison de Montreal[3] (Bordeaux Jail) was the place where they warehoused mentally disturbed inmates. It was called the Bordeaux Asylum for the Criminally Insane. Male nurses, some of whom were actually reassigned prison guards, easily subdued a disturbed inmate by throwing a rolled-up wet towel around his throat. It had the effect of choking him within a matter of minutes; a strait-jacket was then applied to keep him quiet.

The arrangement between the Canadian Penitentiary Service and the Province of Quebec at the time stipulated that convicts who were declared insane within three months of their admission to the penitentiary were wards of the province; those who became mentally ill three months after their admission were a federal responsibility. An alienist would visit the inmate who had been referred to him by the doctor; he would declare the convict insane if he considered it valid, with a recommendation that he be transferred to Bordeaux Jail. The inmate languished often in his cell at Saint Vincent de Paul Penitentiary awaiting a transfer because it was always delayed by bureaucratic red tape pending a decision as to who should accept responsibility for the cost of maintaining him.[4]

Léo Gendreau was sensitive to this problem. He wanted to build medico-correctional institutions in every region of Canada so that CPS would assume the responsibility of treating mentally disturbed inmates. But that decision was a long way in the future, given that the government of the day (Treasury Board) was niggardly when it came to providing budgets for building correctional institutions; more so for building facilities for treating mentally disturbed inmates. At the time CPS, rather than build new facilities from scratch, converted unoccupied structures to fulfill its need. Late in 1956, headquarters decided to renovate the old keepers' hall, a two-story building, by converting it into a psychiatric and psychological centre to replace the psychiatric ward below the hospital infirmary.

The centre was destroyed during the June 1962 riot. Custodial staff accused Cormier of being one of the factors responsible for the riot because mentally disturbed inmates allegedly enjoyed special privileges resulting in a breakdown in discipline (Committee of Inquiry, 1962). Their complaints referred to the loss of "walking an inmate" (Jacobs, 1977) to the dissociation cells (punitive segregation or the hole) whenever he caused a disturbance. This was a baseless accusation and an example of scapegoating to restore power to custody staff.

The "temporary" facility was a haven laid out in the midst of Canada's largest maximum security prison (which had over 1,100 inmates at any one time). An ex-convict paid the treatment centre the supreme compliment. He called it "liberated zone." The ground floor was a unit with eighteen hospital cells, of which two were padded to accommodate inmates whenever they were self-destructive. Interviewing offices were on the second floor, as were the two large rooms for conducting group psychotherapy.

The centre operated as an active treatment hospital; in- patients were admitted and treated with a combination of medication, psychotherapy, and occupational therapy. Occupational therapy, given the constraints imposed within a penal institution, included pottery, weaving, painting, and leather work. An out-patient clinic offered inmates the opportunity to consult either the psychiatrist or the psychologist; the out-patient clinic also dispensed medication every morning to ambulatory patients (Cormier, 1959).

Gendreau stated that this was only a temporary facility, but he omitted putting a time frame to it. Early in 1960, Cormier got another jolt when he was refused one of the wings that he had been promised in the new facility, the Leclerc Institution being built next door to Saint Vincent de Paul Penitentiary. It would have been one of the first regional psychiatric centres.

By 1958, the CPS faced the serious problem of overpopulation in every region of Canada; it was most acute at Saint Vincent de Paul Penitentiary. There were many convicted offenders awaiting transfer from provincial detention centres and they were causing problems to provincial authorities who threatened to dump them at the front gates of the penitentiary unless federal authorities sped up the admission process.

In 1959, Davy Fulton, Minister of Justice, appointed Allan MacLeod, Chairman of the Correctional Planning Committee, charging him with the objective of developing an immediate plan to deal with the problem of overpopulation as well as implementing the recommendations of the Fauteux Committee's Report (1956). When MacLeod announced that his committee would visit Saint Vincent de Paul Penitentiary in the summer of 1959, he invited senior penitentiary staff to a meeting to consult them on future requirements. Cormier, facing the problem of managing mentally disturbed inmates in inadequate facilities, was keen on expressing his urgent need for new quarters. His expectation was high. He was sadly disappointed when MacLeod arrogantly declared at that meeting that his immediate concern was to find a method of liberating cells at Saint Vincent de Paul Penitentiary so that it could receive newcomers awaiting transfer to the penitentiary. This experience embittered Cormier. MacLeod became irritated, accusing psychiatry of trying to be the tail that wags the dog.

Cormier aroused MacLeod's animosity once more when the latter announced his ten-year prison construction program in 1962. The master plan called for the construction of multiple facilities in every region of Canada: minimum, medium, maximum, and super-maximum security institutions. Overall the plan was a good thing. But the designs for the proposed super-maximum institution (the Special Correctional Unit) and the proposed maximum security institution (the Archambault Institution) in the Quebec region were deemed unacceptable as facilities for carrying out rehabilitation programs.

Cormier and Ciale led the opposition against these proposed designs. The designs were rejected on numerous grounds:

1. The maximum security design featured an increased number of locking devices, reducing opportunities for interaction between staff and inmates considered essential for creating a correctional atmosphere.
2. It featured separate passageways for inmates and guards, potentially increasing the alienation between staff and inmates.
3. It featured four domes, one of which would operate as a main control of inmate movement, again increasing the ubiquitous sentiment of being "watched" from above.
4. The living units contained over fifty cells, a number considered too large to implement therapeutic communities, according to Maxwell Jones' (1953) treatment modality.
5. Since its location was approximately forty-five miles away from the city, it was not conducive to form convenient links with university departments which might have had an interest in using the facility for teaching and research purposes.

6. The super-maximum security design featured window-less cells, a principle that had been condemned by the 1938 Royal Commission.

7. Every cell in the super-maximum design had a large window in the ceiling which allowed a guard patrolling on a raised catwalk above to "watch" the inmate inside; his privacy was subject to involuntary violation twenty-four hours a day.

Cormier and Ciale were not alone in opposing the proposed program. Bill McGrath, Executive-Director of the Canadian Corrections Association, and his Board of Directors joined the campaign to fight against building these monstrous prisons as soon as they became aware of the constraints these designs imposed on carrying out rehabilitative inmate programs.

In the summer of 1965, Cormier and Ciale, in a last-ditch effort to prevent the building of these two institutions in the Quebec region, joined a large delegation organized by McGrath that met with Guy Favreau, Minister of Justice, in Ottawa. The delegation assembled many professional associations, including the Canadian Psychiatric Association, the Canadian Psychological Association, the Canadian Association of Social Workers, and the Canadian Bar Association, amongst others. Favreau listened carefully to petitions calling for a halt to the construction of these prisons. Although he was sympathetic to the pleas expressed by the delegation, he declared that since the contracts had already been awarded to build the SCU at Saint Vincent de Paul, Archambault Institution at Sainte-Anne des Plaines, and Millhaven Institution in Ontario, it would be too costly to cancel those contracts.

To appease the angry delegation, Favreau declared that he would appoint the Canadian Committee on Corrections (the Ouimet Committee) to examine the criminal justice system with special emphasis on the process of designing penal institutions and the requirements for the treatment of offenders in keeping with the standard minimum rules advocated by the United Nations.

In 1967, the Canadian Committee on Corrections (1969) succeeded in persuading the government to appoint a Joint Committee of the Senate and the House of Commons to examine the penitentiary plans and correctional treatment. After several months of hearings, the Joint Committee concluded by recommending a moratorium on construction of super-maximum and maximum security institutions based on existing CPS designs.

By 1970, owing to the need for maximum security cells by CPS and to develop a maximum security design acceptable to the correctional community, Jean Pierre Goyer, the Solicitor General appointed the Mohr Committee (Canada, 1971) to develop an alternate design for maximum security institutions.

CPS implemented the recommendations of the Mohr Report (Canada, 1971) by building the Kent Institution at Harrison Hot Springs and the Sharpe Institution in Edmonton. Both these maximum security institutions respected the principles of the Mohr Report. Small in size (not greater than 300 inmates), they provided for living units assembling less than twenty inmates; neither had a dome around which every inmate must pass. There were other desirable features which shall remain unmentioned.

Although the Quebec region, to Cormier's everlasting chagrin, would be stuck with both the SCU, now a Special Handling Unit,[5] and the Archambault Institution for the next fifty years, he played a key role in successfully halting the construction of Archambault-Millhaven type institutions in other regions of Canada, as well as condemning the construction of super-maximum security institutions. He made the correctional community aware of the evils of sensory deprivation, the stifling boredom and paranoia, the natural result of imprisonment in concrete wombs bereft of human contact. He aroused the correctional community to take action and compelled bureaucrats to take another look at the process of building maximum and super-maximum security institutions.

Cormier was a pioneer in clinical criminology in Canada; it was a new discipline at the time; he defined it as integrating all available knowledge for the purpose of diagnosis, prognosis and treatment of the offender.

In pursuit of that goal, he organized the first Conference on Current Research that was held at the Federal Training Centre in Saint Vincent de Paul, March 13-14, 1959. The participants were the Department of Psychiatry, McGill University, the treatment team of Saint Vincent de Paul Penitentiary, and the treatment team of Kingston Penitentiary. The McGill University team included Miriam Kennedy, social worker, Michel Trottier, psychologist, Jadwiga Sangowicz, psychiatrist; the Saint Vincent de Paul treatment team included Justin Ciale, Marcel Fréchette, and André Thiffault, psychologists; the Kingston Penitentiary treatment team included George Scott, psychiatrist, Maurice Gauthier and Joseph Csank, psychologists. It marked the beginning of a long tradition.

The success of the first conference incited the organizers to add an extra day to the Second Conference (May 4-7, 1960), as well as invite professors from several faculties of the University of Montreal to participate. Two years later, the Quebec Society of Criminology assumed the responsibility of organizing the Third Research Conference (November 20-24, 1962); thereafter conferences were scheduled on a biennial basis.

By 1964, the research conference became an anticipated event in the scientific world of criminology. It included researchers from McGill, Montreal, and Toronto Faculty of Law, the faculties of Psychology of Montreal and McGill, the treatment teams of McGill, Saint Vincent de Paul Penitentiary, the Clarke Institute of Psychiatry, the clinical staff of Boscoville, a juvenile treatment centre, as well as social agency workers from Montreal and Toronto. Senior officials from the National Parole Board and the Canadian Penitentiary Service attended these conferences.

Cormier presented his "Basic Classification for Research and Clinical Work in Criminology" at the First Conference on Research (Cormier et al., 1959). It was a brilliant synthesis that integrated personality theory (Freud's structure of the psychic apparatus), psychopathology, patterns of criminal behaviour, of a repetitive, episodic or incidental nature, as well as the age of onset of criminal behaviour (linked with Erikson's developmental stages (Erikson, 1950). Equally important in the observation schedule were the frequency and duration of the offender's pattern of criminal behaviour. The degree of ego awareness of feeling either guilt, disgust, shame, or fear for committing a criminal act was another factor. Basically it was and is a frame of reference useful to systematize clinical observations.

His method adhered to the hypothetico-deductive process of generating hypotheses and testing and refining them through continual experimentation. But in contrast to the experimentalist in the laboratory who has quasi-total control of his variables, Cormier could only control his method of observing his clients, inmates, ex-inmates, and clients with criminal tendencies seeking treatment. Errors are corrected by continual clinical observations as are confirmation of hypotheses.

The classification yields several types of delinquents:

1. Primary delinquency is a fixated pattern of delinquency that begins in latency, continues into adolescence, and transforms itself into persistent adult criminality.
    Offenders of this type are called primary delinquents.
2. Secondary delinquency is a fixated pattern of delinquent behaviour which begins in adolescence and, like the type above, transforms itself into persistent adult criminality.
    Offenders of this type are called secondary delinquents.
3. Late delinquency is a fixated pattern of criminal behaviour which begins after maturity without any significant early history of delinquency. There are three subtypes within this class: Those with persistent patterns of criminal behaviour are called late delinquents; those who recidivate but have significant crime-free periods between offences are called episodic offenders; those with incidental patterns of criminal offences are called late offenders.

It was a first and unique Canadian construction that oriented Cormier's research team for the next three decades. There were precursors, of course, that guided him to create this remarkable typology. The follow-up studies of Eleanor and Sheldon Glueck (1930, 1937) on aging and maturation of offenders, persistence of criminal patterns, and careers inspired him to extend their work. Following in their footsteps, he used the same methodology; he partitioned items for analysis gleaned through interviews and submitted every one to statistical analysis using the chi-square to tease out insights.

Raymond Boyer a former professor of chemistry at McGill University, was his statistical consultant. Because of his interest in criminology, Boyer wrote two fascinating books, the first describing life at Saint Vincent de Paul Penitentiary in the modern era (Boyer, 1966), the second tracing punishment during Quebec's early days (Boyer, 1972).

Two books that deeply influenced Cormier's outlook on penology and corrections were Sutherland and Cressey, *Principles of Criminology* and Barnes and Teeters, *New Horizons in Criminology*. He thoroughly identified with Thorsten Sellin's *Humanity, Scholarship and Diligence* (1976).

He was also conversant with sociological studies by Clemmer (1940) on the prison community, Sykes' (1958) social system and prisoners' roles, Sykes and Messenger's (1960) inmate subculture and the pain of incarceration, Goffman's (1961) modes of adjustment to total institutions and relationships between staff and inmates. He was equally conversant with the psychiatric literature, Guttmacher's (1960) study on the murderer and his motivation, Karpman's sexual offender and his offences (1954), among many others. He was very sympathetic to Marguerite Q. Warren's interpersonal maturity levels and differential treatment which bore resonance to his basic classification (Warren, 1966, 1977).

But his interest lay in developing a diagnostic tool and linking it with an appropriate treatment modality. His fundamental approach was one of unconditional acceptance of the offender-inmate. It was an approach that shunned the use of force to control a disturbed inmate. He was like the doctor who facing a mysterious bacteria was unyielding in his probing until he discovered the source of the infection and found an antidote. He sought methods that would allow him to cure patients who suffered from the stresses and strains that bedeviled and disturbed their mental equilibrium.

By 1964, Montreal had become a world centre in criminological teaching and research: Father Noel Mailloux, O.P., directed the Institute of Psychology at the University of Montreal; he was also clinical director of Boscoville and le Centre d'orientation de Montréal. Denis Szabo had recently established the Department of Criminology (1960). Bruno Cormier was well engaged in research at the McGill Forensic Clinic and at Saint Vincent de Paul Penitentiary. Together they were a driving force in extending an invitation to the American Society of Criminology to hold its annual meeting in Montreal in December 1964 (Reckless and Newman, 1965).

They had also succeeded in inviting the International Society of Criminology to hold its Quinquennial Congress in Montreal in 1965, the first time the society had approved a North American site.

He was an equal-opportunities employee. His clinical research team at Saint Vincent de Paul included Miriam Kennedy and Dr. Jadwiga Sangowicz. He practised that same policy when the McGill Forensic Clinic expanded its personnel in the 1960s.

With Miriam Kennedy, he pioneered some of the first clinical studies on family offences at a time when this was a taboo subject. In those days, people whispered in hushed tones when talking about incest; it was a conspiracy of silence. It was not unlike whispering about a family that had a family member, either a schizophrenic or a manic-depressive, removed to an insane asylum. Miriam Kennedy was a Social Worker and team member who had written widely on patterns of incestuous relationships; her findings are valid today for those who are interested in acquiring knowledge in diagnosing and treating problem families.

Cormier's policy towards the crime of incest went against the current politically correct trend of banishing the sexual offender to a penal institution. His preference was to refer the whole family, victim(s), and aggressor to a community clinic; it was his opinion that condemning an offender to a penal institution created more problems for everyone concerned.

His intuitive spirit enabled him to empathize with inmates and understand their paranoid reactions and accompanying terror; more often the paranoia was a valid reaction on the part of inmates. Many stole dinner trays to be used as armor underneath their shirts as protection against would-be attackers or knife-wielding aggressors during the walk to and from work, to lunch, or back to their cells (Laflamme, 1991).

The frequent prison disturbances, some of which were quite violent in the late 1950s and early 1960 at Bordeaux Jail, provoked a great deal of turmoil to provincial prison administrators and raised a public outcry for solutions (Hebert, 1959); recall that an entire wing of the jail was a facility for the criminally insane.

Given the crisis of the moment, the Provincial Attorney General appointed the Mailloux Committee[6] to investigate the situation and propose recommendations to remedy the problem of frequent riots at Bordeaux Jail. The Mailloux Committee was quick to condemn the multiple functions[7] for which Bordeaux Jail was called upon to fulfill and for which it was not designed to do. Moreover, the custodial personnel were untrained in corrections, the majority of whom had been hired because a relative or a friend knew the sheriff of Montreal who was responsible for hiring people. Some were former provincial police constables.

At the same time, the Commission for Investigation of Psychiatric Hospitals Committee created in 1961 also condemned the deplorable condition within Bordeaux Jail. It recommended the immediate and urgent construction of a new hospital; the

Commission added that it should be built on a site away from Bordeaux Jail (Gervais, 1965). The Commission appointed a working committee composed of Drs. Bruno Cormier, Camile Laurin, and Lucien Panaccio who were charged with the task of formulating a policy and an organization for the new hospital. The hospital should admit only those patients presenting severe behaviour disorders, including those who presented dangerous or criminal behaviour which had proved uncontrollable after all therapeutic methods in ordinary psychiatric institution had been tried. It should conduct the most up-to-date therapies and be oriented towards the rehabilitation of patients; it should be affiliated with universities to provide training to students from different faculties in the field of medico-legal psychiatry.

The Ministry of Health acted with celerity in proceeding to the construction of L'Institut Philippe Pinel. The Institute began receiving its first patients-inmates in 1969.

Ciale met Bruno Cormier for the last time at the annual meeting of the American Society of Criminology in Montreal in 1987. He showed no signs that he was ill and had only a few more years to live. His eyes were still bright, his complexion healthy-looking. News of his passing away several years later after came as a shock, more so because Ciale was unable to attend Bruno's funeral in Montreal.

Cormier was small in stature, about five feet two inches tall. Inmates towered above him, yet none repelled or frightened him because of viciousness, crimes, or attempts to manipulate or intimidate him. No pejorative or opprobrious label, such as psychopath, dangerous offender, or con, ever escaped his lips. He was loved and respected by all who came in contact with him. It is a tragedy that the Canadian Penitentiary Service did not provide him the opportunity to set up a therapeutic community in the Saint Vincent de Paul region. Sadly, he had to go to another country to prove its worth as a therapeutic modality (Cormier, 1975). It is ironic that both John Kidman, who wrote *The Canadian Prison:*

The Story of a Tragedy (1947), and Bruno Cormier experienced a similar fate. Kidman was the principal driving force that established the Canadian Penal Association in 1935 (Ciale, 1998). It moved the government to appoint the Royal Commission Investigating the Penal System of Canada (Archambault Commission) in 1936, the Bible of Canadian penal reform.

Cormier deserves a place in the pantheon of stars for his contribution to the psychology of the individual experiencing the terror and trauma of incarceration: for his work on aging and maturity; his monumental book, *The Watcher and the Watched* deserves close reading by all correctional workers who plan to work in prison settings.

Justin Ciale, *Ph.D., Emeritus Professor, Department of Criminology, University of Ottawa, 1989. Director, Department of Criminology, University of Ottawa, 1981-1988; Interim Director, 1987-1988; Professor of Criminology, 1971-1981; Director of Research, Solicitor General of Canada, 1968-1981; Senior lecturer and Assistant Professor, Department of Criminology, Université de Montréal, 1963-1968; Consultant Psychologist, La Société d'orientation et de réhabilitation sociale, 1961-1963: Doctoral Studies, Université de Montréal, 1963-1968; Psychologist, St. Vincent de Paul Penitentiary (with Dr. Bruno Cormier), 1955-1960; Armed Forces, Canadian Artillery, 1941-1946.*

Notes

1. According to the late Leo Plouffe of the Sûreté de Montréal, it was rumoured that Houde preferred seeing French-Canadian girls coming to Montreal giving pleasures to men in the red-light district, where they picked up easy money, rather than seeing them exploited in sweat shops in the garment industry. Houde had concluded a deal with a Mr. Lupo (Wolf) to ensure that the brothels would remain open.

2. The late Father Bernard Mailhiot, O.P., once stated to the author in a personal communication that the administration of the

University of Montreal had refused a $75 million grant from the Ford Foundation in the immediate postwar era. The University was free to administer the scholarship fund as it saw fit, the only condition being that the recipients would have had to acknowledge that they had received a Ford Foundation grant whenever they decided to publish any results. The administration refused it, declaring that the University was a professional school and not a research organization.

3. Montreal Prison in 1960 was mainly a provincial prison for incarcerating convicts sentenced to one day up to two years less a day (Prisons and Reformatory Act); it also served as a remand centre, a detention centre for those awaiting transfer to the penitentiary, a detention centre for escapees from juvenile training institutions, a centre for carrying out executions in the District of Montreal, and a hospital for the criminally insane.

4. It should be pointed out that sentences of two years or more are served in penitentiaries while sentences of one day up to two years less a day are served in provincial prisons.

5. The Special Handling Unit holds in custody those who require administrative segregation. Jacques Mesrine and Coco Mercier attacked this institution in the mid-1970s. Mercier was killed in a shoot-out with the Police in Montreal. Mesrine was killed in Paris in the Spring of 1978 in an ambush set up by the police.

6. Justin Ciale, psychologist with la Société d'orientation et de réhabilitation sociale, and Steven Cumas, Executive Director of the John Howard Society of Quebec, were members of this committee.

7. Refer to note 3 (above).

Bibliography

Barnes, E.H., Teeters, N.K. (1959). *New Horizons in Criminology.* Englewood Cliffs, N.J.: Prentice-Hall, Inc. Third Edition.

Borduas, P.E., (1977). *Refus global, projections libérantes.* Montreal: Les éditions Partis Pris.

Bourassa, A., Lapointe, G. (1988). *Refus global et ses environs.* Montreal: Editions Hexagone.

Boyer, R. (1966). *Les crimes et les châtiments au Canada français du XVIIe siècle au XXe siècle.* Montreal: Cercle du livre de France.

Boyer, R. (1972). *Barreaux de fer, hommes de chair.* Montreal: Editions du jour.

Canada. (1938). *Report of the Royal Commission to Investigate the Penal System of*

Canada (Archambault Report). Ottawa: King's Printer. Canada

Canada. (1956). *Report of a Committee Appointed to Inquire into the Principles and Procedures Followed in the Remission Service of the Department of Justice of Canada* (Fauteux Committee Report). Ottawa. Queen's Printer and Controller of Stationery.

Canada. (1960). "Report of the Correctional Planning Committee of the Department of Justice: Summary of Recommendations" (MacLeod Report). Ottawa: Unpublished.

Canada. (1967). *Report of the Special Joint Committee of the Senate and House of Commons on Penitentiaries.* Ottawa: Queen's Printer and Controller of Stationery.

Canada. (1977). *Report of the Sub-Committee on the Penitentiary System* (MacGuigan Report). Ottawa: Queens Printer.

Canada. (1971). *Design of Federal Maximum Security Institutions* (Mohr Report). Ottawa: Department of the Solicitor General.

Canada. (1979). *Report of the Canadian Committee on Corrections* (Ouimet Report). Ottawa: Department of the Solicitor General.

Canadian Penitentiary Service. (1962). "Committee Inquiring into Disturbance and Fire at the Saint Vincent de Paul Penitentiary, June 17-18, 1962." Ottawa: Unpublished Document.

Ciale, J. (1997). *Tales of Saint Vincent de Paul Penitentiary.* Ottawa: Legas.

Ciale, J. (1998). *The Contribution of the Canadian Penal Association to the Penal Policy in Canada.* Ottawa: Legas. (In press).

Clemmer, D. (1940). *The Prison Community.* New York: Holt, Rinehart and Winston, Inc.

Cormier, B.M (1959). "The Psychiatric Hospital in a Maximum Security Hospital." *The Canadian Journal of Corrections.* 1, (4). pp. 3-14.

Cormier, B.M. (1959). "Some Rights, Duties and Responsibilities in Penology and Suggested Changes." *The Canadian Journal of Corrections.* 1, (4). pp. 70-79.

Cormier, B.M. (Ed.). (1975). *The Watcher and the Watched.* Montreal: Tundra Books.

Cormier, B.M., Kennedy, M., Sangowicz, J., Trottier, M. (1959). "Presentation of a Basic Classification for Clinical Work and Research in Criminality." *The Canadian Journal of Criminology.* 1, (4). pp. 21-34.

Erikson, E.E. (1950). *Childhood and Society.* New York: Norton.

Gervais, L. (1965). "Philippe Pinel Institute." In *Proceedings of the 4th Research Conference on Delinquency and Criminology.* Montreal: Quebec Society of Criminology and L'Institut Philippe Pinel.

Gibson, R.B. (1947). *Commission on the Penitentiary System of Canada.* Ottawa: King's Printer.

Glueck, S., Glueck, E. (1930). *Five Hundred Criminal Careers.* New York: A.A. Knopf.

Glueck, S., Glueck, E. (1937). *Later Criminal Careers.* New York: Kraus Reprint Corporation.

Goffman, E. (1961). *Asylums.* New York: Anchor Books.

Guttmacher, M. (1960). *The Mind of the Murderer.* New York: Farrar, Straus and Cudahy.

Hebert, J. (1959). *Scandale à Bordeaux.* Montreal: Edition de l'homme.

Jacobs, J.J. (1977). *Stateville, The Penitentiary in Mass Society.* Chicago: University of Chicago Press.

Jones, M. (1953). *The Therapeutic Community.* New York: Basic Books, Inc.

Karpman, B. (1954). *The Sexual Offender and his Offenses.* New York: Julian Press, Inc.

Kidman, J. (1947). *The Canadian Prison: the Story of Tragedy.* Toronto: Ryerson Press

Laflamme, A. (1991). *Creation d'un criminel: récit autobiographique.* Ottawa: Les Editions du Vermillon

LeBeuf, M.E., Gauthier, D. (1986). *Penser la criminologie: propos recueillis sur 25 ans de criminologie au Quebec.* Montreal: Ecole de Criminologie, Université de Montréal.

Reckless, W., Newman, C.L. (1965). *Interdisciplinary Problems in Criminology: Papers of the American Society of Criminology, 1964.* Columbus, Ohio: The College of Commerce and Administration.

Sellin, J. T. (1976). *Humanity, Scholarship and Diligence.* New York: Elsevier Scientific Publication Company, Inc.

Sutherland, E.H., Cressey, D.R. (1960). *Principles of Criminology.* Chicago: J.B. Lippincott Company. Sixth Edition.

Sykes, G., Messinger, S. (1960). *Inmate Social Systems.* Social Sciences Research Council pamphlet.

Sykes, G.M. (1958). *The Society of Captives.* Princeton, N.J.: Princeton University Press.

Warren, M.Q. (1966). "Classification of Offenders as an Aid to Efficient Management and Effective Treatment." Mimeographed Document Prepared for the President's Commission on Law Enforcement and Administration of Justice, Task Force on Corrections.

Warren, M.Q. (1977). *Correctional Treatment in Community Settings: a Report of Current Research.* Rockville, Md.: National Institute of Mental Health. Superintendent of Docs., US Govt. Print Office, Washington.

Zilboorg, G. (1941). *The History of Medical Psychology.* New York: Norton.

Renée Fugère

Bruno never asked me to
do anything he himself would not do.

 It was my curiosity about Bruno Cormier's connection to the arts as well as his reputation as a forensic psychiatrist that led to our initial meeting.

I had been trained in the late 1970s in the Department of Psychiatry at Laval University in Quebec City. After a few rotations, and at the suggestion of two senior psychiatrists in that city, I decided to focus my sights on forensic psychiatry. The doctors, being clinicians rather than academically oriented, observed that the forensic field was not as developed locally as it was elsewhere in the province. It would be worthwhile, they said, to pursue that course. Seeing as I had my eye on a future appointment in Quebec, I could train wherever I chose, then return to the city and develop a program there. They recommended I visit three places. The first was the Philippe Pinel Institution in Montreal, the hospital responsible for providing psychiatric services for mentally disordered patients who had committed a crime and were found not guilty by reason of insanity. Also on the list was a good program offered by the University of Toronto, and Dr. Cormier's clinic at McGill, described to me as being "the English equivalent to Pinel."

After visiting them all, I applied to McGill University's program in psychiatry as a resident in psychiatry. On what did I base my choice? For me it was a combination of intuition and curiosity. I was quite confident in my ability as a general psychiatrist and a therapist. I felt my training in Quebec was solid and that time and experience would expand the knowledge I would need in the future. What piqued my curiosity was Bruno himself. I knew very little about him as a psychiatrist except that I had been told he was the Father of Forensic Psychiatry in Canada. Anyone taking on the challenge of building a field had to be exceptionally knowledgeable and a visionary, as well, I reasoned. At that point, my own vision was very narrow. I saw forensic as the interaction between law and psychiatry concerning mentally ill people involved in committing crimes. I restricted my definition of mental illness to suffering from a psychosis and/or affective illness. It never occurred to me that there was a whole field of personality disorders or that forensic, rather than being limited to criminal forensic psychiatry, also included civil aspects, correctional forensic psychiatry, ethics, dangerousness and the making of laws, policies and programs. Because I was not trained to be an academic, neither had I given much thought to research or teaching.

Aside from what I knew of Bruno's professional interests, I was aware of his devotion to the arts. I knew he was one of the signatories to the *Refus global*, an anti-clerical manifesto that had raised a storm of controversy during the Duplessis era and given birth to Montreal's Automatiste movement. I was fascinated by those years and eager to hear about them first-hand from someone who had been part of the history. To me that was better than simply reading books.

Our first encounter was an emotional one. Bruno was the third psychiatrist to interview me for the selection process, the third one to sift through the details of my longitudinal history, the third one whose interpretation of my life and evaluation of me could prove unsettling, even destabilizing. I entered his office prepared to put my foot down and reverse the interview tables. This time I would ask the questions. He smiled at my tactic and played along, explaining why he believed McGill rather than the University of Montreal or Toronto should be my choice. Well, he passed the test and the rest of the time in his company went rather smoothly. I trusted him. He respected my privacy and accepted my blunt remarks. He was even able to contain my arrogant attitude that I would work with him not exclusively for what he could teach me as a mentor, but as someone who could also broaden my views of Quebec history, painting, and modern art.

I was introduced to a few of my colleagues, including social worker Baila Markus and, later, Ingrid Thompson-Cooper, a professor of social work, and criminologist Yann Bobopolsky.

I trained with Bruno from 1980 to 1982. During my first year I learned how to assess different types of individuals involved in various crimes. We would receive a substantial number of new referrals, a reflection of the fact that Bruno was the only psychiatrist combining administrative directorship with clinical and academic leadership. Also, our staff was limited. The other psychiatrist saw private patients, having relinquished the clinical side of his work after a period of involvement. We had one research assistant, hired with private funds remaining from unused grant money, who saw patients clinically; one social worker from Ville Marie Social Services, who devoted most of her time to clinical matters; and one McGill-based social worker involved in the training of field placement students. Until the mid-1980s, we had two full-time secretaries who were kept constantly busy due to our tremendous number of new and on-going cases. Over the period of a year it was routine for us to assess more than one hundred and fifty new cases for reports dealing with issues of responsibility, sentencing, and progressive versus full-parole considerations. These patients had to be seen on the premises where they were to serve their time or where they were detained while awaiting trial. Since the clinic's mandate was to provide service not only for court-related issues and administration of sentences, but also to treat the individuals, a great deal of flexibility in the professionals' schedules was required.

During my first year of training I was exposed to a large number of individuals and received intensive supervision. For every case, all the history and data analyses would be discussed with Bruno and either supported or corrected by him. We normally received cases at the beginning of court procedures and would follow them through the criminal proceedings. The sheer variety of problems gave me broad exposure to the field of penal forensic psychiatry. For a trainee such experience was unique. The approach at the clinic (the clinic being Bruno in our minds) went far beyond psychiatry. Rather, it combined various disciplines, each contributing to an understanding of the human being that was considerably more comprehensive than what psychiatry alone could reveal. I am referring specifically to sociology, anthropology, social work, psychoanalysis, and clinical criminology.

Bruno often repeated his philosophy to me and other students arriving to be trained at the clinic: "To practise forensic psychiatry, it is not sufficient to be a psychiatrist. We need to know much more than the average professional. The clientele we serve has many needs that can't be answered through one single mode of intervention or just one theoretical model. To be effective, we have to be creative in our recommendations." Living with this philosophy, I not only consolidated my knowledge in general psychiatry, I also learned how to analyze the longitudinal aspects of a criminal career, how to assess the subtleties of dangerousness, and how to analyze a delictual state by taking into account its phenomenological aspects.

Every patient we saw was assessed extensively and understood from a global perspective. We studied each one as an individual with his own psychology and psychiatric problems, as a perpetrator whose particular offence could be examined through clinical criminology and as a citizen whose culture was part of a society. We looked at how that citizen interacted within his entire social network, from family to community to North American society at large. This latter we would compare to the culture of his family's country of origin.

This first year of training was very rich and stimulating, although I felt the pressure of there being so much to learn and so little time to integrate it all. Aside from the clinical work, which sometimes took as much as 80 and even 90 hours a week, we were asked to reflect on research proposals and presentations of papers. And, if time allowed, we were reminded not to forget about publication. With our limited staff, we were busy days, nights, and weekends. Our secretaries never had a free moment.

Learning with Bruno was not easy. He was a high achiever with a brilliant mind and obsessive traits in his personality. He also had an idiosyncratic way of talking and not infrequently people on the receiving end had to struggle to decipher what he meant. In essence, he spoke in free associations, calling in references from his vast knowledge of other disciplines. Unless you knew him well, or knew as much as he did, or made your own attempt at free association, the end result could be utter confusion.

Bruno never asked me to do anything he himself would not do. I took it for granted that, not having his experience or knowledge, I had to work harder, but despite my deserved reputation as a workaholic, I more than met my match in him. I could not always understand why we had to work as much as we did. It was never enough. I was left with a keen sense of limitation as my complaints evoked neither guidance nor sympathy. I could not expect praise either, since Bruno felt we should all be content doing what we have to do. For him that was reward enough. In retrospect, I would say this was his way of considering someone a mature worker, self-sufficient, confident, able to set his or her own limitations.

There were some fights between us that first year. Essentially they related to the writing of reports and my lack of understanding of what he expected of me. I can testify that he was the only teacher I ever had who was able to tolerate my most intense feelings of discontent. I could approach him with anger, even fury. He never lost his objectivity or his capacity to respond humanistically. He was also quite willing and able to admit any responsibility he may have had for my outbursts.

Much to my surprise, in February, 1981, mid-way in my training, Bruno approached me to do an extra year of training with him. This opportunity was equivalent to a Fellow and it came with an irresistible proposal: a position at the clinic. To say I was excited is an understatement. I jumped at the offer and, after my certification, was accepted on staff at the Allan Memorial Institute. I continued to work under Bruno's directorship until 1988. We were constantly busy, more often than not, putting our mandate to offer clinical services ahead of publishing papers. We did make our opinions known, however, at conferences world-wide, where we presented on a variety of topics in psychiatry, criminology, and mental health. On a number of occasions we were invited to speak publicly on issues relating to society's hardening attitudes towards rehabilitation. The ever-harsher decisions of sentencing judges ran counter to the approach favoured by Bruno and his colleagues, an approach based on extensive research studies among sexual offenders in particular. We added our names to a petition against the Port-Cartier Institution, which we believed did not meet the best clinical rehabilitation standards or serve society's needs, but had been built solely through political expediency.

At the clinic, our workload grew steadily heavier as the first cutbacks began. Bruno supported our Ville Marie social worker in her battle to preserve her job, which had already been reduced to a part-time position. That she was permitted to retain her part-time status is a credit to the woman's fierce determination to remain at the clinic and pursue her clinical work as a therapist there. What was so commendable in Bruno's attitude was the respect he showed for each worker, regardless of training. On more than one occasion, professionals who did not work with us hinted that he was totalitarian, something of a dictator. I respectfully disagreed. Strongly opinionated, yes, but Bruno was fair enough to consider any point of view that was shared with him or the staff.

We continued to be involved at the Allan Memorial throughout the 1980s, offering residents an introduction to forensic psychiatry. Through our teaching, we hoped to be able to recruit future candidates for the clinic. Those were the years I witnessed a growing interest in forensic concerns. McGill's Department of Psychiatry became eager to expand its Diploma Course program for residents by establishing a core block of teaching in forensic, ethical issues, and quality assurance. This became a *fait accompli* in 1993 and was the first of its kind in Canada.

In the late 1980s, cuts by McGill and the Allan began to seriously affect clinic operations. A series of losses decimated our staff: the university secretary, the research assistant, the social worker, one full-time hospital secretary—all gone. During those difficult times, Bruno never felt discouraged. Or, if he did, he never showed it. He continued to defend the importance of our work, pointing out the uniqueness of our approach, the potential we offered for training and research, and how well our service complemented the mandate of the Philippe Pinel Institute.

He envisaged taking progressive retirement while still remaining on staff. At this point, from 1987 to 1991, I became his acting director and, in 1988, director of the clinic. In effect, our roles were now reversed. At this late stage of his career, Bruno continued to see patients for treatment purposes, but would also take time off to pursue his writing projects. He continued at the clinic longer than he had anticipated, due largely to my unsuccessful efforts to secure the appointment of one or two candidates to our staff. The Allan Memorial Institute, it appears, had other, more urgent needs to address. Bruno worked on a paper right up to the very end. The paper was published after his death in the *Canadian Journal of Psychiatry.*

Bruno Cormier was an original: innovative, creative, and visionary. He was committed to a humanistic approach in the understanding and treatment of offenders. He believed strongly in the potential of each individual to change. He treasured and defended freedom of speech and thought. I can count at least sixty new concepts in clinical criminology that he was responsible for developing during his career. Fortunately he worked during an era that was open to the acceptance of new disciplines. This period saw the growth of such forensic legal services as legal aid, probation, and improved medical and psychiatric treatment in penal institutions.

In my opinion, the impact of Bruno's thinking on more than one generation of professionals is still under-recognized. This is not an intentional slight, but due largely to a limited perspective in the longitudinal transmission of knowledge and the tendency towards homogenization in present-day thinking, particularly in psychiatry. I agree with Bruno that if forensic psychiatry is to survive and thrive, it will need to see itself in much larger terms than it does at the moment. University programs in forensic psychiatry will have to revert to a teaching approach that is less compartmentalized, more multi-disciplinarian. As Bruno used to say: "In the practice of forensic psychiatry, to be a psychiatrist is not enough ..."

Renée Fugère, *M.D, FRCP(C), Assistant Professor, Department of Psychiatry, McGill University, 1993-present.*

Senior Psychiatrist, Allan Memorial Institute, Director, McGill Clinic in Forensic Psychiatry, 1988-1997; Acting Director, McGill Clinic in Forensic Psychiatry, 1987-1988; Assistant Director, 1982-1987; Resident in Psychiatry, McGill Clinic in Forensic Psychiatry, 1980-1981; Certification in Psychiatry, 1981; Fellow in Psychiatry, 1981-1982.

Pierre Gagné

Cet homme extraordinaire à la réputation internationale
était demeuré d'une simplicité admirable.

 Vingt-cinq ans se sont déjà écoulés depuis ma première rencontre avec le professeur Bruno Cormier. J'étais résident en troisième année de psychiatrie au Clarke Institute à Toronto. C'est à l'initiative de mes professeurs du temps, Basil Orchard, Robert Coulthard et le regretté Ken McKnight que j'avais sollicité une rencontre avec le Docteur Cormier pour explorer la possibilité de faire une année de spécialisation en "Forensic Psychiatry." On me l'avait présenté comme celui qui avait fondé la première clinique externe de psychiatrie légale au Canada et qui avait introduit les services psychiatriques dans les milieux carcéraux, celui qui avait écrit extensivement sur la problématique de l'inceste, celui qui avait depuis quelques années été impliqué dans le "Clinton Project." En somme, un incontournable, celui avec qui je devais faire une résidence.

Je n'en savais pas plus. Je n'avais aucune idée de la personne que j'allais rencontrer en cet après-midi de mars 1972. Jamais je n'aurais pu imaginer quelle influence déterminante il aurait dans ma vie personnelle et au niveau de ma carrière.

La "Forensic Clinic" de l'avenue des Pins avait de quoi surprendre à première vue. C'était une ancienne demeure à trois étages qui devait n'avoir subi que des modifications mineures depuis que ses derniers habitants avaient quitté. Je me revois, accueilli par la très digne Louise d'Amour, secrétaire exécutive, puis conduit tout au haut de l'escalier au bureau du professeur Cormier. Je fus d'emblée fasciné par cet homme qui me recevait chez lui comme quelqu'un qui est heureux de revoir un vieil ami. La poignée de main ferme, le sourire engageant, l'oeil vif et inquisiteur, tout était là pour à la fois rassurer et impressionner le jeune médecin que j'étais. Assis sur son tabouret, je l'observais à m'observer, à m'écouter lui dire ce que je savais de la psychiatrie légale, ce que j'avais appris à Toronto et du pourquoi j'envisageais passer une année avec lui et son équipe. Puis, il commença à parler comme lui seul pouvait le faire. J'ai eu droit à un cours sur l'histoire de la psychiatrie légale, l'organisation de la "Forensic Clinic," de son implication dans les milieux correctionnels, de la recherche au niveau de la famille, des adolescents meurtriers. Il s'interrompait pour en savoir un peu plus sur moi, mes origines, mes intérêts, mes objectifs. Plus le temps passait, plus j'étais certain que la prochaine année de ma vie se passerait à ses côtés. Tout en l'écoutant, je regardais furtivement autour. Derrière lui, des centaines de livres dans des étagères remplies du plancher au plafond, à côté de moi, le fauteuil de l'analyste; devant la fenêtre donnant sur le Molson Stadium, son bureau de travail jonché de dossiers, par terre d'autres dossiers, des sacs remplis de documents avec lesquels je deviendrais si familier. Sur les murs, des tapis, des peintures. Au cours de l'année qui devait suivre et des multiples rencontres que j'ai eues par la suite, je devais revivre la même expérience enivrante. Bruno Cormier c'était le professeur, l'humaniste, l'artiste, le philosophe, le politicien, le guide, l'ami.

Lorsque dans les premiers jours de juillet 1972 je me suis présenté à la clinique pour entreprendre mon année de résidence, je sentis qu'il se passait quelque chose d'important, quelque chose de grave. L'annonce que le budget relié au projet Clinton n'était pas renouvelé avait provoqué un état de choc. Cette vieille maison avec toutes ses figures tristes et préoccupées m'apparaissait encore plus ancienne. L'heure n'était certes pas à la réjouissance et je me demandais ce qui allait advenir de mes projets personnels. Le Docteur Cormier me présenta ceux et celles qui allaient devenir mes compagnons de tous les jours: Colin Angliker, Josh Zambrovski, Ingrid Cooper, Lorna Graham, Madeleine St-Germain. J'appris ce jour-là du Docteur Cormier qu'on venait de se faire confirmer la fin du projet Clinton qui était devenu l'activité principale de l'équipe. Sa préoccupation concernait ses collaborateurs. Il se laissa aller à me parler du financement de cette fameuse clinique qui ne recevait pratiquement rien de l'Université McGill dont elle portait pourtant fièrement le nom. A part la bâtisse dont on n'avait probablement jamais repeint les murs et le salaire de sa secrétaire administrative, aucun fond universitaire. Tout fonctionnait grâce au projet de recherche, aux expertises médico-légales, trop peu payées, et aux maigres sommes rapportées par l'Assurance-maladie. C'était la crise économique en plus de la fin d'un rêve. Chez le Docteur Cormier, de la tristesse évidemment, de l'inquiétude mais pas d'amertume, pas de panique. La clinique allait survivre. Elle en avait vu d'autres et lui aussi. Jamais je n'avais rencontré quelqu'un avec une telle force de caractère.

C'est dans les semaines qui suivirent à travers de nombreuses rencontres tantôt dans son bureau, tantôt dans un restaurant ou dans son automobile qu'il sentit le besoin de me faire part de ce qu'avaient été les grandes lignes de sa vie. C'est ainsi que j'appris qu'il était originaire de Plessisville, qu'il avait bien connu le député provincial Tancrède Labbé et mon grand-père Wilfrid Labbé qui avaient fait partie tous deux du Gouvernement Duplessis. La conversation glissait tout naturellement sur la politique qu'il affectionnait sans se commettre par l'appartenance formelle à un parti. Il me parlait de ses amis co-signataires du *Refus global*, de son amitié avec Pierre-Elliott Trudeau, de son engagement social, de l'importance pour le psychiatre de voir l'humain dans toutes ses dimensions, du concept de la liberté de pensée qui est fondamental et qui permet de survivre dans des périodes de déprivation de liberté physique. Il me transmettait par ses paroles et par son attitude avec tous ceux qu'il rencontrait, son plus grand respect pour leur opinion, même lorsqu'il ne la partageait pas. C'est ainsi qu'il m'écoutait avec sympathie parler de mon admiration pour mon grand-père qui avait été ministre dans le cabinet de Maurice Duplessis, un homme pour qui il n'avait sans doute que bien peu d'affinités. C'est aussi avec beaucoup d'amusement qu'il me présentait à l'occasion aux membres de la clinique comme un admirateur de John Diefenbaker et un des rares membres, à l'époque du parti Conservateur. Il faut dire que Pierre-Elliott Trudeau était alors Premier Ministre libéral et au zénith de sa popularité.

Bruno Cormier était aussi un artiste. Il concevait l'art comme l'expression des sentiments humains cachés. Les peintures qu'il avait à son bureau avaient été peintes par des gens qu'il connaissait bien. Il en était de même pour celles qu'il avait à sa maison et qui prenait l'allure d'une galerie d'art. Il m'introduisait à son épouse Ruby de qui il me parlait avec beaucoup de tendresse, la décrivant comme une femme de tête, elle aussi, une grande fervente des arts. Il faisait souvent référence à elle comme l'organisatrice de sa vie et nul doute qu'elle était responsable du maintien de la structure socio-économique de ce grand penseur.

A l'occasion d'un congrès auquel j'assistais avec lui à Chicago, je découvris l'ampleur de ses connaissances au niveau des arts. Alors qu'on passait d'une salle à l'autre du Musée des Beaux Arts, je l'écoutais avec émerveillement me décrire les oeuvres, des impressionnistes français qui faisaient l'objet de l'exposition. Il savait tout de l'homme, me décrivait les circonstances de la vie de l'artiste au moment où il avait peint sa toile, me brossait lui-même en quelques phrases un tableau des différentes phases de sa carrière, de ce qu'avait été l'homme. Il connaissait même l'histoire du musée, pouvait me parler des philanthropes qui avaient rendu sa construction possible. Il racontait tout cela avec la verve qui lui était caractéristique mais sans aucune trace de vantardise.

Vers l'heure du midi, il suggéra qu'on aille dîner au musée. Alors qu'on était à la toute fin du repas, en train de prendre le café, l'alarme d'incendie se déclencha. Après quelques instants d'hésitation, le personnel indiqua aux clients qu'ils devaient quitter la salle. On nous dirigea prestement vers une sortie de secours. C'est ainsi qu'on se retrouva sur le trottoir sans avoir payé. L'honnête homme, qu'a toujours été Bruno Cormier, n'arrivait pas à se faire à l'idée qu'il quitterait la place sans avoir payé son dû. C'est à mon insistance qu'il s'éloigna à regret, promettant de revenir plus tard pour régler la note. Je ne sais pas s'il le fit jamais. Chose certaine, plusieurs années plus tard, lorsqu'on se rencontrait à l'occasion de congrès, il me rappelait toujours cet amusant épisode, me rendant responsable en riant de l'avoir influencé à commettre un délit.

Cette grande honnêteté se reflétait au niveau de sa probité intellectuelle. Dans ses rencontres avec ses collègues, il savait écouter les points de vue avec le plus grand respect. Même lorsqu'il était visiblement en profond désaccord je ne l'ai entendu exprimer des propos blessants. Il fronçait plutôt le sourcil et sa jambe pouvait s'agiter plus rapidement que de coutume. Lorsque l'autre s'arrêtait de parler, il exprimait sa position en incorporant ce que l'autre avait dit dans un exposé qui, avec quelques retouches, aurait pu faire l'objet d'un article. Jamais il ne déviait de ses principes basés sur sa croyance en la valeur intrinsèque de l'homme, de sa capacité à s'améliorer. Il refusait qu'on porte des jugements à l'emporte-pièce sur le comportement des individus, même ceux qui avaient commis les pires crimes. Le message était que nous étions là pour les comprendre et pour les guider à travers le chemin tortueux que la vie leur avait imposé. Il cherchait avec eux et pour eux la solution la plus profitable, la plus susceptible de faire ressortir l'honnête homme derrière le masque du délinquant, qu'il soit meurtrier ou père incestueux.

Les solutions qu'il suggérait n'étaient pas toujours les plus faciles et ne rencontraient pas toujours spontanément l'assentiment des accusés ou de leurs avocats. Ses négociations avec eux les amenaient graduellement à comprendre que le débat ne se

situait pas fondamentalement autour de l'issue d'un procès, mais
bien comment le procès devenait pour l'accusé l'occasion d'une
prise de conscience, la première étape dans un processus de réhabilitation. Je l'ai vu s'asseoir et discuter pendant des heures avec
les plus grands criminalistes de l'époque, leur faisant partager sa
vision de la problématique du client, leur exposant comment par
exemple un séjour en milieu carcéral pourrait, bien davantage
que dans un hôpital psychiatrique, restructurer l'individu, lui donner l'occasion de reprendre contact avec lui-même et reprendre
un fonctionnement psychique normal. C'est alors que son talent
de communicateur se manifestait de façon spectaculaire. Les avocats ressortaient de la clinique satisfaits, probablement convaincus
d'être devenus partie prenante de la solution d'un conflit humain
aux dimensions qu'ils ne soupçonnaient pas, prêts à convaincre
leurs clients de l'à-propos d'aller passer plusieurs années en
milieu carcéral plutôt que de se voir acquittés pour aliénation
mentale.

Je l'ai vu défendre avec la même âpreté, la même intégrité
intellectuelle les théories qui étaient siennes devant les tribunaux.
Il y exposait ses points de vue avec éloquence en utilisant les
mêmes arguments que lors des discussions de cas à la clinique ou
pendant ses rencontres avec l'avocat. Encore-là, on retrouvait le
respect de l'opinion de l'autre, avec la même détermination
farouche à faire triompher non pas sa vérité mais la vérité. Tous
devenaient partie prenante du débat. L'accusé, dans ses exposés,
n'étaient plus l'individu solitaire au pilori. Il était issu d'une
famille, il était intégré dans une dynamique où il se retrouvait au
centre d'un méga système auquel la victime était intégrée et où
temporairement étaient impliqués les différents intervenants qu'il
s'agisse du médecin, des avocats, du juge, du système carcéral. Le
procès n'était qu'un moment de l'histoire de l'individu, une étape
de son cheminement.

C'est sans doute là que son talent se manifestait de façon spectaculaire. Sa réputation le précédait de sorte que dès que son nom

était appelé, tous les yeux se tournaient vers lui et le suivaient jusqu'à la boite aux témoins. Cet endroit devenait pour lui une tribune. Il savait utiliser avec un art consommé le pouvoir du président du tribunal afin qu'on le laisse exposer sa compréhension de la situation de l'accusé au moment du délit, les facteurs sociaux et familiaux et la dynamique sous-jacente. Pour lui, pas de référence au bottin des diagnostics psychiatriques (DSM), pas de citation savante. Son langage était celui du scientifique de l'esprit, du criminologue et de l'humaniste. L'accusé prenait une dimension nouvelle, agrandie. Le Docteur Cormier le replaçait parmi nous. Accusé sans identité propre, il redevenait tantôt un père, tantôt un fils, tantôt un époux. Les explications qu'il fournissait étaient basées sur sa profonde connaissance de l'humain et des vicissitudes de l'esprit. On ne retrouvait pas chez lui de déclaration à l'emporte-pièce, de jugement ex catédra. C'était une longue et patiente reconstruction du cheminement de l'accusé à travers la vie, une analyse détaillée de ses relations interpersonnelles. Son objectivité ne laissait aucun doute. Il établissait d'emblée, lorsqu'il était questionné sur qui avait retenu ses services, que son témoignage était le même, qu'il soit là à la demande de la défense, de la Couronne ou du juge. Lors des procès auxquels j'ai assisté, je n'ai jamais vu son objectivité ou son honnêteté intellectuelle être questionnés. C'était à regret qu'à la fin de son témoignage on le voyait quitter l'enceinte. Il s'engouffrait alors dans un taxi ou dans son automobile, silencieux, encore pris dans sa recréation psychologique du crime. Dès qu'il revenait à la clinique, la machine se remettait en marche à une cadence accélérée. C'était les téléphones à retourner, le document à relire que lui apportait Lorna Graham, la réunion d'équipe qu'il convoquait pour discuter d'un cas.

Cet homme extraordinaire à la réputation internationale était demeuré d'une simplicité admirable. Devant lui, le récidiviste, le déficient, le ministre de la Justice, la serveuse, étaient traités avec le même empressement, la même courtoisie. Il était visiblement à l'aise dans tous les milieux, qu'il soit en train de dîner au Faculty

Club de McGill ou à la taverne d'Henri Richard située à quelques pas de la clinique. Jamais de signe d'impatience à cause de la lenteur du service ou de la désinvolture du serveur. La période du repas était pour lui l'occasion de faire le point sur une problématique, de continuer l'élaboration d'une nouvelle politique, de demander l'opinion de ceux qui partageaient sa table. Cette extraordinaire machine à penser ne s'arrêtait même pas pour manger.

A mesure que mon année de résidence s'écoulait, il m'introduisait graduellement aux différents rouages des grands systèmes. Je participais à ses rencontres avec les responsables de la psychiatrie du système correctionnel canadien, les avocats fondateurs de ce qui allait devenir le bureau d'Aide juridique, la direction de l'établissement Parthenais, les fondateurs de l'Institut Philippe-Pinel, les Béliveau, Laberge, Morant, Maufette, Talbot, qu'il admirait tout en divergeant d'opinion sur leur vision de la criminologie clinique. A l'occasion des congrès, il m'introduisait comme son jeune collègue à tous ceux que nous rencontrions. Tous ceux qu'il croisait le reconnaissaient spontanément. C'était l'éclat de rire, l'accolade et la conversation qui reprenait son cours après parfois trois ou quatre ans d'interruption comme s'ils s'étaient quittés la veille. Il vouait pour tous ces gens une grande admiration et tenait à ce que je fasse leur connaissance. Etre résident en psychiatrie avec Bruno Cormier, c'était avoir l'opportunité d'entrer par la grande porte dans un club très sélect. Les collègues qu'il affectionnait étaient comme lui des maîtres à penser, des créateurs.

Vingt-cinq ans plus tard, je revois encore le Docteur Cormier engagé dans des discussions animées lors de congrès de l'American Academy of Psychiatry and the Law côtoyant les Herbert Thomas, Jacques Quen, Jonas Rappaport, Bernard Diamond. Issus de milieux différents, ils partageaient le même enthousiasme pour leur travail de cliniciens, d'éducateurs et de chercheurs. Dans leurs discussions, il y avait cette soif d'en savoir toujours davantage sur l'humain en utilisant une approche analytique associée à des données en provenance de la criminologie, ou de l'anthropologie. Pour le Docteur Cormier et ses collègues de l'époque, il n'était pas question d'emprisonner le patient et sa criminalité dans des critères diagnostics étriqués et froids.

Sa soif de liberté se manifestait de plusieurs façons. Il était clair d'une part qu'il ne supportait pas se faire dicter sa conduite par qui que ce soit. Sa démarche rapide, son air déterminé, son timbre de voix était la manifestation visible du besoin d'assurer son autorité, de définir son territoire et de décourager la moindre tentative de contrôle de sa pensée ou d'intimidation. Dans les présentations qu'il faisait lors de congrès scientifiques, il arrivait mal à se limiter à ce qu'il avait lui-même écrit. Il annonçait souvent après quelques minutes qu'il mettait son texte de côté pour livrer à son auditoire ce qu'il voyait comme une pensée plus élaborée, plus complète, plus à jour. Il se lançait alors dans un exposé complexe à partir d'un thème central où venaient s'accrocher différentes parties d'un tableau qui ne devenait souvent compréhensible que vers la fin quand il dévoilait sa réponse à la problématique exposée au début. Sa grande éloquence, sa capacité de développer en parallèle deux ou trois thèmes pour les fondre dans un concept unifié et adapté à une réalité pratique en laissaient plus d'un médusés. Il cherchait à communiquer à travers ses présentations, sa compréhension de la liberté qui, pour lui, se situait à l'intérieur de l'individu de sorte que pouvait être davantage libre le prisonnier dans sa cellule que celui chargé de le garder. Cela l'amena même à écrire un livre *The Watcher and the Watched* qui développe cette notion.

Pour le Docteur Cormier, l'individu qui avait commis un crime, pouvait pour des raisons sociales se voir placé dans des conditions de déprivation de liberté tout en poursuivant son cheminement, l'amenant à reprendre contact avec lui-même et à réintégrer sa place que ce soit dans la famille ou dans une notion de famille élargie. Sa croyance au droit fondamental à la liberté faisait en sorte qu'il s'acclimatait mal à l'idée de l'hospitalisation prolongée pour un criminel, l'hôpital psychiatrique étant pour lui un milieu éminemment asocial, favorisant la régression. Il voyait en ce sens le milieu carcéral plus humanisant parce que plus près du fonctionnement réel dans la société. La prison était ce microcosme où l'individu pouvait reprendre des habitudes de vie normales en acquérant la notion de sa liberté par rapport à celle de l'autre.

Il encourageait son entourage à exprimer leur point de vue de la façon qu'il l'entendait dans un contexte idéologique qui ne pouvait cependant par la force de son influence, qu'être un développement de sa propre idéologie. On pourrait parler en ce sens de l'influence de Bruno Cormier comme de celle d'un Rubens avec ses élèves.

J'ai vu sa tolérance testée à la limite lors d'une cause célèbre où il m'avait fait participer à la rédaction de l'expertise demandée par l'avocat de la défense. C'était vers la fin de mon stage à la clinique. Suite aux discussions que j'avais eues avec le Docteur Cormier et par ma compréhension du cas, il me semblait que les conclusions devaient aller dans un certain sens. Soit qu'il était pressé par le temps ou qu'il avait fait une lecture en survol de mon texte, il laissa partir un rapport qui ne correspondait pas à sa pensée. L'avocat de la défense l'ayant présenté à la Couronne, le Docteur Cormier se vit obligé à l'occasion du procès, de corriger le tir. Son habilité fit en sorte que ni l'accusé, ni lui, n'eurent à subir de préjudices à cause de mon erreur. Il ne s'emporta pas et se contenta de me dire qu'il était surpris de voir les conclusions auxquelles j'étais arrivé.

Durant les dernières semaines de ma résidence, on passait de plus en plus de temps ensemble à discuter de ce que serait ma carrière. J'avais pris la décision d'aller m'établir à Sherbrooke, une jeune ville universitaire où je comptais bien ouvrir un service de psychiatrie légale. Je ressentais beaucoup de tristesse à quitter le Docteur Cormier et les gens extraordinaires qui composaient son équipe. C'était bien davantage qu'un groupe d'individus travaillant à une même cause. C'était une famille qui m'avait donné un modèle, qui m'avait fait croître. La tentation était forte de rester dans ce milieu sécurisant. On m'invitait à le faire mais en même temps je sentais que j'avais atteint tous mes objectifs et que je devais fonctionner de façon autonome. La confiance que me témoignait le Docteur Cormier, son enthousiasme à me voir me lancer dans un travail de pionnier m'inspirait la confiance dont j'avais besoin. Nos dernières rencontres servaient à nous rassurer qu'il n'y aurait pas de coupure, qu'un travail de collaboration se poursuivrait. On se parlait du prochain congrès à venir, de la visite qu'il ne manquerait pas de me faire à Sherbrooke, du prochain article à publier. On allait à nouveau dîner ensemble.

Nous sommes effectivement toujours demeurés en contact. Il m'appelait pour s'informer de moi, de mes enfants. Il voulait savoir quelle avion je prenais pour aller au prochain congrès. Pour moi, il était le consultant dans les causes difficiles, la mémoire encyclopédique qui me donnait instantanément accès à la référence cherchée. Il était devenu au cours des ans un confident dans les périodes difficiles, un ami avec qui on pouvait partager sans avoir à tout dire.

C'est avec une infinie tristesse que j'ai appris la nouvelle de son décès à la radio alors que je m'en allais témoigner dans un procès à l'extérieur. Le vide n'a pas été comblé. La douleur persiste. Son influence demeure. Lorsque je me vois avec les résidents et résidentes qui font des stages avec moi en psychiatrie légale, je réalise bien que le modèle que je leur donne n'a rien d'étranger à celui que j'ai reçu du Docteur Cormier. Il ne serait pas fâché de lire ça.

Pierre Gagné

*For Dr. Cormier, prison was more humanizing
than a psychiatric hospital because it was a microcosm of society,
closer to real life.*

 I first met Professor Bruno Cormier twenty-five years ago when I was a Resident in Psychiatry at the Clarke Institute in Toronto. At the time, I had no idea how much he would come to influence me personally and professionally.

Through contacts at the Clarke, I was able to secure a placement at his Forensic Clinic in Montreal, beginning in July 1972. Over the year I spent there, I came to know Bruno Cormier as a teacher, humanist, artist, philosopher, politician, mentor, and friend. I learned that he was originally from Plessisville and that he had known the MPP Tancrède Labbé, as well as my grandfather Wilfrid Labbé, who had both been members of the Duplessis government. He spoke to me of his associates and co-signatories of *Refus global*, his friendship with Pierre Elliott Trudeau, and his commitment to social change. He taught me that psychiatry must see all sides of a patient and that freedom of thought is critical to survival during periods of incarceration.

Bruno Cormier was also an artist. He viewed art as an expression of hidden emotions. Once, while attending a conference in Chicago, we visited the Art Institute, and I discovered how knowledgeable he was about painting. As we dined in the museum restaurant that day, a fire alarm went off and we had to leave without paying our bill, which troubled Bruno. Years later, he still joked about how I had led him to commit a theft. His wife Ruby, whom I had occasion to meet, and of whom he spoke with great tenderness, was also a patron of the arts, as well as being the organizing force behind the great thinker that he was.

The Chicago incident illustrates for me Bruno Cormier's total honesty, which permeated his dealings with colleagues. No matter how much he might disagree with someone, I never heard him make a disparaging remark. He never strayed from his belief in the intrinsic goodness of people and their ability to change for the better, even those who had committed the most heinous crimes. He taught us to understand and to guide our clients. His goal was always to find the outcome most apt to bring out the human being in an offender, whether he be a murderer or an incestuous father.

The solutions he proposed for offenders were not the easiest, and they did not always appeal to the accused and their lawyers. However, he would gradually bring them to see beyond the outcome of the criminal trial. He viewed the trial as a process by which an offender could come to terms with his offence, a prerequisite to true rehabilitation. I recall him talking for hours to some of the greatest criminal lawyers of the day, sharing his vision of the offender's situation and outlining why a prison term could be more beneficial than a stay in a psychiatric hospital. Lawyers would leave the clinic convinced and ready to persuade their clients of the value of spending several years in prison, rather than being acquitted on grounds of insanity. For Dr. Cormier, prison was more humanizing than a psychiatric hospital because it was a microcosm of society, closer to real life. In spite of having gained an international reputation for his work, Dr. Cormier remained unpretentious. He treated everyone, from a recidivist client to the Minister of Justice, with the same attention and courtesy.

As the end of my year at the Forensic Clinic approached, I was tempted to accept Dr. Cormier's offer to stay on with his outstanding team, which had become almost a family to me. At the same time, I was inspired by his confidence in me as I considered setting up a forensic service in Sherbrooke. We kept in touch and Dr. Cormier assisted me with difficult cases. He had become a friend and confidant.

So it was with great sadness that I learned of his death. Nowadays, though, as I work with residents doing placements in forensic psychiatry, I realize that the model I offer them reflects what Dr. Cormier provided for me many years ago. I like to think that would please him.

English Summary: Lesley Benderavage

Pierre Gagné, *M.D., FRCP(C), Head, Department of Psychiatry, Faculty of Medicine, University of Sherbrooke, Que.; Chief, Forensic Service, Centre Universitaire de Santé de l'Estrie; Adjunct Professor, McGill University.*

Following his graduation in Medicine at Laval University, Quebec City, in 1969, Dr. Gagné was the first resident in psychiatry at the University of Sherbrooke. Pursuing a career in forensic psychiatry, Dr. Gagné trained at the Clarke Institute of Psychiatry, University of Toronto, and at the Forensic Clinic, McGill University, with Dr. Bruno Cormier. He is a Consultant to the National Parole Board and Ministry of Justice, Canada. He has also served as President, Section on Forensic Psychiatry, Canadian Psychiatric Association. Dr. Gagné was the recipient of the 1996 Bruno Cormier Award of the Canadian Academy of Psychiatry and Law.

Baila Markus

*In thinking about Bruno's words—humanity, self-worth,
and dignity—a poignant scene comes to mind.*

 In the summer of 1971 I was interviewed by Bruno
Cormier for a position within his clinical staff. I had
despaired of ever hearing from Dr. Cormier, who had
received a letter of recommendation on my behalf
from a mutual friend several months before. But
there I was, sitting opposite him in his wall-to-wall, book-lined
office on the second floor of the McGill Forensic Clinic. He apolo-
gized for the long wait and actually said in a distracted way (I did
not know then that he would have a multitude of thoughts and
ideas simultaneously buzzing around in his head) that he had carried the letter of recommendation around with him in his pocket
for the past three months. Surely it was a way of speaking.

After a question-and-answer period in which the emphasis was
on my vital statistics, the horrid subject of qualifications came up.
Horrid, because I had none. Dr. Cormier later provided me with
them for his curious staff. He attributed three qualifications to me,
different but as many as anyone else had. First, I was a mature
woman with life's experience; second, I knew the working-class
poor and welfare recipients through my political involvement with
Citizen Committees in underprivileged neighbourhoods in and
around Montreal; and third, I spoke French. I should not have
told him that my involvement with the underprivileged was "political" because it became a bone of contention between Bruno and
me until, many years later, I learned to avoid the subject as best I
could.

As a psychoanalyst treating offenders, Dr. Cormier naturally emphasized the behaviour problems of the individual in criminal acting out. Although he certainly took into account the environmental influences, especially the influence of the family, Bruno would more than cringe at those who blamed crime exclusively on society. At that time I had recently completed the translation of a book on a Marxist interpretation of the history of Quebec. As a radical of the far left, I believed in it. Bruno had tried to read it, probably because it became a whopping success, hated it, cursed it out for lack of documentation, false notions, and "threw it away." It looked like it was all my fault. He never let up on it.

Despite our different socio-political views, it always struck me how radical Bruno was in the field of criminology and even in psychiatry. He often said, with that mischievous grin, "The shrinks would shake their heads if they witnessed my interviews." Despite his background of intensive training and study it seemed to me that Bruno relied less on the books than on his intuition. He did odd things with his patients. It was told to me that once when a patient had a breakdown in his office, Bruno stuck out his middle finger and placed it on the patient's forehead. The response was immediate. Total recovery. A miracle! Maybe there *was* a scientific theory for Bruno's action.

Bruno was not predictably one of your silent "uh huh" therapists, intolerable to most of our clientele. He could be heard behind closed doors from the top floor to the bottom, yelling at certain interminable patients who kept coming back for more. Where else would they get such attention? And how Bruno persisted in pursuit of changes in his patients' behaviour. I once said that I admired his incredible patience in his impatience. He smiled knowingly. I never knew Bruno to laugh outright. He seemed uncomfortable with glee, so all you could get from him was a little gurgle.

But how gentle he really was with his "birds." He spoke their language, listened intently to them no matter where they'd drift off. Once when I told him of a boring patient I was tired of seeing, he said, "No such thing as a boring patient. You can learn something from all of them. How do you think I learned to build a stone fireplace in the country?" Treatment was all about establishing a working relationship with the patient. To almost every "how to" question regarding therapeutic intervention, Bruno's answer, "Establish a relationship," made it so much easier for all of us, students and professionals alike.

I was fortunate to be hired in the summer since most of the staff (including myself there were ten clinicians) were on vacation. I had the opportunity to spend a good deal of time with Bruno and (in my mind at least) he became my private tutor. For Bruno, vacations were an unnecessary evil. He only absented himself from the clinic in the capacity of work, conferences, and meetings. He grumbled endlessly and promised himself that he would disallow all vacations in the future. The biggest problem was that he couldn't find anything and it was all the fault of his vacationing staff. It was left to me, during that time (my initiation), to drop everything at regular intervals and search for missing papers, files, his glasses, his briefcase. I soon learned (and what a useful lesson) that the work at the Clinic involved fulfilling several tasks simultaneously. It was not likely that a piece of research could be completed before having to start another. At first it was stressful, but in the end I was grateful to Bruno for piling on the work, teaching me to stretch my mind—a new challenge and I enjoyed it!

Bruno invited me to sit in on his interviews, the optimum learning experience in my formation as a clinician. He advised me to pursue a degree in the social sciences, as certification would eventually be necessary for official purposes, whatever they may be. He suggested that I register in the School of Social Work at the University of Quebec at Montreal, but he was not too enthusiastic some years later when I asked for shortened hours to do my Master's at McGill. He was not concerned with the time off to attend classes (at five o'clock) but he thought it was unnecessary because by that time I had co-authoured several published papers which he believed carried more professional weight than a postgraduate degree. Actually I was not that enthusiastic myself. If not for the convincing pep talk from Ingrid Cooper, who was also on staff in the Social Work Department at McGill University, I probably would have passed up the Master's plan.

I was disappointed in the M.S.W. program at McGill. What I had learned at the Clinic spoiled me, so to speak, for higher education in the social sciences, and, even though I risked telling Bruno for fear of hearing "I told you so," he just passed it off as an "experience." One of the most important lessons I learned from Bruno, more so as the years passed by, was the ability to live without regrets. How often he said to me in troubled times, "It was an experience," and sometimes, "it was an adventure," and he eased my pain. Bruno was not one to brood over trouble. He didn't laugh out loud, but what a sense of humour!

Bruno started me on my own caseload *tout de suite*. If the phone rang while I was sitting in on the interview with his patient, it was almost a sure thing that the patient would be mine. Bruno's philosophy for neophytes was to throw them in the lake and they were sure to swim. His way, as my colleagues well know, was to tell the patient in his office to accompany the lady to her office because she was nicer than he was. Of course, the perplexed patient acquiesced and the new therapist was left to bungle through the rest of the session.

I soon learned that Bruno delegated responsibility without hesitation and certainly took risks. I recall that in the years I worked at the Clinic I would have reservations about certain offenders who had committed violent acts, but Bruno's reports to the courts recommended sentences of non-deprivation of liberty (probation and treatment). Every offender was assessed on his own merits and not on the offence. Those who did manage to avoid incarceration kept coming to the clinic and did not recidivate. Bruno just knew.

In my second week at the clinic I went along with Bruno to the super-maximum penitentiary at Laval. Some of the staff not on vacation were involved in the activities at the Clinton penitentiary in Dannemora, so it was left to me, the newcomer, to accompany Bruno. The purpose of the visit to the Correctional Development Centre, which was condemned even before it was built, was to evaluate the institution, a request from the Solicitor General of Canada. As we sped along the route, with Bruno in the driver's seat, I was too overwhelmed with curiosity by the new adventure that awaited me to ask any questions. I had never been to a prison before. Bruno chit-chatted, light talk, becoming somewhat agitated as, unexpectedly, that awful Marxist book without documentation came to his mind. I asked how far it was to the penitentiary.

The director of the prison introduced me to the administrative staff and returned to his office to learn from Bruno how we were about to conduct the evaluation. The staff was not too friendly, and did not like the idea that we would be snooping around their prison. They were intimidated by the prestigious Dr. Cormier, but a mere social worker like me was easy prey to impress with their cynicism. No holds barred, they informed me that this institution was a boarding school; it held the worst of the worst criminals from all over the country, and it was their task to *break the spirit* of these dangerous, incorrigible criminals. In their view I was a naïve do-gooder thinking I could make a difference. I had no intention of making anything other than trying to make friends with them. The evaluation would include months of interviews with all of the seventy-two inmates, excepting one, an F.L.Q.-proclaimed political prisoner, the one prisoner I would have liked to interview, as would my colleagues who joined me later. The so-called political prisoners were off-bounds, *verboten*.

The staff of the CDC had no choice but to open their doors to us since the orders came from the highest of authorities. Nevertheless we struck up an amicable working relationship through conversation over lunch. I listened with rapt interest to their anecdotes of fishing and hunting trips, and they reciprocated by listening with courteous patience to my family stories. Access to inmate files and to unescorted interviews were offered without hesitation. Almost thirty years later I can recall some of the faces of those correctional officers, as they were later called, and remember how helpful they had been.

On our way to the cell block, Bruno and I walked slowly along the broad corridor, me with my knees shaking and trying to be nonchalant. I heard only the crashing sounds of automatic gates opening and closing for us and the click-click of my high heels on the cement floor. There were no guards in sight.

"This silent world gains an astute ear," Bruno remarked, really musing to himself. (I memorized those words and jotted them down soon as I had a chance.) I smiled, not knowing how to respond and besides, this adventure into a world as foreign to me as outer space left me speechless, awestruck! Dr. Cormier waxing poetic in a joint like this? It came to me that in his younger years he wrote poetry and belonged to the group of intellectuals, artists and poets of the *Refus global*. Once a poet ...

Finally the long corridor opened up to a large rotunda where a guard was stationed in a glass cage. He came out, and shook his head when asked to open interview rooms for us. He said it was lunch-time. Rocking back and forth on his heels Bruno said that we'd wait right there but the guard said no can do. We did anyway. The guard returned to his cage and the door swung securely shut behind him. He turned to a panel of instruments, no less complicated than a supersonic airplane, and pushed some buttons which lit up miniature flashing lights. The gates of the cell block opened wide, letting through another guard wheeling in a huge canteen and immediately passing back through the gates, safely to the other side. The gates clanged shut, hermetically sealed. In this institution any physical contact between guards and prisoners was not to be seen.

At the push of a button a cell door slid open releasing a prisoner to pick up his lunch tray from the canteen and then to return to his cell. One by one they emerged separately, and in the split seconds before returning to their cells, they managed to cast an inquisitive glance our way. Towards the end of the line one prisoner did not appear when his cell door was opened. He called out, *"Je ne suis pas prêt. Je fais ma toilette."*

To myself I said, "Bravo." Bruno was more eloquent, "That one is a prisoner whose spirit they won't break," he said.

For the remainder of that summer we interviewed the inmates. I was hoping to be supplied with a questionnaire for comfort, but essentially the only question we had to ask was what they thought of that particular institution, most of the inmates having done time in various other penitentiaries across the country and some in foreign countries. As they stepped into the interview room, I had the impression that the inmates blended into the antiseptic atmosphere of the institution—spanking clean, slicked-down hair, chalk-white sneakers. Not one of them looked scary to me, although one asked if I was scared. They were all co-operative, happy to be out of their cells. I asked the question about the institution and took notes from their barrage of complaints—from inedible food to isolation, twenty-three hours a day locked up in their cells. Only one inmate did not complain, the notorious internationally known criminal, Jacques Mesrine. A brilliant escape artist, he didn't waste his time thinking about the rigorous conditions in this super-maximum penitentiary. He had seen them all and simply said, *"Une institution vaut une autre, sont toutes les mêmes."* He could not have seen many more, for I had later read that Mesrine was gunned down in Europe.

At eight o'clock Saturday and Sunday mornings, Bruno and I met at the Clinic to compile the statistics for the report to the Solicitor General. I considered it a privilege to work with Dr. Cormier and not for a minute did I shy away from weekend or any-hour work. Nevertheless, Bruno had a way of evoking traditions, policies, ethics, anything to justify after-hours work. Sometimes we were a research clinic and sometimes a service clinic depending on the priority at the time. When we were a service clinic we did research on our own time. When we were a research clinic we saw our patients at night. Finally, Bruno was gifted at inspiring loyalty to himself or to the Clinic, which is to say, one and the same, and no matter how surly he could get, there was always a sense of pride in all of us who worked at the Clinic.

As I worked only on the statistical aspect of the report to the Solicitor General, and as I had temporarily left the Clinic before the report was drafted, I have no knowledge of its recommendations nor how it was received in Ottawa. Unfortunately, no important (or otherwise) changes were instituted for the benefit of the inmates of the Correctional Development Centre. Suffice it to know that Bruno Cormier fought hard for the establishment of a therapeutic community inside the prison walls. He believed that imprisonment without rehabilitation, which is generally the case in penal institutions in Canada, can have severe negative effects on the personality of the criminal who more likely than not will return to a life of crime when he is free. Punishment in the form of lengthy sentences as well as the construction of more prisons is being increasingly promoted by politicians. Bruno was quick to point out that a government policy of longer sentences serves no purpose but to make criminals worse. As for the so-called hardcore criminals, Bruno did not deny that society must be protected, but shorter sentences with meaningful therapeutic programs in prison would be a much better alternative. Treating hard-core criminals with humanity, giving them self-worth and dignity was a step in the right direction. For Bruno no one was totally bad or forever bad. He did not use the term psychopath because he believed that if we look deep enough into the human psyche some goodness will be found. He preferred to describe serious criminal behaviour in terms of a personality or character disorder.

In thinking about Bruno's words—humanity, self-worth, and dignity—a poignant scene comes to mind. One morning Bruno and I arrived at Archambault maximum penitentiary to interview some inmates for parole evaluation. It took a very long time until

we were set up for the interviews. We sat silently in the entrance-
way of the institution, observing the come and go of guards who
never gave us a second look. When the prison gates opened we
expected that it was our cue to see the inmates to be evaluated.
Instead, a tall slim figure followed by a guard came through the
gates. We immediately recognized that this was an inmate being
released after serving his sentence. He wore a dark green suit
meticulously pressed, tie and shirt of a lighter green, and mirror-
shiny brown shoes. I wondered if the correctional service offered
these clothes or were they brought in from the outside. He looked
straight ahead and walked stiffly as if with purpose, his eyes glued
to the door to freedom. The guard waved to the waiting driver of
the car marked Correctional Service of Canada and returned to
the interior of the prison. Not a word or a handshake to the
inmate who had been in the institution for at least two years and a
day and possibly many years. It passed through my mind that a
dog being released from a kennel would have received at least a
pat on the back. A few inmates working outside on the grounds
approached the released inmate, some with handshakes, one with
a hug and although we could not hear what they said, it was evident they were wishing him good luck. The driver got out of the
car, motioned the inmate to get in and entered the car again. As
the freed man struggled with the door handle, an inmate
approached to help out, but the driver jumped out of the car and
told him to get back to work and then spat out some words to the
man in the green suit. They drove away, and as far as we could
see, the newly released prisoner never looked back.

An important factor that Bruno wrote about in his voluminous
papers on the deprivation of liberty is the concept of responsibility in regard to the criminal. In a talk that was transcribed he said,
"In freedom, offenders have serious problems dealing with
responsibility, yet we place these individuals with this problem
into an environment which takes away any opportunity to learn
responsibility. They become totally dependent on the institution

for all their needs. They are told when to eat, sleep, get up, go to work. In summary, we are placing psychologically damaged individuals in an environment which not only fails to deal with the emotional problem that led to criminality in the first place, but actually damages him further, sometimes irreversibly."

In an aside after his talk, Bruno remarked, "I always find it ironical that when these individuals are children and are abused, they arouse sympathy and understanding; however, when they are adults, we fear and reject them and make no relation to the rejected child we failed to help."

In regard to the persistent offender, whose delinquent behaviour starts in pre-puberty, *i.e.*, truancy, theft, fire-setting, running away, if punishment did not work for him then how is it expected to work for him when he is a full-blown adult criminal? Institutions like the CDC that operate solely on the principle of punishment, in all likelihood, ultimately fail to protect society. How can we expect to rehabilitate people with multiple imprisonments who are thrown into more extreme conditions of deprivation? Twenty-three hours a day in a cell with only one hour a day to stretch their legs in the prison yard; walls within walls blocked not only from the exterior but also from the interior by heavy sliding cell doors with a square foot of window looking out on nothing but the cell block corridor; indeed conditions like these guarantee a very bleak and hopeless outcome. In recalling the experience of the CDC, I wonder about the cruel and unusual punishment clause in the Criminal Code.

I left the clinic after a year because of a budget cut. Bruno arranged for me to work at the John Howard Society under the direction of Steve Cumas, and a year later I went off to France to work in community psychiatry. Upon my return in 1975, I went to see Bruno at the Clinic. The familiarity of his office, the precarious way he rocked on two legs of his chair, the books piled in disarray: This is where I belong, I thought. I told him that I'd like to come back to work, not really expecting an opening. He gave me a hard time, asked what made me think he could pay me. And then he found something to challenge me on. This time it was community psychiatry and not the terrible Marxist book with no documentation. He said they tried community psychiatry fifty years ago and it never worked; that the services of the Centre de Santé Mentale in the Troisième Arrondissement in Paris where I worked was just another pilot project that does not work, etc., etc. And again, I never heard the end of it.

If that day I had defended what I thought were the most comprehensive psychiatric services at that mental health centre in Paris, pilot project or not, I'm sure Bruno would have gone on and on with his criticism: His patience within his impatience. Wherever did he get the energy? In any case, the digression was worth it because it appeared to give Bruno time to assess my request for a return to work. He asked if I wanted to do some research because there was some money in a research fund. I offered to do anything as long as I could work at the Clinic. Bruno said, "Welcome home," and I did everything.

In the late seventies, Bruno and I plunged into a research project on adolescent homicide. With the help of a couple of students, I ploughed through stacks of *plumitifs* (ledgers) at juvenile courts in search of names of adolescents who had killed during a time-period of twenty-five years from 1950 to 1974. I studied the files, compiled the data, read and summarized the literature, mostly mechanical work—and then, a major breakthrough. We snagged our first live case.

With his casual display of enthusiasm, Bruno came to my office waving a sheet of paper. He handed it to me, a request from the Parole Board for an evaluation of a man serving a life sentence for a murder he committed as a teenager. When Bruno saw my delight in having the opportunity to study and treat our first case of adolescent homicide, he smiled, a wisp of a smile, and said we should be ashamed of our professional deformation. I laughed but I knew that our new patient, Daniel, would not be just a statistic in our research. (The case history of this subject is described in the second volume of this book under the heading, "A Longitudinal Study of Adolescent Murderers.")

Bruno interviewed Daniel for the first few sessions in order to complete the evaluation for parole. Daniel had been before the Parole Board on several occasions during his incarceration, and the refusals to grant him parole were based on his lack of social integration. Since he was somewhat of a loner, the authorities were not convinced that Daniel would not recidivate. According to Daniel he had avoided establishing close friendships in the penitentiary because inmates came and went and he was there on a life sentence. But the Parole Board interpreted this as fear of rejection, the very reason he killed in the first place.

Bruno not only described Daniel differently, but his report was a brilliant thesis on the aetiology of murder, the psychodynamics, and the recuperative possibilities. The members of the Parole Board must have been impressed because they released Daniel to a half-way house, with the condition to follow treatment at the Clinic. I was to be his therapist, Bruno his ultimate support. Daniel had heard about Bruno Cormier in the penitentiary and expressed relief that he was to be treated at the Clinic.

After Daniel had settled down during the difficult task of reintegrating into society, I asked him, and with some trepidation he agreed to be a subject in our research project. He was not the least reluctant to tell his story. Of course, he had told it so many times, from the day of his arrest, to the trial, to the several parole hearings, and now again. We found that Daniel had an air of sincerity about him, and his seemingly rehearsed account of the murder was a way of suppressing the painful memories. Besides, he well knew that we already knew about the crime.

Daniel was released from the half-way house after a year, and conditions to follow therapy were removed. However, he continued to come to the Clinic on a voluntary basis, and in all he was with us for five years. For much of the time he talked trivia incessantly and was seldom interrupted. He had the need to buttress himself up by educating me about his new discoveries—where to shop and eat inexpensively and how to cook. His was the best recipe for stew. Having spent half his life in the penitentiary, Daniel was given the freedom to express himself at will in a supportive type of therapy.

The therapeutic goal was for Daniel to discover, express, and understand his feelings and to establish a trusting relationship with his therapist so that he could eventually repeat the experience outside the Clinic. Daniel's early childhood was devoid of warmth and affection. In particular, the mother who adequately performed her role as homemaker to a large family, had no time or no need to give affection or even attention. The father was absent most of the time. Daniel, whose only delinquency before the murder was to play hooky from school, was placed in a series of foster homes. He struck up a close relationship with a young foster brother who was an invalid but recovered shortly after Daniel moved in. As the boy's health improved, he began to socialize with his peers, leaving Daniel out in the cold, so to speak. Swamped with overpowering feelings of rejection, really the tip of the iceberg, Daniel stabbed and killed the boy. Rejection from a good object transformed itself to a bad, persecutory object in the murdering moment.

It wasn't until five years into therapy that Daniel had a deep emotional reaction when recalling the murder. Instead of using euphemisms like "the thing that happened" or "the thing I did," he could finally say, "I killed the boy." In the next couple of interviews, without prompting, he talked about how he hated the person he was then. He asked himself where he would be now if he had not committed the crime, and he thought that he would still be that same person. Now he had his own apartment, a steady job and a few friends. He became aware that he would never have approval from his family for the gains he had made. In his perception, the family saw him only as a murderer; however, he understood that they have their own lives to deal with. He said that he tries not to dwell on the remorse he feels nor the memories of his childhood and the crime he committed, but he cannot erase those memories. As part of the process of reparation, Daniel could put those memories to use. He said that the memories served a purpose, a guard against other mistakes which could have other consequences. Daniel saw himself as evolved and having made progress in his social integration. He asked what "the Clinic" (euphemism for his therapist) thought about his progress.

That first day I met Bruno, when he interviewed me for a post at the Clinic, he warned me that I should not think I could cure anyone, and that if I actually did cure someone I should not expect any thanks. This is to say that in the case of Daniel, when he asked to be seen less frequently, Bruno and I, more so Bruno, agreed to extend the sessions to once a month instead of weekly. In a couple of months, Daniel, dewy-eyed, recapped his interviews of the past five years, saying that at first he kept them superficial so that he would not feel ridiculed, but now he was sure that his therapist would not reject him. He asked again if I (not the Clinic this time) was happy with his progress. He was ready to terminate. It was wrenching to let him go. I enthusiastically acknowledged his progress and mistakenly asked what he attributed it to. He smiled, a huge smile, and said, "My girlfriend." I felt a pang of jealousy. So much for expectations. I should have listened to my boss.

Bruno teased me about curing my "bird" and told me to write it up now. Many of us, old or new clinicians, were a little nervous before discussing a case with Bruno outside of case conferences at the Clinic because he would always ask us to write it up. One former colleague, it was said, crossed the street when he saw Bruno for fear he would be asked to write something up. However, write it up we did, all forty-one cases of adolescent murderers. We did not see them all because some could not be located after their sentences or juvenile detention had terminated, some, many years ago, but we had access to legal and institutional documentation. Although Bruno, and I myself too, preferred to work with adults I was touched by Bruno's approach with the teenagers we saw together. He immediately inspired confidence, spoke so gently and as if he had always known them. He related to them on an adult level but also as the good father. It was not an easy task to get them to reveal anything about themselves, which is generally the case with adolescents, but these boys had the added burden of guilt and shame. Most adolescent murderers in the juvenile detention centres tended to retreat to the background.

We completed our paper on adolescent homicide and presented it at various conferences. It drew large audiences and was well received; in fact, it made quite a sensation when it was published. We received commendatory letters from the experts in Canada, the United States, and even from Australia. Involved in similar research, they wrote of their own experiences and commented on ours.

Bruno and I were interviewed and photographed, and our paper was reviewed in psychiatric bulletins and journals. Neither of us liked what we looked like in the photographs, but we both thought the other looked better. Following a presentation, a television person came running after us asking for a live interview. Bruno suggested, or rather, he *made* me do the interview. He was not a man to chase the limelight, always ready to give his staff exposure and credit. What was remarkable at the Clinic was the absence of a hierarchy. As a multi-disciplinary team we were all involved in the same work, clinical and research. When we attended conferences, Bruno was always surrounded by members of his staff, psychiatrists, criminologists, and social workers alike. We sat at the same table at the banquets unless of course Bruno was being honoured. I must say he made me feel mighty important!

In the early eighties I left the Clinic again for a spiritual experience in New York. Bruno was not at all pleased with that decision. For him it was a descent into hell. I had given three months' notice and he chided me all that time. He warned me that I was burning my bridges behind me but, throwing caution to the wind, I left anyway. Six months later I was back in Montreal begging again for my job back. Bruno asked me if I had learned anything in New York and I told him, flippantly, that I learned about love. Much to my surprise he said, "Good, now you can apply it here." He offered me the post at the Miriam Kennedy Youth Clinic adjacent to the Forensic Clinic. Besides working with adolescents, I could see my old patients and do research. By this time I was a government employee integrated into the Ville Marie Social Services (now Batshaw) and paid by them.

No sooner did I get back to work than the public servants went on strike. I picketed along with my social work colleagues in front of the Clinic. Bruno, wildly antagonistic to unions, although he considered himself a socialist, passed me on the sidewalk without a nod on his way to lunch. For some days after, the sight of me provoked a sneer. But Bruno did not hold a grudge for long; he even let me have the biggest office at the youth clinic, where I was to be in charge of the staff of three psychiatrists and a secretary. Bruno warned me that it would be a challenge and indeed it was.

We planned to have our regular Friday didactic case conferences at the youth clinic, with the intention of inviting workers from youth courts to present their cases and receive input from our staff, chiefly from Bruno our teacher. The Friday conferences were one of Bruno's favourite and sacred Clinic activities. "You must attend Friday conferences even if your grandmother dies" sounded startling at first but again it must have been just an expression. Fortunately it was never put to the test. We had a good attendance the first Friday but no one came with cases, so we presented our own in the hope that it would catch on. Gradually as the weeks passed, the attendance dwindled down to one social worker who was attentive, interested, but still did not present a case. As far as the psychiatrists of the youth clinic were concerned, they came late or not at all. These psychiatrists, competent in their field, were used to working on their own and did not present a team or, I may say, a family as we did at the Forensic Clinic.

All this may not sound very interesting except for the fact that I had never put so much effort into making a success of something. I had to prove to Bruno that I could meet the challenge. Every week I wrote letters to the supervisors at the juvenile courts reminding them of the next meeting. Gradually those letters had a tone of cajoling, pleading, begging, and all to no avail. Before these meetings I would carry chairs up three flights of stairs from the basement and set them up in a circle in the conference room. The youth clinic psychiatrists *en passant* watched. Headed by Bruno, the staff of the Forensic Clinic was the first to arrive. We waited for the psychiatrists of the youth clinic. Bruno bounced and twisted in his chair. Scowling at me, he asked where "they" were and that I should go get "them." The shrinks, as Bruno collectively called them, were with their patients.

It was no surprise that Bruno shut down the youth clinic and integrated services for juveniles into the Forensic Clinic. Of course that left me in limbo. I never got an answer when I asked Bruno what I should do. He asked where I was going when teary-eyed I put my coat on to leave. He told me he wanted to talk to me, which he didn't but probably intended to. I followed him to his office. He answered the phone, turned to me, and asked if I was free to come to dinner. I thought it was a consolation prize but said yes because I liked going to his house for dinner. He gently put the phone down, always gentle with Ruby Cormier. Well, it turned out that he had a document that said the Department of Social Affairs had a post at the McGill Forensic Clinic, but he had never been able to fill that post. Now that I had the government post at the youth clinic, they would be obliged to keep me at the Forensic Clinic, but I would have to write them a letter. I asked Bruno what I should say and his answer was, "Use your imagination," another important lesson from Bruno.

I wrote about Bruno Cormier's worldly renown as the foremost forensic psychiatrist; about the Clinic functioning on a shoestring; about the need for professional staff to serve our community; and about how I could fulfill that need with my experience and (at last I could say) with my qualifications. I received a response from one official who passed the buck to another who advised me to arrange a meeting with Bruno Cormier and the chief of all officials, who as it happened, wanted to see me alone. It took many weeks, but step by step I built up my case, and in the end I must have exhausted the entire hierarchy of officials. I received a phone call. A tired voice said, "You have the post. I'm sending you a letter of confirmation."

In order to satisfy the requirements of the government, I had to be affiliated with an agency of the Ville Marie Social Services. Paul Williams, the director of the John Howard Society who was well acquainted with Bruno Cormier and the Clinic, graciously accommodated me, and for awhile I had an office there as well as at the Clinic. Eventually I was able to see my clients from the agency at the Clinic where I was installed full-time. Now I was at the Clinic for my longest stretch until 1989, when at sixty-five years I retired.

In reminiscing about Bruno I think about the impact he had on me with just a few words. He was not one to inquire about our personal lives but somehow he knew us so well. When I was about to make changes in my life that he objected to, I always thought it was for the sake of the Clinic. That was partially true but in thinking back on it many years later I was able to see the wisdom of his objections on my behalf. One difficulty Bruno had with me was my lack of confidence and my indecision when it came to writing papers. I had a hard time getting started. He would be impatient when I asked too many questions. I expected him to tell me what to write but instead I only ruffled his feathers. I remember that in the end he would smile up at me from behind his desk and say, "Use your imagination."

Bruno was not generous with compliments. Maybe he thought it would go to our heads and slow down our performance. The best I could ever get out of him was that I was a good therapist because I kept my patients. However, he did comment favourably when I stopped dying my hair. I walked away thinking, "He noticed!"

I cannot fathom what were the best of times with Bruno Cormier. Working with him had been exciting much of the time, frustrating some of the time, and stimulating most of the time. His perspicacious mind asked questions and answered them almost simultaneously. Outside of the Clinic he changed personality, that is to say, he was able to detach himself from the demands and pressures of his work. He disagreed with the reputation he had of a shy man, and rightly so. Bruno was not shy. He was a quiet man (socially) taking in everything around him. Somehow he shone in his silence.

At one of his Christmas parties at his home, I have a vivid memory of him dancing with the rest of us, a very rare thing for Bruno. He was a good sport and a charming host, always. Bruno's classic invitation to the Christmas parties, year after year, included husbands and wives of the staff and, "You can even bring your lovers." Some of us smiled, others rolled their eyes. Another little ritual speech was given before a vacation. "Have a good time and don't think about us at the Clinic." But as mentioned earlier, if many of the staff took off at the same time, Bruno was, at the least, disgruntled. He could have (if he was that kind of man) regretted the warm farewells. I do not recall any organization around vacations. Everybody seemed to be doing their own thing. Maybe because of the lack of a hierarchy!

I remember the lunches we shared at Schwartz's deli where he liked the smoked meat sandwiches but had to forego his midday beer, or the restaurants on the Main where he could have his beer. At noon Bruno would come to my office and ask if I was going for lunch, never if I would like to have lunch with him. Those lunches, which he called having a sandwich, involved his going to the bank first and sometimes to his barber for a haircut and once shopping for a suit before we sat down to a hearty meal at his favourite restaurant. We talked shop over lunch, and subtly I was able to get all the information I needed to help my next patients. A bit tipsy (a glass of wine for me), I'd clear my head walking back to the Clinic to work until evening.

After Friday case conferences, Bruno, Ingrid, and I would walk (he strolled) over to Park Avenue for what Bruno called a *détente*, a drink in the hotel at La Cité. How good it was to see him relaxed, able to forget the Clinic for that interval anyway. Ingrid and I contributed little to the conversation, always wanting to learn more about Bruno, the private man—his interest in art, in architecture, the movies he saw, his country farm. It seemed to me that Bruno lived very much in the present.

Best of all were the unexpected invitations to dinner at the Cormier home. As I drove Bruno home from work from time to time, he would phone Ruby to say I was coming to dinner. I'd go through the motions of "please, no fussing" and "are you sure," and I was always met with the response I cherish most from both Ruby and Bruno, "Baila, you are family."

When I retired from the Clinic and moved to New Mexico to be with my family and to write my memoirs (using my imagination), Bruno had already taken sick but was out of hospital and, as I later learned, was semi-active at the Clinic. I would regularly return to Montreal twice a year, which gave me the opportunity to keep my ties with the Cormiers. The last time I saw Bruno, he greeted me warmly and asked, "How is the life of Baila?" I was briefly puzzled by the way he asked how I was until it came to me that he was referring to my book. Leave it to Bruno to recall it. He had a most unusual memory even when confronted with a fatal illness. His last words to me were. "That's what I want to do. I am looking forward to writing poetry after I finish this pedophelia paper."

Sadly, Bruno Cormier was not given the time to write his poetry, but what a legacy he left—an amazing collection of papers and for me, personally, memories of an exciting period of my life working with this very smart, innovative, dedicated, and charismatic man.

Baila Markus, *M.S.W., Royal Victoria Hospital, Forensic Psychiatry Clinic, retired, 1989.*

The McGill Clinic in Forensic Psychiatry and the John Howard Society of Quebec, 1982; Miriam Kennedy Youth Clinic of Ville Marie Social Services and McGill Clinic in Forensic Psychiatry, 1978; McGill Clinic in Forensic Psychiatry, 1975-1978; The Office of the Rights of Prisoners, League of Human Rights, Montreal, 1974-1975; L'Association de Santé Mentale du Troisième Arrondissement de Paris and Dispensaire d'Hygiene Mentale de Villeurbanne (Lyon), 1973-1974; John Howard de Society of Quebec, 1972-1973; McGill Clinic in Forensic Psychiatry, 1971-1972.

Guy Mersereau

*But far more than the sum of these memories, what
Bruno Cormier gave me was what good art gives,
a great expansion of experience.*

 How did I miss so much? Never notably quick on the
uptake, was I that slow or maybe not even very
bright? Or was it him?

These thoughts came to me during the memorial
service for Bruno Cormier, September 24, 1991, as
speaker after speaker spoke of his involvement in *le Refus global*
and the art world from which it came. Sure, I'd been to his home
several times and noticed how well-appointed it was with various
objets d'art. I'd even heard he was somewhat of a collector of such
things. But how any of this other life of his, past or present, could
possibly relate to our work at the Clinic, I had no idea.

Curiosity grew from this, however, and beside the obvious task
of collecting Bruno's works it seemed reasonable to try to relate the
earlier art to the later science. At Cyril Greenland's instigation, such
an attempt was made on April 22, 1994, at the Toronto Queen
Street Archives on the History of Canada, under the rather unlikely
title of "The Anti-forensic Psychiatry of Bruno Cormier."[1] A clumsy
effort illustrated with Automatiste art, it did at least draw some
attention to that period of Quebec history. And it educated me.

With Ruby Cormier's invaluable help, I was able to interview
Bruno's schoolmates, Pierre Gauvreau and Jean-Louis Roux, co-
signatory Magdeleine Arbour, Bruno's sister, and Ray Ellenwood
of *Egregore* (Toronto: Exile Editions, 1992) fame.[2] How can one
express the insights gained from these glimpses into this world?
Pierre in the midst of his work and with his flair for dramatic por-
trayal. The profound cultured expressiveness of the future senator

and Lieutenant-Governor. The feminine fabric of Mme. Arbour's insights. The family view of Bruno as a child. And the studied passion of that gang of artists that shook the Quebec establishment.

Memories of my old chief were awakened. Sometimes they would awaken themselves. "Myth(e)" resonated with Borduas' "magi(e)c," while it echoed Bruno's response to my excited report of what to me was a group delusion at Dannemora. This last had originated from inmates' complaints about the lights and requests for "shades" (sun-glasses). In the regular therapeutic meeting a suspicion emerged that the standard fluorescent lights were part of an experiment by an administration complicit with the university. Arguments to the contrary were ineffective. If this had happened in an individual case, I maintained, it would be considered a delusion, so why not report it as a *folie à plusieurs?* Bruno replied that this was rather a not-so-unusual instance of myth formation. Nothing to bestir our readership. Although I still felt we were on to something, his view, of course, prevailed.

In my now-tortured retrospection, I'd like to have argued that our public may not have shared his sophistication on the madness of crowds. And he, having gone from "all the world's a stage" to its prison microcosm, and then having brought prison to the criminologic stages of the world, could hardly share my personal enthusiasm at the discovery of so well known a phenomenon.

Bruno was remarkably—if not always—patient with his diverse crew. I don't know why I went to him for my first job as a fully trained psychiatrist. I had seen and heard him once before this: his lecture on persistent criminality in the McGill diploma course. When I went for the job, it was mainly just that: something to keep me and my young family alive while I thought about what I might do with the rest of my life. (Such thoughts as these never having come to any conclusion, I've stayed in jail ever since.)

He had two jobs to offer, one doing clinical psychiatry in the maximum security St. Vincent de Paul Penitentiary, the other on the professional team for his new therapeutic community at Dannemora, N.Y., for the Clinton State Prison. He said while I'd make more money at the first, he wouldn't advise doing it full-time for long. I took both jobs part-time and never regretted the decision. At the same time he warned me that he wasn't easy to work for. I was never quite sure what he meant by that.

The basic-training ground—our "boot camp," if you will—was the Penitentiary. I learned how to read a criminal record, not as confirmation or disconfirmation of the patient's history, but as an aid to developing it. The examining orientation was phenomenological, time divided by the crime, distinguishing pre-delictual, delictual and post-delictual states. Psychodynamics were seen, of course, in Kleinian terms derived from depressive or paranoid positions.

But advanced teaching tools, like words, whether spoken or written, are not as basic to medicine as are more primitive, imitative methods. Watching Bruno at work was to see a style not commonly taught. However psychoanalytic his formulations, his interviewing style was hardly passive. Luckily most of the work was in French, for some important meanings suffer in translation. An interjection like *"Ecoute!"* won't work as well rendered as "Listen!" I once tried a Cormier interpretation on a bilingual patient in a Hamilton hospital: *"Aimes-tu le gout de la merde que tu le manges tout le temps?"* The response, while it missed the point, was quite idiomatic: "Well fuck you too."

Little psychiatry by psychiatrists at the penitentiaries was done outside of interview rooms, but Bruno made a point of visiting each psychiatric cell before Christmas. At one such visit we saw a painting done by the inmate. Bruno flew into a rage and ordered it removed. I'd never seen him so angry. The picture was mainly of a blue sky with two beautiful boys. These I learned were of two of the inmate's murder victims pictured by him as in Heaven. It was one of the cases we used to illustrate semi-specific homicide in the paper under that title.[3]

Staff were all-important to Bruno. To him they were "family," and they responded in kind. Whether at the Pen, at Dannemora, or at "Five-oh-nine" (Pine Avenue, "the Clinic" in Forensic Psychiatry), whether squabbling among themselves or not, a fierce loyalty remained. In this they resembled the Automatiste *égrégore* and the (now only partially infamous) group around Ewen Cameron at "the Allan" (Memorial Institute). Inter-disciplinary team-mates, Bruno would quip that they were qualified as "sociable workers."

Our training, of course, was basically by doing the job, then discussing it. The watcher-watched dynamics at Dannemora were such that the main discussions were with all concerned and so held there on site. If issues were being avoided, Bruno would raise them, sometimes as much to our surprise as to that of the inmates. I remember squirming when he dropped such a bomb at a community meeting on the topic of masturbation.

Report-writing, especially for the New York State Parole Boards, was another important school. We were repeatedly reminded of the need to address effectively both options before the board, including specific pre-delictual warning signs under the "street" option.

But it wasn't all work. Lunches or just a beer, parties anywhere but usually at one of our homes, and the day at Bruno and Ruby's country place. Politics was a favourite topic, usually much broader than that of the justice system. It's known, of course, that Bruno was no stranger to the corridors of power, but this was another part of his life which he didn't advertise to us. He had tried to get a therapeutic community in a Canadian prison but was repeatedly rebuffed, even after the Dannemora project began and David Orlikow, M.P. (Winnipeg North, 1962-88) asked in the House of Commons why there instead of here. And the politics of Canadian psychiatry was not a favourite forum, though he presented his findings at many of their meetings. This relative neglect was reciprocated by their finding other, usually less qualified, official spokesmen on justice matters. A more congenial forum was in the criminologic circles where he gained international prominence. We'll see how this played out in the Canadian Corrections Association over the Special Detention-Correction Unit at St. Vincent de Paul.

My own outside interests came to Bruno's attention when I

suggested to him I might be better employed in Viet-Nam. This reminded him of the Spanish Civil War and he said it made more sense to fight for the Viet-Cong than do medical work there. If I were looking for causes, he added, he could provide plenty closer to home for which to fight.

But far more than the sum of these memories, what Bruno Cormier gave me was what good art gives, a great expansion of experience. I had already gotten some such expansion coming back to McGill to finish my training in psychiatry. The Department was in a "thousand-flowers" period, and Bruno just happened to be the one I picked. My earlier, half-baked dialectical views got transformed by his interactive concepts, which I later tried to reformulate in terms of general systems theory. Now, working with a more modest language-based model (maybe one-quarter baked), I still find myself going back to things I learned from Bruno, especially *The Watcher and the Watched*.[4]

Quis custodiet ipsos custodes? Other than the title, little survives in print of the important fruits of Bruno Cormier's watching of the watchers. A tough discipline learned from Freud via Melanie Klein and thence via his own analysis, his staff caught some insights from his dealing with them. It is based, of course, on that now-little-taught art, the analysis of transference.

Most of the staff had little formal psychoanalytic training beyond the usual fare then in Psychiatry school. A personal analysis was neither expected nor particularly encouraged. The concepts Bruno used, phenomenologic and as much socio-dynamic as psychodynamic, were learned in our case conferences where they were applied individually before being systematized for the studies that were later reported. Psychoanalese, especially terms like "acting-out," was employed more precisely than was common elsewhere. The field, of course, had its own imprecisions, and Bruno was as guilty as his analytic brethren in other tortures of medical language, e.g., "symptom" as synonym for "manifestation."

Blaming the parents, a common pseudo-analytic sport of the day, was dealt with in the Clinic by analyzing the counter-transference. If he says momma made him do it, how is it that you're buying this? The current "false memory" versus "recovered memory" debate could well benefit from such an *optique*.

"The Watcher and the Watched" entitles much more than Bruno Cormier's one published book. It's also the title of the paper with Paul Williams,[5] and the concept was developed in the earlier "On the history of the men and genocide" paper out of the "classic" observation of *persécuté-persécuteur*.[6] Like another francoformulation, *folie à deux*, it breaks the individualistic bounds of mainstream English adult (non-analytic) psychiatry in reconstructing the "interacting pair" as the basic unit. Such agent-patient, doer-done-to, action-passion talk is more the stuff of French *jeux de mots* than of modern science, whether from a forensic or psychiatric *optique*. Not research to interest drug houses.

But our governments had some money for some non-quick-fix criminology, and Bruno was able to tap into that for quite a number of his lesser works. But not the big one. Then an inmate Johnny in Dannemora State Hospital in the New York State Department of Corrections was judicially found to be one of a class held therein beyond warrant expiry without due cause. The resultant void—with the attendant superfluity of civil servants—led to a sudden interest in a therapeutic community south of our undefended border. Bruno was called and the rest can be read in *The Watcher and the Watched.*

The Word and Bruno Cormier:

"What is he saying?"

"Qu'est ce qu'il dit, lui?"

The English thought it was his second language, the French his McGill ideas. Non-analysts called it analytic mystique or downright nonsense; non-Kleinians blamed Melanie.

Language problems were most evident when Bruno spoke. Many (possibly most) of his papers were rewritten by others more literate—though less literary—in English than he, leaving his readers with other levels of hermeneutic problems. But his speech had to be absorbed, filtered, and contextualized more than most before some glimmerings of understanding could be formed. Working with him was not for the linguistically challenged. (How I survived there as long as I did remains a mystery to me.)

An exercise of limited value has been to compare French and English versions of the same material. A key word is the verb "to watch," *a veiller*—or is it? The English doesn't include the meaning of spending an evening, nor does Cormier, but he does make it clear that he means something more attentive than is usually denoted by either the French or the English used. It may be better described in his *Refus global* essay where he depicts the alert hunter *aux aguettes*.[7] It's usually used nominally, though, and the *résumé* appended to the 1971 Watcher paper uses both *surveillant* and *gardien*. Some consolation is the struggle of so skilled an Automatiste interpreter as Ray Ellenwood with the *double entendre* on the word *experience* in the essay's title which he decides to render "an experiment and an experience." This appears in *Total Refusal* (Toronto: Exile, 1985).[8] More specific insight, however, may be found in the marketing of Foucault's *Surveiller et punir* (Paris: Gallimard, 1975)[9] as *Discipline and Punish* (New York: Vintage, 1979).[10]

The threatening nature of the situation described might bring the word *vigilant* to the English mind that happened to know there was such a word in French, but Bruno studiously avoided any such celestial implications. This avoidance is not so easy in a language so conditioned by King James as is the English. Maurice Duplessis had chased the Jehovah's Witnesses purveyors of *The Watchtower* and *Awake!* from the streets of Montreal, but the biblical connotations of these words hang longer and deeper in the minds of *les anglais*.

And the mind of the psychiatrist, especially if American Board qualified, must necessarily turn to *neurologic* correlates, notably in the brain stem. Clinical paranoia in prison is typically treated by, and frequently responsive to, neuroleptic drugs. Equally typical, however, is poor (or no) compliance with such treatment. Our patients often voice the fear that the drug will impair their ability to respond appropriately. Bruno warned us of a lower tolerance for these drugs than was found in hospital practice. And fear is not an indication for neurolepsis. Psychotic anxiety maybe, but fear, no. Canada would not send soldiers to Somalia or Bosnia or Iraq, or wherever the fighting is now, on those drugs. One needs one's wits, upper and lower, unimpaired just to drive home, let alone to deal with more danger.

Hank Steadman, the other main Johnny beneficiary, reminded us some time ago that one of the most demonstrably dangerous things we do is to find a person dangerous: the endangered "dangerous," *"dangereux" en danger.* (Our current Canadian penal reformers seem to have heard of neither of the sons of Johnny: neither Steadman nor Cormier.) One's wits, particularly the lower, the alerting wit, are there to protect one, but lacking temper they can do one in.

This is not the place to speculate about such things as the function of the reticular activating system, its neuro-vegetative connections, and their chemical regulation in the deprivation of liberty, tempting as they may be at this point. Suffice it that our regular pharmacotherapy at the Pen was well within the range of that practised elsewhere, intramural or extramural, if tending to the conservative. At Dannemora, need for such intervention was an exclusion criterion, so psychotherapy, group and individual, reigned supreme.

Psychotherapy, the talking treatment, is of course a species of dialogue usually involving more listening than talking by the therapist. Sometimes as our conferences became dominated by his monologues, we might wonder how much listening Bruno actually did. Still, the essential reciprocity between the watcher beside the couch and the watched upon it was never far from our deliberations. Part of the training was to learn a different valuation of the spoken word *vis-à-vis* the unspoken act, especially in the reading of the record. We all have our dysphasias (and dysgraphias) but manage somehow to express ourselves, and even sometimes to communicate with another.

Ethics

Forensic Psychiatry
509 Pine Avenue, West
26 May 1965

The Honourable Guy Favreau
Minister of Justice Department of Justice
Ottawa

Dear Sir:

Silence may be the easiest way out of a difficult situation, and many reasons could justify my silence at present. It may be said that as a psychiatrist at St. Vincent de Paul Penitentiary, I go beyond my duties if I publicly express myself on the policy of the Ministry of Justice. I am a physician and researcher, and I cannot accept the argument that because I am part-time psychiatrist at St. Vincent de Paul, I am not to protest against the construction of a penal institution which disregards the psychology of the deprivation of liberty and its effects on the individual prisoner, most particularly the so called "hardened, rebellious" individuals who, without question, need very special care.

The Special Detention Unit which is being built in the Province of Quebec and is designed for this group is not only inhumane to men whom the state justly detains both for the protection of society and for treatment, but it creates a situation which will inhibit treatment possibilities. It will lead to further deterioration of men who are already socially and psychologically ill. I do not hesitate to say that when this centre, as presently designed is in use, a psychiatrist will have the painful task of treating emotional illnesses that are partly the result of conditions created by the

state itself. I have criticized the construction of this special
detention unit from the start and my protests have grown
stronger as further information, though unofficial presented and explained to the National Executive of the
Canadian Corrections Association that I realized their
fullest implication *[sic]*. Till this recent meeting, I continued to treasure the hope that my associates on the Liaison
Committee would succeed in preventing the construction
of this unit. I know now that, having done everything to
state their case, they failed and that the worst seems
inevitable. As my protests could find no echo outside the
walls, I must allow myself, as a professor in charge of
Forensic Psychiatry at McGill University, the right to
address myself directly to you. A career devoted entirely to
research and criminology imposes its responsibility.

I find it hard to understand how, having personally
been in contact with so many inmates, having treated
them inside the penitentiary, followed them on the outside with my colleagues of the McGill research group in
Forensic Psychiatry, I was not at any time consulted about
appropriate plans. It is precisely inmates with character
disorders who, at some time or other, because of their
deeply pathological personality structures, come to the
attention and care of the psychiatrist.

My protest against the special detention unit is founded on ten years of lived experience at St. Vincent de Paul
Penitentiary, where I share the vicissitudes of the prisoners
and of those who have the difficult task of caring for them,
of trying to understand them, and change them. I cannot
put these years out of existence, nor deny the scientific and
human considerations which justify my unequivocal con-
demnation of the special detention unit. My reasons are
based neither on abstract theoretical notions nor on senti-
mental considerations, but on hard knowledge. My experience has also grown out of the clinic in Forensic Psychiatry

at McGill University, where we have worked with ex-inmates for a sufficiently long period of time, and in sufficient depth, to have gained first-hand information about the effects of certain conditions of the deprivation of liberty which may result in a man losing what remaining ability he has to live free. I find it necessary to inform you how strongly my research associates and I condemn this move, and we add our voice to the Canadian Corrections Association that the construction of the special detention unit be immediately halted. We further respectfully suggest that you personally call to your assistance those who are in a position to give you advice and information of which you may not have previously been aware.

Pioneer work on the consequences of sensory isolation has been carried on in Canada so that we are in possession of valid information about its effects. The McGill Clinic in Forensic Psychiatry has also studied the effects of deprivation of liberty as a punishment. Necessary and unavoidable as such punishment is for some offenders, it has, nevertheless, ill effects which we should not overlook. Our main objection lies in the type of cell that is planned for the new special detention unit, but we wish to make it clear that we strongly criticize the whole architectural design, and above all that it is based on no valid program.

The saddest thing I believe I have heard in my ten years of work is the answer given at the last meeting of the Canadian Corrections Association. When a member of your department was asked whether there was a program for this unit, the answer was so vague that it did not amount to the barest sketch. We were informed that such a program would be organized by experts, and when it was asked who were the experts, there was silence. The final statement was that all this was an experimental project. We can only ask—who are the experimenters?

I can assure you, Sir, that I am writing because of my great personal concern in this matter and that of my colleagues. I understand that penologists in other provinces concur with us in condemning this new prison. I can only regret that our province was chosen to be the first for this "experiment," which is a penological anomaly in the 20th Century.

Yours respectfully,
(signed)
Bruno Cormier, M.D.
Associate Professor
Department of Psychiatry

BMC/mp

cc: Canadian Corrections Association
       Quebec Society of Criminology

Ecce homo & res ipsa loquitur. A similar letter from the professional staff of eight (Bruno, Raymond Boyer, Tony Galardo, Miriam Kennedy, Tony Obert, Paul Williams, Carlos Barriga, Siebert Simons) followed five days later. Further efforts to stop the SDU/USD are described in a letter of July 22, 1965, to Lucien Cardin, Favreau's successor. The campaign failed, and we watched the renamed, imperceptibly improved Special Correction Unit rise from the ground next to St. Vincent de Paul. We toured the place, including the concrete block of electrically operated cells. They were indeed windowless save for the ceiling glassed strip beside the catwalk. We were shown a junction of corridors which was explained could be used for a small meeting. We also saw workshops beside the cell block, and a four-stage program was described, starting with full "dissociation" as in similar areas of other prisons, and culminating in a typical maximum security, work-and-play schedule. The whole was enclosed in a sheet-metal structure surrounded by two security fences, the observation tower its landmark.

Protective custody inmates were the first to arrive, some weeks after the inevitable security flaws had been remedied, followed some time later by the hard-core bad guys for whom the place was designed. Not long after this, the first escape occurred, demonstrating the problem of fitting program, plant, and population. As we did not extend our service to include this place, an outside psychiatrist was secured for it, and the only casualties we saw were those transferred to St. Vincent de Paul.

Ethical practice within walls is a constant war with whatever maintains those walls, that microcosm again dramatizing—at least to those within—the larger society it serves. This was the *optique* from which Bruno saw the panorama of the "On the history of men and genocide." The connection was made more explicit in his "Mass Murder, Multicide and Collective Crime" (1975)[11] including a discussion of Henry Dicks' work with SS killers, *Licensed Mass Murder,* London: Chatto, 1972.[12] The co-option of a physician by a more recent murderous regime in Latin America was dramatized by Ariel Dorfman in *Death and the Maiden,*[13] and related to the earlier work in my "Bruno Cormier, *Death and the Maiden*" (Archives of the Health Sciences, 1001 Queen Street, Toronto, 1995).[14] Most recently we have the Ontario mega-jails being questioned by the Canadian and Ontario Psychiatric associations as well as by the Physicians in Corrections of Ontario, with similar results. *L'Unité Spéciale de Détention* remains with us, of course, in the federal SHUs (Special Handling Units) *a mari usque ad mare.* As Bruno counselled me, we don't have to look far for causes to espouse.

Qu'est ce qu'il reste à dire? What's left to say without that restless dramatist to say it in endless obscurity? *Plus ça change, plus c'est la même chose.* We know he had lots more to say than that.

The discussions in recent years found me speculating on what Bruno's reaction might have been to the revival of the defence of automatism. He certainly was aware of its existence, but I can recall only learning at the Clinic the Canadian distinction between it and insanity. Being then totally unaware of his antecedents in the art world (other than hearing that he had played in *Petrouchka*), I had no way of knowing that deep other significance of the word to him. He had no patience with the classical forensic questions like insanity and likened the debates over such niceties to the casuistry of scholastic theology as taught by the Jesuit fathers. Far from the legal category encoded as a more severe derangement than insanity, he knew automatism as a consummation devoutly to be wished by any artist. Both are views of a transport beyond the self, the one morbid the other mystic. In this respect I believe Bruno remained much closer to his religious and artistic roots than to forensic psychiatry.

In lieu of summation, since I find it impossible to sum up the man, may I say that, of his many parts, I was privileged to meet a few. These scattered memories, together with those of others and selections from his writings, will paint perhaps a surreal picture, but one which I hope is more *impressioniste* than *automatiste*. As well as those *taches*, which may punctuate more than portray, I've allowed myself some expression of my own thought as it has developed from the impact Bruno Cormier had upon me.

Basic to his work is the irreducible mutuality of human phenomena and the ethical burden flowing therefrom, but above that and beyond any specific memory of mine, he radiated such a *joie de vivre* that even now I find it hard to believe he's dead. As I concluded in my eulogy for the Canadian Psychiatric Association,[15] a tough act to follow but one that must be followed.

I cannot conclude now without thanking those, too many to name, who helped me when my part of this project was more ambitious. Special thanks and recognition, however, must go to Ruby Cormier for her unstinting efforts, patience, and hospitality.

Guyon Mersereau, *M.D., C.M., McGill, 1959, FRCP(C), Consultant psychiatrist, Niagara and Hamilton Detention centres, Ont. Consultant psychiatrist, Ministry of Corrections and Hamilton Psychiatric Hospital, 1974-1993; Director, Erie County (N.Y.) Forensic Services, 1970-1974; Psychiatrist, Canadian Penitentiary Service and New York State, Department of Corrections, with Dr. Bruno Cormier, 1967-1970; General practitioner, Welland, Ont., 1961-1963.*

Notes

1. Mersereau, G. "The Anti-forensic Psychiatry of Bruno Cormier' Archives on the History of Psychiatry and Mental Health Services, Toronto: 1994.

2. Ellenwood, R. *Egregore.* Toronto: Exile Editions, 1992.

3. Cormier, B., Angliker, C., Boyer, R., Kennedy M., Mersereau, G., "Psychodynamics of homicide committed in semi-specific relationship." *Can. J Criminol and Corrections,* 1972, 14: 335-344.

4. Cormier, B., ed. *The Watcher and the Watched.* Montreal: Tundra Books, 1975.

5. William, P. "The Watcher and the Watched," *Can. Psychiat. Assoc. J.,* 1971, 16:15-21.

6. Cormier, B. "On the history of men and genocide." *Can. Med. Assoc. J.,* 1966, 94: 276-291.

7. Cormier, B. "L'oeuvre pictorale est une expérience." In Borduas P.-E., et al. *Refus global.* Montreal: Maurice Perron, 1948.

8. Ellenwood, R. *Total Refusal.* Toronto: Exile Editions, 1985.

9. Foucault, M. *Surveiller et punir.* Paris: Gallimard, 1975.

10 Sheridan, Alan. *Discipline and Punish.* New York: Vintage, 1979.

11. Cormier, B. "Mass Murder, multicide and collective crime." In Drapkin, I., Viano E., eds.*Victimology: A New Focus*, vol.4. Lexington: Lexington Books, 1975: 71-90.

12. Dicks, H. *Licensed Mass Murder.* London: Chatto, 1972.

13. Dorfman, A. *Death and the Maiden.* New York: Penguin, 1994.

14. Mersereau, G. "Bruno Cormier, *Death and the Maiden."* Archives of the Health Sciences. Toronto, 1995.

15. Mersereau, G. "In memorium: Bruno Cormier," *Canad. Psychiat. Assoc. Bulletin,* 1991: 5-17.

Hans Mohr

*His concern and his work were based on a
humanism, informed as it was by
the life experiences of his generation.*

À La Recherche

I

This title impressed itself ever more strongly in the process of reflecting on Bruno Cormier and his work. What evolved was, and yet was not, a *Remembrance of Things Past*, the customary translation of Proust's *À la recherche des temps perdues*. It was not so much a question of "things" as of "time," not a question of a past that has passed by, but a question of what has been lost *(perdue)* and ought to be recalled so as not to be wasted. More specifically, what emerged was indeed a re-search of the kind of research that was central to Bruno Cormier's work, central to my relationship with him as well as that of many others. It informed not only his work and that of his colleagues but formed a community of interest, indeed shaped it. One looked forward to the research conferences that he initiated and conducted almost single-handedly as a kind of family affair. His wife, Ruby, provided a centre of stability, was a welcoming committee of one, and brought an unexpected sense of coherence to last-minute arrangements, balancing order and spontaneity, adventure and conviviality.

There was a sense of curiosity and excitement at the very beginning of these meetings, surrounded the scheduled sessions, led to heated discussions that went on everywhere. It is almost inconceivable today that conferences which draw together people from across the country and beyond could be arranged without outside assistance and without any money to speak of. Bruno's

137

small staff, in addition to preparing their own presentations which usually included observations of the last set of cases seen, also had to function as guides, bring together people with shared interests. Expenses were minimal and it did not even occur to me to ask for reimbursement of costs from my clinic even though the pay for research positions was poor.

The *temps perdues* to be re-searched is thus not a search for things past, nor even for time lost or wasted, but a search for a spirit that seems to have somehow receded, gone underground, as it were, persists only as a memory of those who have been touched by it. It also represents an *esprit de corps* that needs to be recalled as a marker and trace of the proverbial "Sixties." And thus this particular memory becomes one "De l'esprit," a question *Of Spirit* so tenaciously pursued by Derrida in his attempt to grasp a different time, a different place, a very different person. The time to be "re-membered" here, to be re-searched, is well marked. Bruno founded the McGill Clinic in Forensic Psychiatry in 1955; and it appears to me that the end of this time, the end of its spirit, can be retrospectively marked as 1975, as foretold in the closing pages of *The Watcher and the Watched* published in that year. Bruno always seemed to sense earlier than others the nature of a given time, the demands it makes, the opportunities it provides for the expression of ideas, the performance of tasks. Much of what he stood for may by now seem to be utopian but it is what we too learned to believe, a belief few of us have abandoned despite the coming upon us of a different time. And he, more than we younger ones, knew the obstacles that stood in the way, needed to be overcome, or later resisted when they re-emerged in full strength, when the tide turned.

So, when at the end of *The Watcher and the Watched* he senses that *Closing Time* was approaching, he still insists that there is hope: "In the meantime, I believe as long as prisons exist, independent voices must be heard, not outside the walls but inside." The kind of voice he represented is now barely audible inside and

finds little echo outside. Thus, a re-search of the spirit of Bruno
Cormier must also come to terms with the fact that inspired spirits
so often lead to apparently contrary results. It is not, or so the
assertion will be, because their searches and researches turn out
to be wrong-headed and are thus rejected in time. It is rather that
the very acceptance of their ideas, their professionalization and
institutionalization turn the spirit into instrumental means and
thus tend to produce apparently incommensurable results. This
can be observed, for example, in the case of Sigmund Freud
whose ideas became acceptable to institutional psychiatry at about
the same time. This resulted in a *furor therapeuticus*, as Freud himself had called it, followed by disappointment and rejection when
it turned out that those ideas could not be mechanically repro-
duced and applied and did not lead to instant salvation. Bruno's
search, even if often expressed in the modes of institutional
research, was essentially a search for the contingencies of the
human condition that could not be captured and re-presented in
terms considered to be scientific; nor could his kind of engagement be turned into mechanical manipulative means.

Bruno Cormier saw very clearly that individual therapeutic
interventions were insufficient to achieve any meaningful social
change. But it was essential to understand the particularity of
human experiences to find ways in which to counteract the massive institutional pressures that formed and deformed human
beings subjected to civilization and its discontents. Those pressures were most clearly visible in the norms and practices of the
criminal process. And thus it was those forces he attempted to
identify and change even though his starting point was the experiences of particular persons enmeshed in this process. For him,
and the colleagues he attracted, it was not so much a question of
individual pathology but predominantly a question of social and
institutional responses to what a certain "pathology" signified.
Phenomena, defined as deviant or criminal, were indeed social
pathologies, constituted and re-inforced by a network of social

relations and societal institutions. Dealing with institutions such as those of the law, it became more and more important to Bruno to show that institutional efforts such as imprisonment tended to further re-inforce deviant behaviour rather than to change it. Not that there had not been a range of efforts before to reform institutions such as prisons, as exemplified in the work of John Howard which, with the best of all intentions, led to the *panopticon*, a prison for watchers and the watched, an institutional arrangement Bruno came to know so well. There is no question that John Howard was a humanitarian, and he despaired when he saw the results of what he had propagated. Or think of the efforts of the Quakers to induce penitence by isolation, leading to "penitentiaries" which isolated inmates but rarely induced penitence. There had also been numerous attempts to define and redefine criminality, deviance, or whatever other name had been invented for marking the proverbial black sheep either in terms of their biological attributes (black), or psychological signs (sins fastened to their fur), or in terms of their social usage to produce a catharsis, a communal cleansing (driven out into the wilderness).

Genetic conditions (bad seed) had not yet been seen as subject to change; this is still reserved for a brave new world to come. But their propagation was curtailed by exclusion, by preventing the spreading of bad seed, as it were, calling for segregated holding institutions, as well as massive eugenic movements that reached their epitome in biological fascism. Along psychological lines there had been glimmers of hope of being able to change the mind of the criminal, "the criminal mind" as it was indeed called. Depending on the belief system that supported those efforts, change of mind could be effected by penitence, by work, by means of psychotherapy or rehabilitation. But those were largely ideas that made punishment and revenge more palatable without changing their basic purpose of degradation. Prisons had become the primary mode of exclusion, creating an environment which counteracted any effort to restore people, as *bien pensant* as these efforts may have been. The creation of particular sciences and particular professions analyzing and curing the ills of the human condition in time led to the proverbial story of the elephant and the blind men. Only that this process (often referred to as progress) was not as innocent as all that, and tended to be, like most institutional efforts, largely self-serving.

Even though Bruno started out with an out-patient clinic that provided assessment and treatment for particular cases, he also investigated the nature of police intervention, what happened in the courts, and he was well acquainted with prisons. It was the fullness of all these interactions that gave shape to the research and the work he initiated, encouraging others to take a more holistic stance. It is difficult enough to bring oneself up to date, as it were, if one has been trained in a particular professional discipline, trained to overlook its limitations. To cross boundaries and involve others that had undergone a different form of training is much harder. We still talk about cross-disciplinary and inter-disciplinary education and research but the training of professionals has, if anything, become even more "disciplined" than it was when Bruno began his forensic work, established his clinic. This move not only led to other clinics and psychiatric centres but also to the establishment of centres, departments and schools of criminology across the country which brought together different disciplines. What started as a spirited enterprise to find wholeness and health (both words sharing their origin with "holy") turned into a search for systematic answers, answers that could be adapted to systems. Not only the legal system and its institutions, but also the educational system and systems of health care have become increasingly committed to technological solutions. The spirit turned literally into a ghost, a *Ghost in the Machine* to be managed by *Sleepwalkers* and propagated by *Call-girls* in Koestler's terms. And those terms are not altogether inappropriate for what in fact happened, is still happening, even though the salvational claims made are no longer believable.

It was clearly not what Bruno Cormier had envisioned. His relationship to the growing teaching and research centres, specializing in the application of punishments by yet another name, became strained even though they honoured him as one of their initiators. His spirit of renewal, in fact, turned into a spirit of resistance when he saw that the efforts of discovery he had spearheaded were turning into new forms of cover-up, provided new (and improved) justifications for institutional "solutions." This development, one should add, was not confined to this field and did not just defeat reforms of law as well as increase the extent and power of repressive institutions as answers to all evil.

II

I joined the Toronto Forensic Clinic in 1960 as a Research Associate and I suspect that it was the model of Bruno's work that led to the establishment not only of the clinic but also of a specific research position even though the clinical staff had a mandate to engage in research. The model, as in other clinical departments of the medical faculty, was treatment, teaching, and research, the first providing the justification for the last, a trend towards "practical" application that now seems to pervade all university departments, all educational institutions. At its inception, the staff had little experience in the forensic field and had to learn to adapt their training in psychiatry, psychology, or social work not just to the needs of clients but also to the demand of the legal process and its institutions. The director of the clinic at the time, Dr. R.E. Turner, was himself a neophyte in this field. There had been a small in-patient unit at the Toronto Psychiatric Hospital (TPH) headed by Dr. K.G. Gray who had been trained in psychiatry and law and this was rather exceptional at that time. This was truly, a "forensic" service, a service predominantly for the courts, asked to examine the mental conditions of accused persons, turning on questions such as "fitness to stand trial" or "the defence of insanity." Bruno had from the beginning staked out a much wider field of research and service. Even though his training was in psychiatry and his inclination had favoured psychoanalytic forms of understanding and treatment, he recognized the need to study systemic effects that determined the definition of crime, the selection of certain people and behaviours for demonstration and control. Thus, research was truly at the centre of his operation and it was not limited to any theoretical model nor confined to any field or profession.

From the sociological perspective it had been well established, at least since Durkheim's *Rules of the Sociological Method,* that crime was an integral part of society and essential to its self-definition. The criminal process was first and foremost in the business of producing and maintaining values and norms. The role of accused persons in this process had not escaped thoughtful legal actors, such as Mr. Justice Holmes, who compared the criminal to the soldier who serves his country and at times has to die for it. Those insights had been much earlier sketched out by Beccaria in *On Crimes and Punishment* which is still a very poignant description of the criminal law and its processes more than two hundred years later. The notion of punishment to satisfy *resentiment* and revenge (our highest ideas in Nietzche's term) now determines the system more than ever. It is true that the *Infliction of a Just Measure of Pain,* as Michael Ignatieff put it, has become less visible and less visibly brutal. It is curious that the brutality of punishment had marked a culture that had been deeply determined by a religion whose God on earth was himself subjected to a criminal process, not unlike the one we have now, was convicted to satisfy those in charge of value maintenance as well as "the people," and sentenced to die on the cross. He was sent, not to change the law, but to fulfill it in love.

In this perspective it is foolhardy to expect that any essential change can be effected. But on the other hand, not to call a society to consciousness and conscience, to hold up a mirror, as it were, of what it is doing to "the least of its members," would remove from society any insight into the deeper layers of self-understanding. Bruno was seen as being foolhardy by many, as one who could not let things well enough alone. But he was by no means naïve about the nature of the process even though his enthusiasm had a child-like quality, a quality he maintained despite the dismal fairy tales played out by mature adults. And it was not that he was not fully aware of the enormity of the task, in particular as a psychiatric consultant to the penitentiary service. Even physical conditions there were still far more graphic than they are now in places such as St. Vincent de Paul with its slop buckets. We have succeeded in making pain and degradation less obvious, have learned to *Discipline and Punish* by other means. And even though Bruno argued for improved conditions in prisons, as anybody who remembers the old prisons (as well as mental hospitals) would understand, he was under no illusion that this would do. The very point of establishing an out-patient clinic was to see what could be achieved outside holding institutions in the very social context in which those accused of a crime lived or to which those convicted and sentenced to prison returned.

Neither did he have any illusions about the sequence of "re-words" that had already shown their fallacy in re-tribution *(sic!)*, and when there was no tribute, turned into re-habilitation which literally was a redressing. And re-conciliation is yet again a counselling that is addressed to some and not others. The present call for restorative justice must also consider whether it makes sense to restore conditions that led to the crime in the first place. It too may well lead to the repetition of offences and renewed efforts to store offenders in holding tanks to pacify an un-restored community. The kind of search Bruno was engaged in, the kind of research he envisaged, was less of a theoretical or disciplinary kind, not even inter-disciplinary in the present sense, but used all available means to challenge the purported purpose of institutions and their "treatment" modalities. What was important was to show their negative effects and to demonstrate how these could possibly be overcome. And although he drew on a wide range of available knowledges, it was his humanistic and artistic spirit that determined the nature of the work to be accomplished. It went well beyond the application of any given treatment modality, focused on exploring the nature and context of behaviours defined as criminal, questioning the rationale of legal-institutional responses. It was an approach that had a measure of public support at the time as well as capturing the interest of some professionals who had begun to question the use of repressive practices in the name of doing good.

From a strategic point of view, an out-patient clinic offered some protection from institutional demands which govern prisons as well as hospitals. And this was clearly appreciated by Bruno who knew that some independence was needed to make one's voice heard, not to be silenced and/or excluded. But despite his charisma, such an achievement would not have been possible without public support. Consider that the establishment of the Toronto Clinic came in the wake of a series of sex-related murders which one would believe would have led to the establishment of another holding facility rather than an out-patient clinic. Such a development is by now rather inconceivable when public pressures seem to demand immediate and prolonged incarceration. There had been some recognition that tragic events were the outcome of human and social processes which had a history and could, perhaps, be detected and treated before they resulted in explosive events. And it was appreciated that prevention could only be achieved if one knew the sources of a sickness, the causes of psychopathology.

Sex had become a central concern to a society caught between the need for control and repression on the one hand and an increasing demand for sexual liberation on the other. Psychoanalysis, particularly of the Freudian kind, had postulated that sexual desires were formed early, were preconditioned by the initial relationship to mother and/or father. If these "libidinal" desires did not mature through various ages and stages, neurosis or deviance would be the result. Permissible expression of desires, the pleasure principle, was limited by a reality principle which confined the expression of sexual desires to socially and legally sanctioned monogamous heterosexual units. Medical as well as legal prescription and proscriptions were detailed and extensive to an extent no longer believable. It is no surprise that those that had been exposed to psychoanalytic thinking would be attracted to a clinic that explored phenomena that constituted the limits of sexual liberation, of the free expression of desires. Official action against homosexual behaviour "between consenting adults in private" had already diminished before criminal sanctions were lifted and the limits of what was considered to be obscene had been shifting for some time. Much of this "liberation" was reserved for the private realm. Public behaviour such as exhibitionism frequently came to the attention of the courts. Age limits to consensual sexual behaviour in private, "carnal knowledge" which "protected" females up to the age of twenty-one no longer represented social realities. Still, limits were demanded and so the question of pedophilia came to the foreground. Questions of consent in cases of unwanted approaches, in the definition of sexual aggression, also had to be redefined. These were indeed the bulk of cases that legal institutions referred to forensic clinics for advice when the application of a punishment tariff seemed to be an inappropriate response.

Bruno Cormier had been committed to psychoanalytic understandings and the first director of the Toronto Clinic, Peter Thompson, became a practising analyst. But Bruno knew from the start that intra-psychic perspectives were not sufficient to explain the singling out of certain forms of behaviour for control and punishment. The major theoretical battles in Toronto were between analysts and behaviourists, whereas for the Montreal contingent the focus was on the nature of social and institutional responses and their effects. As a researcher in the Toronto Clinic with little knowledge of law, courts, and prisons, I started with a systematic analysis of the definition of cases and then proceeded to explore further those cases that were most frequently referred to the clinic, which turned out to be pedophilia and exhibitionism. And although I was committed to a phenomenological perspective, I learned from Bruno and his work to appreciate the nature and effect of institutional responses which I found more and more baffling. The legal process and its assumptions were particularly confusing, and so a lawyer was added to the research team. Much of my later work was determined, not so much by Bruno's research as by his *recherche* in the Proustian sense of finding ways to see (the Greek's sense of *theorem*), his attempts to raise personal consciousness and shape a social conscience.

III

And so, thinking of Bruno Cormier, his spirit and his work, at this point in time, one is invariably led to a *recherche des temps perdues*, less in terms of a *Remembrance of Things Past* as in terms of the loss of a certain spirit. The point is not to bemoan this loss, sad as it is, but to engage in a re-search *de l'esprit des temps*. The ambit of the criminal law has grown progressively since then and so have prisons. Forensic services, on the other hand, have all but disappeared in terms of providing independent voices, have at best returned to serving the system as have most of the educational institutions which sprang from this development. This, too, Bruno had already foreseen in 1975. Now, twenty years later, this process is barely abating despite renewed efforts in terms of restorative justice and community involvement in the process, such as in sentencing circles. There are short-term historical developments but also a *longue durée*; and even if such a perspective may lead one to see only an eternal recurrence of the same, it is nevertheless informative in terms of particular understandings.

Following the Second World War there was on the one hand a need to return to some kind of normalcy which occupied the remaining years of "the Forties" and reached its full expression in "the Fifties." But on the other hand, the experience of the war, preceded by the "Dirty Thirties," could not be set aside for long.

The First World War had already led to an abundance of slaughter between "civilized" nations. It was to be the last of all wars. But after the initial euphoria of "the Twenties" there followed a Depression that was largely interpreted in economic terms, but nevertheless led to a recognition that more radical social changes were necessary, that times of peace, too, demanded moral attention. The war that followed could well be seen as the result of, as well as a reaction to, ideas of radical social change. These ideas sought salvation in various ways. They either banked on a nationalism to re-establish the power of a nation-state in the idea of a *Volk* that was purified; or they pointed to a new internationalism and Communism that would re-distribute the fruits of labour by controlling capital and the ownership of the means of production. The idea of a National Socialism was roundly defeated but led to a Cold War between ideas of Capitalism and Communism. The very commitment to such ideas may by now seem strange even though Capitalism has emerged as the apparent winner.

Bruno's ideology, if one can call it that, did not fit any of these categories. His concern and his work were based on a humanism, informed as it was by the life experiences of his generation. Not only was his work not determined by any particular ideology, he also distanced himself from the kind of scientism that promised the production of positive knowledge. This idea was in fact the predominant ideology everywhere, based on assumptions that this kind of knowledge would make us free, lead to never-ending progress. A further assumption was that this progress would be all for the good, for the good of all. When this did not happen, one had to find ever-new scapegoats to account for the continuation of miseries. Science and technology indeed made it possible to control internal experiences of misery by drugs, avert external threats by unprecedented forms of power. This development was based on a kind of prelapsarian stance that assumed that paradise was possible if it were not for ... the poor, the sick, the mad, or the bad inside society as well as evil enemies threatening from outside.

Experiences such as a Great Depression and a Great War tend to recede and their lessons are forgotten by succeeding generations. Bruno had been a political activist when he was still a student, albeit not in terms in which we tend to understand "politics" now. As a medical student in "the Forties" he was one of the signatories of the *Refus global*, a movement spearheaded by artists concerned with social and cultural as well as political conditions. It was truly an attempt to renew the human spirit, and although it was rooted in the particular history of Quebec, it foreshadowed the spirit that characterized "the Sixties" everywhere. It demanded an examination of repressive factors in one's own "system," of one's history and tradition. Repression and domination came to be seen as outcomes of social arrangements, of power relations that had to be made conscious to become *maître chez nous*. This call for renewal of self and human relations in time also turned into blaming others, called for the liberation from others rather than oneself. The spirit of renewal, the renewal of spirit was exactly what informed Bruno's work. And even though he saw systemic features as being in the foreground, he also was intent to make sure that patients as well as offenders understood that assigning blame to others left them incapacitated. They had to recognize their background and circumstances but then had to address their own deficiencies in their relation to self and other. It seems that this attitude became too demanding for a society increasingly conditioned towards ease, defining problems as a form of "dis-ease" that could be magically cured. And so, it was the notion of separation that carried the day, separation from self to reduce internal pain, as well as separation from others that caused pain, particularly in intimate relations, let alone others for whom one did not care. And one cannot help but suspect that the helping professions, with the best of intentions, contributed to this development by their promise of pain reduction by technological or institutional means.

The incisive experience of Bruno's generation was not only growing up in the shadow of a Great Depression and a world war that outperformed the previous one by far. This experience had shown (again) that apparently "normal," ordinary people could engage in behaviours which under other circumstances would be seen as wanton crimes. Under conditions of war it was possible not to see them as "senseless," a term frequently applied to such acts in times of peace. Almost anything could be justified under conditions of war—at least by the victor. In addition there were revelations of brutalities and atrocities sanctioned by an apparently civilized and learned nation that were not directly related to war, the wholesale extermination of undesirables such as Jews, gypsies, and others defined as persistent criminals, as an insidious poison destroying the social fabric of a nation. In the light of these revelations it was difficult to return to business as usual, to see "madness" just as an individual pathological phenomenon, a "mental illness" from which some people suffered, people that were "abnormal." Nor was it possible any more to ignore the inhumanity of prisons after the awareness of concentration camps, after the experience of "ordinary" people having been prisoners of war or of conscience. Psychiatrists in particular had been exposed to the kind of breakdowns previously termed "shell-shock" that were more often than not the result of a moral awakening in becoming conscious of killing another human being, dropping bombs on women and children. When officially sanctioned rationalizations no longer worked, participation in atrocities were no longer possible for many, even though the result was that they were then declared to be criminals or to be mentally ill.

These phenomena had already emerged during the First World War but were soon set aside in the euphoria and manic liberation associated with "the Twenties," were driven underground by the threats of the Great Depression and another war. The point of reiterating these experiences once again is to draw attention to the massive forgetfulness which allows notions such as "civilization" and "progress" to persist even when they produce ever-larger calamities. The atom bomb may well have speeded up the end of the Second World War but then emerged as a new threat, not only because the world became divided into two opposing camps threatening mutual destruction, but also because it constituted a threat to the very foundation of human existence in this world. The Cold War has by now receded, the ideologies that divided West and East, Capitalism and Communism, have apparently led to the victory of the first. Remember, one had sponsored liberty with the hope of bringing about equality—fraternity be damned; the other had promised the production of equality, expecting that fraternity would come in its wake—liberty be damned. But since these concepts are interactive and in tension, it should be no surprise that the systemic production of liberty should lead to ever-increasing forms of confinement, matching those found necessary to produce equality in opposing regimes. With the disappearance of this official dialectic, both, liberty as well as equality, are endangered everywhere.

The after-war years were also the time of the inception of large-scale studies in social psychiatry such as the Stirling County Studies under the leadership of Alexander and Dorothy Leighton. The title of their first volume was indeed relevant: *My Name is Legion*. It was also the time of experiments with therapeutic communities, particularly in regard to behaviour disorders, "psychopaths" who seemed to be resistant to individual treatments, including psychoanalysis. The term, "sociopath" was to express a new understanding but came to mean essentially the same. Social work was no longer restricted to the poor but was charged with the diagnosis and treatment of social conditions of individuals and groups that did not fit normative perceptions. In the general trend towards professionalization it developed its own analytic and therapeutic commitments such as casework, group-work, and community organization. And although psychology was largely employed to carry out testing procedures to assist in diagnostic work and to contribute to the formation of categories that would permit categorical treatments, psychologists also expanded their role, invented their own therapeutic interventions such as behaviour modification, particularly of the "aversive" kind. Rewards, as a form of positive conditioning, were—as always—more difficult to define and to apply outside controlled settings. In all this *furor therapeuticus* there was also a serious questioning of received wisdom in the various disciplines, and boundaries between the professions began to break down in terms of practices, if not status.

In clinical settings identified as "psychiatric," psychiatrists obviously played a leading role. But in other settings such as the administration of sentences, in the enormous growth of probation and parole, in the new classification procedures, social workers assumed a leading role. Prisons were fair game for all, with psychiatrists and psychologists usually functioning as consultants and social workers charged with the actual work of classification and rehabilitation. "Research" which had been a central part of academic endeavours became an activity that would show avenues of change. But to the extent it was sponsored by institutional regimes it also tended to provide justifications for the maintenance of regimes. It is still inspiring to consider how Bruno was able to protect his research endeavours not only from institutional pressures but also from the pressures of a professional scientism that increasingly became the preferred mode of academic institutions.

It is ironic that the "humanities" had come to imitate the methods of the "natural" sciences, the "hard" sciences, when assumptions underpinning these methods were already in doubt. It had become quite apparent that Science (capitalized) was not informed by eternal verities but depended on the acceptance of paradigms which defined and confined its parameters. The power of these sciences and the technologies they spawned rested exactly in their ability to ignore idiosyncratic features, to ignore particularities of nature including human nature. I once raised doubts about the research of a psychologist who then told me in no uncertain terms that I should go to the prisons to look at the facts; I replied that I had been in many prisons but had never seen his "facts." He no longer appreciated that "facts" were literally "made up" *(factus)* according to certain recipes which may and may not shed light on the conditions they are supposed to represent.

Bruno's notion of research was much more concerned with showing than telling, whether it was to shed light on conditions defined as "mental illness" or "crime" (there is a limit to the use of inverted commas). It was clear to him that those were not natural facts but were constituted and interpreted by what a given society accepted as "normal." Although biological and psychological factors could serve as signs, they did not determine signification. Signification, although associated with particular signs, be they bumps on the head, certain neural connections, intelligence quotients, or social positions, cannot be derived from facts but depend on the grammar of a given structure. Sociology, engaged in defining social norms and their distributions, does not rely on "empirical" facts but on composites, generalities forming a structure that can only accommodate individuals defined in this way. Such a structure can be informative in general but can never assign any particular person to its categories beyond a reasonable doubt. Scientific psychology is in an even more difficult position, deriving most of its norms and distributions from experimental procedures that calibrate instruments such as tests. And the signification of diagnostic categories in psychiatry are almost exclusively determined by social/structural conceptions. Bruno, although he made use of statistical procedures, and was attracted to narrative procedures more akin to his artistic temperament, preferred ways of accounting that would tell the story of individuals and their forms of relations as perceived by them, as well as others with whom they interacted.

IV

The major theoretical battles from "the mid-Fifties" to at least "the mid-Sixties" were between psychoanalytic and behavioural understandings. In the Toronto Clinic, the former were mainly represented by consulting psychiatrists, and the latter by clinical psychologists. Social workers tended to align themselves more with the analysts but less in terms of intra-psychic perspectives than in attempting to understand the nature of primary relationships. As was traditionally the case, social workers tended to see "significant others," such as family members and partners, psychologists tested, and psychiatrists tended to make the final assessments and recommendations. Comparing the research papers that emanated from the McGill and the Toronto clinics, one can see a significant difference in what were identified as subjects for research. Toronto concentrated mainly on nosology, identifying groups such as pedophiles and exhibitionists, focusing on diagnosis, forms of treatment, and their results. In addition to individual therapy there was an extensive experimentation with groups and various forms of behaviour therapies. The work of the Montreal Clinic, on the other hand, even though it obviously included clinical assessments and recommendations, had a much wider range in exploring the perceptions and action of other agencies and institutions of the criminal justice system. Bruno was well versed in the various clinical orientations and treatment modalities but it is fair to say that his main interest was in shaping appropriate institutional responses to problematic behaviours, to show their genesis and how they were socially maintained.

This is not the place to make comparisons of research styles, only to highlight that the Forensic Clinic in Montreal under Bruno Cormier's guidance had from the beginning avoided, as much as possible, the impact of theoretical divisions between various schools. For Bruno, there were just too many blatant misperceptions of the nature of criminality to engage in finely calibrated distinctions. These misperceptions were not just those of a public that was divorced from the actual processes and had derived their images mostly from the media. Neither were they just those of administrators and professionals who could not see their own marks on these images. They were also shared by offenders as well as those offended, were largely produced by the process itself. Anybody who observes the courts or enters a prison with open eyes, cannot help but be impressed by their irrationality as described by Kafka (who was trained in law and worked as a legal analyst). Neither offender nor victim has a prominent place in the courts, and prisons are clearly designed to de-face personal features, to produce a grey in grey that enfolds the keepers as well as the kept, the watchers as well as the watched. Prisons not only keep inmates inside to be watched, but also keep the public outside so as not to see what is obvious to anyone who has not yet become used to the sights, sounds, and smells of prisons, does not yet "understand" the behaviour of keepers and kept.

To pious statements that "prisons do not work," Michael Foucault has given the most appropriate answer by stating that they in fact work very well by making sure that criminals conform to the images a given society has of them. Those involved in the process tend to take institutional behaviour for granted. But if they are at all reflective, they will admit (alas, only in private) that the stated purposes of courts and prisons, such as the reduction of crime and the protection of the public, are not what the system is about. But in anyone's particular position there is little room for manoeuvre. Everyone must conform to systemic expectations, even if apparently in charge of a given process, such as judges and prison administrators. And thus their consciousness as well as conscience is curtailed by what they perceive as the limits a system will tolerate. There are, of course, differences in terms of harshness but they count for little compared with the character formation and the impact of the system as a whole.

Bruno would argue again and again that it was not so much a question of treatment modalities, not even that of a therapeutic community, that informed his commitment. It was the blindness and the inhumanity of the process that he could not and would not accept. On the one hand, he worked in the context of an outpatient clinic to examine what can be done in the community itself; on the other hand, he worked with persistent offenders to see whether one could break their addiction to prisons that had become the most congenial environment for them. Manipulative

behaviour based on power allowed these offenders to be successful in prison where such behaviour is the best, if not the only, way
to survive. Despite the fact that for those offenders prison tended
to become the home to which they again and again returned,
Bruno had a deep belief that human beings, given a chance,
would prefer to live in a context of care and positive relations if
they were able to do so. He had maintained this spirit even
though he experienced the inevitable disappointments. But these
very disappointments showed what needed to be overcome,
showed the nature and depth of the damage done, a damage that
in some cases indeed seemed to be irreversible under prevailing
conditions. He had no illusion and accepted that control and confinement were necessary for some when they were indeed a danger to others. But prisons as a means of punishment make poor
selections in those terms and tend to further endanger the community when those confined come back even less able to cope
with life outside than before. There is no actual purpose for prisons other than the administration of sentences handed out by
judges as a kind of tariff of punishments. What is expected from
keepers is literally to keep those handed over to them for safe-
keeping. All other measures, such as rehabilitation or treatment,
are after-thoughts. This purposelessness pervades all prisons,
infects prisoners as well as staff. A "good prison" is an oxymoron.

Another interaction between law and psychiatry has to be
addressed. The movement against confinement of the mentally ill
was indeed successful, as can be documented by the reduction of
beds in mental hospitals. For those that were less troublesome,
asylum was provided in rooming houses and hostels; but for those
who displayed offensive or threatening behaviour there was no
other place than jails and prisons. Increasingly, disturbed
behaviour could be observed more frequently in jails than in psychiatric facilities which could no longer accommodate people that
were, or were perceived to be, a threat to others. And thus, even
this form of liberation turned out to be a kind of a shell-game,

shifting confinement from one definition to another. The legality of psychiatric forms of confinement by "jailors in a white coat" was successfully questioned but judicially sanctioned confinement under the rubric of criminal law, resisted reform. In the end, as of now, there are many more in confinement than have been before.

It is a further irony that Bruno, even in the middle of "the Sixties," had to go to New York State to conduct his major experiment of producing human openness in a closed institution by turning it into a therapeutic community. Although the "helping professions" by then played an increasing role in Canadian prisons and assumed leading positions, there was in fact less and less willingness to accept the kind of spirit Bruno represented. Prison hospitals such as the Oakridge unit at Penetang conducted similar experiments, but it was removed from the prison system even though the facility itself was indistinguishable from other carceral institutions. The project for persistent offenders at Clinton, N.Y., on the other hand, was a shared undertaking between the Dannemora State Hospital and the New York State Department of Corrections. The group selected were persistent offenders with a background of violent crimes. Their self-definition as well as their definition by prison authorities was based on repeated offences as well as previous confinements even though they were relatively young, between the ages of twenty-five and thirty-five. There was some notion at the time that persistent offenders began to reconsider their life in their early thirties, were getting fed up with the cycle of incarcerations and were open to change their lives but needed some insight and skills to accomplish such a feat. Because of his previous intense and intensive clinical commitment to individuals, Bruno was well aware that significant changes could only occur if ingrained habits of relation were understood and worked out. It was not a question of mechanical deconditioning in terms of aversive therapy, or any other form of punishment, nor was it a question of deep psychoanalytic insights which tend to reinforce self-centredness, but a question of facing oneself as perceived by others.

Bruno was eclectic in his methods and drew from whatever source to create a situation in which open exchanges were possible. It is exactly what prisons in general do not permit because in their context there are serious repercussions for inmates as well as staff. And thus in his project, staff too had to change their habits, had to learn to function in a different climate. What stands out in the account of this project, is not so much methods and the nature of the regime but an account of people, their very particular perceptions and ways of changing—or resisting change. And even though these kinds of programmes have largely disappeared, the account Bruno gave of this work still makes for fascinating reading. One is reminded of the fact that although crimes, and in particular violent crimes, are considered to be abhorrent, there is an extraordinary public demand for crime stories. One can observe, particularly in the visual media, that the violence portrayed for the purpose of entertainment goes far beyond the amount of violence involved in actual crimes, or in prisons, for that matter. The relationship between fear of crime and fascination with it, is obvious. Trials were indeed a form of theatre, with their costumes and formal procedures, and court houses could accommodate most members of the community who were indeed there to watch. Rules of procedure and evidence were carefully worked out to distance the trial from communal assumptions and knowledges. There can be little doubt that those are mainly dramaturgical devices holding the legal actors to their script. There was no such subtlety in sentencing. As in any good story, it was more convenient for the villain to die.

What is exciting in reading the account of Bruno's experiment is the nature and intensity of relationships between inmates, inmates and staff, as well as consultants. Conducted over a period of six years, from 1966 to 1972, on a follow-up visit before publication in 1975, it was clear that institutional features were re-asserting themselves. Bruno saw this as a result of the taxing features of the programme, and although this is certainly the case, subsequent developments have shown that it was also part of a general trend that not only reduced all therapeutic interventions but represented an increasing reliance on "human warehousing." What is described at the end of Bruno's account in *The Watcher and the Watched* we can now see as the end of an era, the beginning of a reaction that still goes on unabated. Bruno fought what largely amounts to a rear-guard action from then on, as in his opposition to the construction of new penitentiaries, which was gaining momentum. He also had to watch how "the system" absorbed his best ideas and his best people and managed to sterilize the human concerns that had inspired him and with which he inspired others. In a sense, his was the last independent voice that was heard in the corridors of power, and for a time he was still able to retard its worst excesses.

On a personal note, due to the influence he still had in the corridors of power, I was asked in the early Seventies whether I was interested in the position of commissioner of penitentiaries and when I declined was then asked to chair a committee on the design of maximum security institutions. Because I had become convinced that there had to be basic changes in law and the legal process before there could be any changes in the nature and purpose of sentencing, I had joined the Law Reform Commission of Canada. Bruno again foresaw that this particular effort would not yield the expected result.

V

The more I re-search, re-consider, remember Bruno Cormier, his commitments and ideas, the more it occurs to me that he indeed represents what is most memorable about the years from 1955 to 1975, five years before the proverbial "Sixties" and five years after. The twenty years that followed are still difficult to assess although it seems quite clear that the spirit of those years has somehow disappeared from public view. Not only has the criminal justice system grown beyond all envisaged proportions, the very notions of a liberal liberty have become legalized in the form of "rights," have become a matter of charters and legal processes rather than being realized in any visible way. The world representative of liberty and the world watchdog of human rights, the United States, by now has over a million and a half persons behind bars at any given time. Canadians are somewhat slower and a little bit behind but well on the way within their means to practise "zero tolerance," to threaten everyone who steps out of line with exclusion. We have seen the crumbling of the coercive order of Communism but seem to be quite comfortable with the growth of our own coercive orders, indeed seem to demand more of it. What seems to have been forgotten is that those are the methods of totalitarianism, of an authoritarianism that has brought about the major evils in this century. Science and technology have introduced ever more rapid changes which threaten social cohesion and increase feelings, of anomy, feelings of insecurity, of being beleaguered by evil forces in the midst of plenty. The poor and the weak are, as always, the most obvious victims. But the threat goes much further and deeper as humans are progressively considered to be means rather than ends, become "human capital" and "human resources," appendages to efficient economic functions.

And so, it is not just a form of piety to remember Bruno Cormier, his convictions, his work, and his influence on others. As one of them, in remembering Bruno, I become increasingly agitated that his very spirit needs to be re-discovered if there is to be any change in how we treat each other and in particular the most exposed ones among us. It behooves us to pay attention to the past, to a spirit of search and research that must not be lost. The unexamined life is not worth living, as the sage of Athens said. And the commandment to love one's neighbour as one loves oneself still stands. It cannot be fulfilled by any one without an other, only by one-an-other. I take this to have been the *daimon* of Bruno's life, his *esprit*, his *Geist*, a sign that carries its own signification beyond the boundaries of a lifetime, indeed constitutes "our world" rather than "the world" as some kind of objective notion. "World" as the word tells us is literally "human-time" *(wer-eld)*, the way we live.

Johann W. Mohr, *M.S.W., Ph.D., Professor Emeritus, Osgoode Hall Law School and Department of Sociology, York University, Ont., 1969-1989.*

Research Associate, Forensic Clinic, Toronto Psychiatric Hospital, 1960-1966; Head, Section of Social Pathology Research, Clarke Institute of Psychiatry, Toronto, 1966-1969; Consultant, Clarke Institute of Psychiatry, Forensic Services, 1969-1972; Commissioner, Law Reform Commission of Canada, 1972-1976.

Anton Obert

It would probably not be far wrong to say
that most of us at 509 Pine worked there
because we liked the atmosphere and
the way things were done there.

The Forensic Clinic was the only place at McGill University where services and training in Criminology were provided, not to mention the extensive research work which had brought international repute to the University in this field. This international respect for the Clinic's work was brought home to me when, in 1970, I visited Japan and representatives from the Ministry of Justice not only wined and dined me for a week but also showed and discussed with me their institutions and ways of dealing with lawbreakers.

I joined the Clinic in 1960, the year of the Quiet Revolution in Quebec. I was always attracted to pioneer situations, working, as it were, at the edge of the known. The McGill Research Unit and Clinic in Forensic Psychiatry at 509 Pine Avenue West in Montreal was definitely such an enterprise, its existence being entirely due to its founder Dr. Bruno Cormier's creativity and persistence against, at times, considerable financial and other odds. These qualities were also reflected in the staff of the clinic, men and women of various ages and from different disciplines. Ours was very much a multi-disciplinary approach. In addition to the permanent staff members, there were always two or three psychiatrists-in-training from the nearby Allan Memorial Institute of Psychiatry. As well, we had at the Clinic students from the McGill School of Social Work and the University of Quebec who were doing their fieldwork at 509 Pine and the prisons and penitentiaries around Montreal. In many instances, such as the ultra-modern Montreal Women's Jail at Bordeaux (stainless steel benches, if I remember correctly), our team and students were the first professional social workers that the inmates had ever met in prison.

It would probably not be far wrong to say that most of us at 509 Pine worked there because we liked the atmosphere and the way things were done there. One was given a great deal of freedom with respect to one's work. This left the staff with the feeling that this was a place where each could fully contribute and go as far as he or she wished. From the outset this spirit appealed to me greatly. It was a lively, stimulating working environment. Often it felt that the new and unexpected was just around the corner—and it often was. In the weekly case conferences, and generally, there was a great deal of free-flowing interchange between the disciplines and among the members of the team. This spirit and climate was in large measure due to the personality of the director of the clinic, Dr. Bruno Cormier.

Bruno was a man of many facets, interests, and contacts. An example of this was perhaps the large Riopelle canvas which hung for many years in his relatively unprotected office at 509 Pine. Unfortunately, Riopelle's mounting prominence and insurance concerns eventually led to its removal. However, the Cormier residence on Côte St-Antoine, where some of our best parties were held, remained a veritable smorgasbord of canvases by contemporary Quebec artists, a reflection of the many sides of Dr. Cormier.

In this context it may be interesting to mention that our paths had crossed many years before I ever contemplated a correctional career. We had met at the Allan Memorial Institute where I worked as technician and photographer in Dr. Bernard Grad's gerontology laboratory. Bruno, fresh out of the diploma course and about to leave for overseas, wanted a photograph of the AMI as a background for his collection of paintings done by schizophrenic patients. I was able to provide him with the required photograph. Following this initial encounter, our paths diverged and we might never have met again had it not been for yet another series of quirky changes in direction to which the course of my life is prone. In fact, we would probably never have met at all had it not been for yet another of those unforeseeable turns of fate, namely, the outbreak of World War II and the invasion of the Low Countries in Europe. But for this I would probably never have come to Canada, a country where by now I have spent by far the greatest part of my life.

My own path to the field of crime and corrections, too, was somewhat circuitous. Growing up in Austria between two world wars and during the tumultuous Twenties, I had more than a conventional share of "trades": aircraft construction and flying, when the airport of Frankfurt am Main, now the largest in Europe after London, was still a grassy meadow; lumberjack in the snowy forests of Norway; tourist guide in Europe, until Hitler's rise to power and my refusal to become a citizen of the Thousand Year Reich put an end to my mobility. This led me to England and to work at Summerhill, the well-known experimental school established by A.S. Neill.

World War II brought me to Canada and to a return to the technical field as head of the electrical department of a machine tool plant in Ville LaSalle. In 1959, I fulfilled a long-standing interest in the social sciences and rehabilitation with the completion of my Master of Social Work studies at McGill University. Following brief stints with a family agency and the Constance Lethbridge Rehabilitation Centre on Ottawa Street in Montreal, I applied for employment at the Forensic Clinic when a job opening there was rumoured. My first contact was with Mrs. Miriam Kennedy, followed by an interview with the director. I was accepted on May 30, 1960, with the proviso that money for my modest beginner's salary could be found among the research grants which at the time constituted the main source of the Clinic's income. Miriam Kennedy, a many-talented, capable woman, was quite a force at the Forensic Clinic and in its research work. Knowledge-able and always ready to help out, she represented a kind of mother figure at 509 Pine. It was not long after my induction that I realized that the climate of this establishment and the work there suited me beyond expectation. I had found my niche! In age I was probably the oldest of the Cormier Team; at the same time, I was in my "professional youth," having only recently completed my M.S.W. studies.

A detailed overview of the Clinic's work and accomplishments, I feel, should be left to people better equipped than I at this stage. At eighty-six years of age, the recollections of my years at 509 Pine are rather incomplete and sketchy. As far as I can remember, certain research work, like the Genocide Study, was done by Dr. Cormier exclusively. Much of our work was group projects in the sense that each research team that collected material for its project shared its fairly uniform, many-faceted files with other teams. Thus over the years we accumulated large amounts of information of all kinds, which greatly facilitated longitudinal and other studies. Furthermore, these files were frequently up-dated, last but not least, by the clinic's open-door policy. Our good reputation among the inmate population prompted many of them to visit 509 Pine after their release. There was usually someone to discuss a man's current situation over a cup of coffee. For some visitors this was often a "consulting before collapsing" and may well have made the difference between early reincarceration and a solution inside the law. In short, the work at the Clinic gave one contact and wide experience with all kinds of offenders in and out of prison. We studied the characteristics and problems of many law-breakers, persistent and incidental, young and old, as well as their families. We also investigated the effects of deprivation of liberty, sentencing, the "black sheep" in the family, and the multi-delinquent family where every son landed in the penitentiary.

The clinic had also an enviable record of success in treating behaviour problems outside of penal institutions. We had our share of violence and pedophilia referrals, requests for presentence reports, assessments, follow-ups of parole risks and many more. The Clinic's incest research had a striking influence on Quebec judges' sentencing practices. Instead of giving the father, usually a good provider, two or more years in the penitentiary and putting the family on welfare, the case was referred to the clinic for assessment and many judges let their sentences be guided by our recommendations, which often kept the offending father working and earning the family's livelihood.

I remember being myself mainly active in research with multi-delinquent families. We presented papers at congresses and conferences and contributed to journals in the field. The yearly McGill Criminological Conference was one of Dr. Cormier's innovations. Drugs were hardly a factor on the crime scene in my days at the clinic. I recall meeting one of the very first drug dealers in Montreal in the penitentiary. He was a young repeat offender who had been attracted by the easy money. In Eastern Canada this was a relatively new area of criminal enterprise where huge profits could be made easily. One day on one of his errands he came face-to-face with the gun of an unexpected rival; it was an "I or he situation," he told me, happy to have survived with only a murder sentence. There was no danger of him recidivating.

The vexing question of recidivism sooner or later touches all of us in the field of corrections. Anyone involved with offenders, particularly those who constitute the vast majority who fill our penitentiaries and institutions, is keenly aware of this seemingly insoluble problem. The recidivism rate and the number of prisoners are increasing faster than the population as a whole. Is there anything beyond aging that can terminate criminal careers, one asks oneself? Is there really nothing effective that we can do beyond the present expensive "warehousing" of law-breakers? I had for some years been interested in this question of recidivism and, therefore, responded readily to the late Dr. Robert Shepherd's request to join him in setting up a half-way house for released and paroled prisoners in Montreal. With the help of church groups, businessmen, judges, lawyers, and other concerned individuals, whom Dr. Shepherd had gathered around him, Saint Lawrence House (Maison St-Laurent) opened its door to residents in 1967, the year of Expo in Montreal.

I was its first director, the man with the know-how and the potential residents. For me this job was merely a new experimental tool, an extension of the work I had been doing at the clinic. Relations and co-operation with the Clinic remained strong. I merely had moved down the slope of the Mount Royal to the centre of the city and lower Mackay Street. I never lost contact and always felt a member of the Cormier Team until my retirement.

Anton Obert, *M.S.W., retired*

Following a varied career which included five years at A.S. Neill's experimental school "Summerhill" in England, Mr. Obert completed M.S.W. studies at McGill University in 1959. Brief stints in a family agency and a rehabilitation centre in Montreal led to the Forensic Clinic where for seven years he worked as research assistant under supervision of Miriam Kennedy, field supervisor of M.S.W. students at the McGill School of Social Work.

Ingrid Thompson-Cooper

Writing with Bruno was an experience, sometimes exhausting,
always challenging, and ultimately fulfilling.

 I started my long years at the clinic as a very "green"
student doing her second and final field placement
for her master's degree in social work. I had wanted
to come a year earlier but my adviser wisely suggested that I wait a year and gain more experience. My
memories of what propelled me towards the clinic are vague—
except I did have an interest in working with offenders: plus I had
heard that the clinic was an excellent placement. For students this
meant interesting and "real" work and good supervision. In my
anxiety I arrived early and waited in the rain for the student
supervisor, Lydia Keitner, to let me in. If anyone had told me on
that rainy day in 1969 that twenty-eight years later I would assist
Dr. Fugère in closing the doors of the clinic for the last time, I
would have been astonished. The reasons for this longevity are no
doubt complex—but what is clear is that it was the nature of the
clientele, complex and fascinating, but more important, the
approach to their problems taken by the clinic's director, Bruno
Cormier; and the purpose of telling this story is not to focus on
me, but hopefully to reveal aspects of the man and his work.

Initially my contact with Dr. Cormier was very limited. I was
certainly aware of him but, as with the other four students, most
of my contact was with Mrs. Keitner who took us under her very
capable wings. In later years I used to joke with Dr. Cormier that
we had never actually been introduced. As a result of my wait in

the rain, I caught a severe cold and missed the next few days of placement, also missing being introduced to Dr. Cormier with the other students. So for that first year at least, and perhaps longer, when we met in the hall or his office, we would smile and nod, I with awe and he probably wondering which one of the large group of students was this one!

One cannot talk about the clinic without describing the building. "509 Pine" is a three-story Victorian building and part of a row of similar houses from a more elegant age. Although an office, it was also a house, with all the charm, familiarity, comforts and discomforts associated with a home. Every possible space was used for offices which ranged from large elegant rooms with fireplaces, large windows and wood trim to small poky spaces. At one time my office was what I thought must have originally been the maid's room! Eventually, when I divided my time between the School of Social Work and the clinic, I had two offices—but the clinic always felt like my "professional home." Certainly it never felt like an institution and the clients responded to its homey atmosphere. (This atmosphere even seemed to affect clients who had never seen the building. Once, an inmate from Dannemora, New York, addressed his letter to me "c/o Friends at Clinic" instead of the Forensic Clinic!)

Dr. Cormier's office was, appropriately, in the centre of the building—on the second floor. The book-lined walls, fireplace, big window and comfortable chairs created an atmosphere of security and intimacy where hard work could go on. Everyone congregated here for the Friday afternoon case conferences which ran from 2:00 o'clock until 5:00 or 5:30, depending on his energy. It was usually the later time in the early years. Attendance was an unspoken but cardinal rule. While occasionally some of us, comparing ourselves with colleagues from other agencies who would have Friday afternoon off, would gripe about the compulsory attendance, eventually we realized their importance. Besides their obvious value in discussing cases and teaching, the meetings allowed us to ventilate and "tie up" any unfinished business that the week's work had left, leaving us with renewed energy for next week's work.

When I first arrived at the clinic, the building was bursting at the seams and very busy. There were many research grants and projects, with the staff organized in various teams, with Dr. Cormier at the centre of them all. He seemed to rely a great deal on Miriam Kennedy, "Mother Kennedy" as the inmates called her. Added to the mix of psychiatrists, social workers and criminologists were the six students from social work and criminology. I later realized that besides research and clinical work, teaching was the third priority at the clinic. Students were included in everything. We saw cases (research and treatment) at the penitentiary as well as at the clinic. I was quickly made aware of the importance Dr. Cormier and his staff placed on being non-judgmental with the clients. In general discussion Mrs. Keitner had with us the subject of homosexuality came up. When I mentioned that I had some gay friends, she immediately assigned me Mr. G., a gay man. Whenever Dr. Cormier referred to the importance of a non-judgmental approach, he would simply state that being judgmental didn't work. It did not mean that acting-out behaviour was condoned; in fact, rigorous, well-timed confrontation was an important part of the intervention. But so was respect and acceptance of the whole person.

As students we were expected to present our cases at the Friday conference, and I recall that the first presentation I made was of a young man whom I was seeing in the penitentiary who had "fallen in love" with me. As part of the presentation I had to read out his love letter to me (written with the help of an anglophone inmate, as my client could not write English!). I was embarrassed but ploughed on. I have no recollection of what Dr. Cormier said, probably something about deprivation of liberty and transference in the institution; but I do remember that I lost my embarrassment and learned what I often heard him say later— that there was virtually nothing that cannot be spoken about, either with a client or with others, as long as it was relevant and done with respect.

At the end of our year of training, three of us students were lucky enough to be hired as clinicians in the clinic's well-known Clinton project in Dannemora, New York. This was a therapeutic community for persistent offenders that Dr. Cormier had set up four years previously at the invitation of New York State and was running with a team of psychiatrists, psychologists, social workers and criminologists from the clinic. Interestingly again, Dr. Cormier and I had no direct contact and I, like the other students, was hired "by osmosis" through Mrs. Keitner. So more nods and smiles when we met! Having the Dannemora program must have been like a dream come true for him; he was able to put into practice what he had learned from his research and clinical experience in St. Vincent de Paul Penitentiary about the different classifications of offenders and their treatment and the effects of deprivation of liberty on staff and inmates. The program involved maximum freedom for the inmates inside a maximum security institution, something Dr. Cormier had to fight for very hard in the initial stages of the contract negotiations. He would not budge and he won with the result that while the institution controlled the physical parameters of the program he, as director of the project, and the clinical staff had complete control of what happened to the inmates while they were in the therapeutic community. Anyone who has ever worked in a correctional institution will realize the rarity of this.

Dr. Cormier did not come to Dannemora very often during the two years I was there (1970-1972), the last two of McGill's involvement with the program. However, when he did visit, there was an electric response. One of his clinical beliefs was that a quiet therapeutic community meeting meant trouble and signified that the community was unhealthy. If he found such quietness on his rare visits, it certainly did not last. Considering that he did not know the men very well, I didn't know how he did it; but he would quickly tune into the issue, intervene, and there were instant and loud interactions which lasted for most of the meeting. Complacency was gone (staff and inmates); large black men leapt to their feet, arguing, gesturing (I got the impression they didn't know what hit them!); he'd respond and so it went. By the end, whatever had been simmering had disappeared, tensions were dissipated; health was restored.

When the clinic's involvement with the Dannemora project was coming to an end, Dr. Cormier started organizing the writing of the book *The Watcher and the Watched* (Cormier, 1975), a collection of papers written by a number of us who were working there. It was at this time that we started to have more contact with each other. He seemed to see me as someone who possibly had the potential to write; I recall once that he said that I "could be creative"—a vivid memory, as he rarely gave compliments. He suggested that I "talk" my ideas into a dictaphone, something I would never have thought of. While I know that I never lived up to his expectations regarding writing (or mine, for that matter), I am equally certain that, without his encouragement, I would never have written what I did.

By now, any reader who did not already know Bruno Cormier is no doubt aware from the other testimonials in this book that he was an exceptional man—brilliant, creative, unorthodox, who applied his inquiring mind and strong personality to expand the understanding of deviant behaviour and society's response to it, all the while supporting the absolute importance of human rights and believing that individuals and society have the potential to change. This was apparent in all aspects of his work—in his clinical work with patients, his teaching, and his writing. One of the most challenging and ultimately rewarding areas of work I did with Bruno was writing papers with him. Writing of some sort or another was always going on at the clinic. Papers were being prepared either for presentation at a scientific meeting or submission to a journal for publication. Each year at least four meetings were attended by Bruno and other staff members—always the Canadian Psychiatric

Association, the Canadian Corrections Association, the American Criminological Association and the Quebec Association of Psychiatry and often others. At various points in the year, usually in the spring, he would hold a special meeting for staff to "brainstorm" and come up with ideas for possible topics to submit as abstracts. Decisions would be made, the abstracts written and sent off. As I recall, our proposals were rarely rejected. Then we would slowly begin to collect material for the papers. As in most clinics there was no time to work on them during the work day—writing was left for evenings and weekends. Invariably when fall rolled around, when most of the meetings took place, there was a rush of activity to complete the papers. It was not unusual for two and sometimes more of them being prepared for the same meeting. Tension could run high when we virtually lined up for work meetings with Bruno and for the secretary to type them. Somehow they always got completed and we could relax until the next round of deadlines!

Writing with Bruno was an experience, sometimes exhausting, always challenging, and ultimately fulfilling. While he initially took the lead, it was a collaborative effort and we developed a process of working that was always the same. First the brainstorming for the initial idea. Then we would sit at his desk and draw up an outline where he would pay meticulous attention to detail. Then the fun would begin. Carefully following the outline he would begin to express his ideas, usually in a stream of consciousness. I have the image of his thoughts flying around the room, with me trying to capture pieces of them! I would interject with ideas of my own, sometimes a query but not too often because that would stop the flow of ideas. I learned not to worry if I didn't grasp everything he was saying. I would write furiously and emerge from the session with a page full of notes written every which way all over the page. Then I'd start writing the material and return with a draft. There would be another meeting where more ideas flowed and the same process continued until there was an almost completed manuscript. (When he prepared a section of the paper on his own, I had the task of editing it—another challenge!) Finally we would go over the paper word for word, checking for nuances and subtleties, many of which I had missed. And at last a finished paper and the sense of having been on a very interesting voyage.

When the Dannemora Project ended, a number of us were faced with having to leave the clinic. However, I was fortunate that Bruno was able to offer me a position as supervisor of a unit of students from the School of Social Work, replacing Lydia Keitner, who had left to assist Guy Mercereau in running the new forensic clinic in Buffalo. Eventually I obtained a tenure-track position at McGill and divided my time between the clinic and the School of Social Work. It was a pleasure to train the students at the clinic. I particularly appreciated how he perceived social workers and other non-psychiatrists and other personnel. Cases were assigned to whomever was available or had a particular interest in the type of problem the patient represented. We were truly a team with everyone's views appreciated. He preferred to do the clinical assessments with students and/or staff and involved us in every aspect of the work. Invariably at scientific conferences when he would be making a presentation, to my dismay, he would always mention those of us in the audience who had worked with him on the project. Initially at least I worried that I'd be asked a question I couldn't answer. The strong team spirit, created and spurred on by Bruno's energy, was perhaps most evident when we attended conferences away from the clinic. These occasions gave us the opportunity to spend some time together in ways that the day-to-day work week did not allow. Thus we would usually gather for lunch or dinner, often joined by former members of staff now living in other cities. There would be lively discussions, catching up on each other's news. On one such occasion when our group was on its way to a restaurant, a psychiatric colleague of Bruno's rather wistfully commented to him how lucky he was to have his staff with him and how close we all seemed.

I imagine this approach of Bruno's was related to his view that to work effectively with offenders, it was not enough to be a forensic psychiatrist. Instead, we must work as clinical criminologists and attempt to understand criminality in all of its social and psychological facets; knowledge was to be gained from every possible source including psychology, psychiatry, psychoanalysis, sociology, anthropology, literature, and history. Bruno also continually emphasized that the main source of information was the criminal himself ("form a relationship" he would tell students) and all aspects of his life were viewed as important, not just the delinquent behaviour. Learning permeated the whole atmosphere of the clinic—the expectation was that all of us, including Bruno, were to continually work at discovering more about the problems of offenders and their treatment. If I had to choose one key clinical principle that operated at the clinic, it would be Bruno's belief that individuals who have acted out in a criminal or delinquent way have the potential to change. This was brought home to me on one of Cyril Greenland's visits to the clinic when he was conducting a small study of professional attitudes about sentencing. After interviewing different staff members about their views of the sentences of various types of serious offenders, he remarked how different the responses of the clinic staff were from other professionals he had interviewed. All of us felt that the offenders might have the potential to be different at some point and did not want to pass lasting judgments on their behaviour. This wasn't a naïve "Pollyanna" approach which failed to recognize the severity of certain behaviours or of the danger of recidivism, but rather a flexible view of the offender, taking into account the positive effects of aging and other factors that might bring about change.

Most of the writing I did with Bruno was on incest, an early and major interest of his. Apparently, prior to his opening of the clinic, when he was at the Maudsley in London, he had treated an incest victim and, touched by her suffering, wanted to have a better understanding of the whole phenomenon. When the clinic opened in 1955 most incest offenders received prison sentences and he started seeing these men in the penitentiary. Miriam Kennedy worked closely with him on this, and they expanded their treatment program to include victims and other family members. This was at a time when the subject was very taboo—it was their seminal paper "Psycho-dynamics of father-daughter incest" (Cormier, Kennedy & Sangowicz, 1962) which virtually opened up the topic. Their research and clinical work in this area actually resulted in an increase in the number of cases that were handled through juvenile court rather than criminal court. A perusal of Mrs. Kennedy's notes reveals the sensitivity, compassion, and understanding she brought to these families. Sadly, she died after a short illness in 1970, just when I was completing my field placement.

My involvement with the incest project occurred quite by chance. I recall that when I arrived at the clinic as a student I had heard about Mrs. Kennedy and her work on "incest," a topic completely new and very mysterious to me. In 1973 I attended the annual meeting of the Canadian Psychiatric Association where one of the papers was on incest. In his presentation the author claimed that there was no such thing as homosexual incest, whereupon I turned to Dr. Cormier and said, "He's wrong! I have a case!" Dr. Cormier replied simply, "Write about it!" The next year at the same meeting we presented a paper on homosexual incest. Ultimately, either together or in collaboration with other staff members, we wrote fifteen papers on incest. We were constantly being consulted by different agencies on their cases and invited to give workshops both in Montreal and throughout Canada. When incest gained greater public recognition and when disclosures became more frequent, mainly as a result of the new youth protection legislation, our views on case management became controversial and "politically incorrect." We were even accused of being old-fashioned! We have always maintained that criminal proceedings should be avoided, if at all possible; the trend, adopted by social workers, is the complete opposite. From time to time

I've become discouraged by my colleagues' punitive approach, yet always marvelled at how philosophical Bruno could be. While he would fight very hard for his views, he always seemed to be able to take a long view of events, knowing that opinion would most likely swing back again. In the few years we had talked about writing a book on incest and were to start when I finally managed to finish my doctoral thesis. He died the year I completed it and up to now I haven't had the heart to write the book on my own.

I have one last "writing story" involving Bruno which I think is illustrative of the impact of his work. Some months after his illness first struck, he recovered to the point where he was able to begin working again. He once again led the Friday conference and researched and wrote a paper on pedophilia. In the spring of 1991 he proposed that we write a paper on the ethical and clinical problems related to the new Youth Protection Act. I was somewhat reluctant because it would be essentially a policy paper and I had always preferred writing on clinical material. However, I knew the topic was important—how important I was only to discover later! We submitted an abstract to the Canadian Psychiatric Association for their fall meeting and it was accepted. Bruno and I had our usual "brainstorming" session and then I left for my annual holiday in the U.K. I was still away when I received the news that he'd died. That summer, with the help of Renée Fugère, I wrote the paper myself. It was a difficult and painful task but completing it had gained even more importance. Presenting the paper was also difficult. Many in the room had known Bruno and were aware of his death. However, with the support of Renée, I managed. As soon as I finished, one of the editors of the *Journal of Canadian Psychiatry* was moved to rise to his feet and exclaim that the paper had to be published! While part of his motivation was no doubt to honour Bruno, I believe his interest was also a genuine reaction to the material in the paper. We had many subsequent requests for it from libraries and clinical centres in North America and Europe. And that's not the end of the story. Many months later I was supervising the research project of one of my master students who was trying to establish a treatment group for incest fathers at a local social work agency. In spite of the agency's agreement to the project, the student was always meeting road-blocks. Finally he was told by a senior manager that one of the main reasons for the lack of co-operation was the fact that I was his supervisor and had written a very upsetting paper. At first I couldn't even figure out which paper they were referring to but then learned that it was, in fact, the paper on the Youth Protection Act. Apparently there had even been discussions about it at the governmental level! The power of Bruno's thoughts was still shaking up the system.

Bruno Cormier was first my teacher and mentor, and eventually a colleague and friend. Working with him was a remarkable experience—sometimes stressful, but always challenging and stimulating and one for which I am deeply grateful.

Bibliography

Cormier, Bruno (Editor). *The Watcher and the Watched.* Montreal: Tundra Books. 1975.
Cormier, B., Kennedy, M., and Sangowicz, J. "Psycho-dynamics of father-daughter incest." *Can. Psychiat. Assoc. J.* 7, 1962: 203-217.

Ingrid Thompson-Cooper, *B.A., M.S.W., Ph.D. (Cantab.), Associate Professor, School of Social Work, McGill University, Montreal, 1985-present.*
Assistant Professor, School of Social Work, McGill University, 1978-1985; Lecturer, School of Social Work, McGill University (half-time), 1974-1978; Intake Social Worker and Research Assistant, McGill Clinic in Forensic Psychiatry, Jan. 1975-June 1975; Research Assistant and Field Practice Supervisor, McGill Clinic in Forensic Psychiatry, 1972-1997, Research Social Worker, Clinton Diagnostic and Treatment Center, Dannemora, New York, 1970-1972.
Thompson-Cooper's book, Child Welfare, Professionals and Incest Families: A Difficult Encounter, *is scheduled for publication.*

Reginald A.H. Washbrook

Professor Cormier was a world figure
who was known to the best in the field,
the likes of whom are sadly mostly not with us anymore.

Introduction

Some number of years ago now I was sitting in the Tea Room at Uffculme Clinic in Birmingham when I mentioned that I was thinking of a post in Montreal at McGill in Forensic Psychiatry. The Director, the eminent psychiatrist Dr. John Harrington, was interested enough to tell me that he knew a Dr. Cormier, whom he had met when they were students together at the Maudsley Hospital in South London. He described him as a friend, considerate, generous, dependable, and a serious and brilliant doctor. There was a genuine appreciation and an affection in the telling, and this encouraged me greatly. Therefore, some two interviews and other formalities later, I found myself on a plane to Canada. The flight became real when through a gap in the clouds I saw the vast expanse of lakes and forests over Newfoundland, my first trip over the Atlantic.

In Montreal, I was rather lost, but through the care of a Dr. MacKenzie, whom I had met in my student days in Scotland, I was found a bed of sorts in an unremembered place in the Victoria Hospital. Next morning I found my way to the department on Pine Avenue West, and I recall my interest in the curved bay windows of the building. No one was about, but after a wait a person appeared smiling and keen to help. This was my new boss, Dr. Bruno Cormier. (I had made an error in my time status.) There followed, after entry, a discussion as to why I wanted to work in that particular place. The chat was warm, friendly, and his interest

183

and impression set the scene for work and involvement in the Department. On recall I can still feel the concern and welcome.

Following On

It was a really new experience to be with the team at that time. It was new to me because in the U.K. I had been a busy registrar in wards and clinics dealing mostly with ill psychotics and a semblance of neurotic patients. Now the accent was upon research, and the thrill of the enthusiasm was different and pleasing. The week with plenty of new material to incorporate from several books busied my time, and so did the case conferences, but after a while I missed seeing patients. Thus the move was taken with the Director to the Vincent de Paul Penitentiary, all new and strange. I had a mere smither of French, which didn't help, but there was a friendly aura about all the members of the staff. This eventually extended into social gatherings outside the Department and meetings with other folk, both academics and members of families.

I was introduced to Kleinian psychology and analysis, also neo-Freudian and existential ideas as they applied to the work in hand. Soon I began to feel that I was actually a full contributing member of the research team. Further, I realized that it was the Department of a person who knew his topic and had worked with his subjects face-to-face and not from some academic distance only. There was the evidence from the older, now-gone criminologists and from the more modern workers. After years of interest in the subject, I was at last in an environment that had a vision and a scope for real clinical scientific criminology, with a leader who inspired continually. There was familiarization with the meaning in practical terms of the power of the ego all against and within social cultural forces that formed the milieu for our work. Here was a clarity of approach, a manageable methodology, all novel and refreshingly attractive. The now-famous Cormier Classification of Offenders of all age groups was tested out in practice, and other more specialized groups such as incest and fraud were added to the growing leaps of knowledge. Further, the legal and psychiatric battle was faced, and so were the effects and meaning of sentencing and its effects upon the inmate. The more universal aspect also entered the ambit of work. We were encouraged to attend conferences, and Friday afternoon case conferences were a teaching lesson in themselves, as they tended to weld together the Department. This experience was to shape the course of my life's work from that time on.

Also

The practical involvement played a major role with visits on a regular basis, seeing the ex-inmate at the clinic, and also involvement with new subjects, perhaps referred via courts for treatment. Social visits and family contact added greatly to the ethos being enacted, which of itself provided material to record and often later to be incorporated into learned papers. Always the humanitarian aspect was to the fore, since this was not pure research for the sake of only itself, of which there is much about, sadly even at well-appointed institutions. Professor Cormier was at his best within this direction of investigations, as he worked to help, to classify, to uncover, and to better the pain that was so much a part of the experience of the subjects that we studied. Although serious, it was fun in the best meaning of that strange word.

The Department was bonded together by the leadership and the general level and clinical tone of the work. The lot who worked there were a mixed technical bunch, psychiatrists, psychologists, those learned in sociology and social work, and others with experiential expertise. We were all amalgamated into the mould of a team without obvious rank, and each was measured for his or her contribution and personal values. There was overlap of disciplines to good effect. This was the result of the ethos governed by the most experienced Dr. Cormier who, though strict, was fair and understanding. We often had coffee breaks that went on far too long! Discussion was encouraged and the dictation of our own experiences from the subject contact and the feel of the environment. The breaks welcomed this, as did the mentioned case conferences, presented by each individual in turn. As we thought and worked together, friendships and trust evolved, and so did originality emerge. Nothing was too novel not to be considered, however distant at the time it seemed from the primary subject in hand. Ideas would be thrown this way and that before the final acceptance or rejection.

The secretarial staff were in on the work, and of particular remembrance was Miss Graham, who pushed and managed so many reports and case histories from often scant recorded material. She was a fount of knowledge of all sorts of things, and she held a place amongst the best of the team—she had a steady sense of contagious humour and yet was stalwart in method and order. Learning filled the place and so did knowledge of diverse kinds, including extraneous topics such as cinema and the like. Such was the leadership and the brilliance of the mind of the director as it affected a climate of enthusiasm and co-operational sharing. Basically we were "Cormier's Team" and so proudly we were fully aware.

Thus

The greatest contribution, to me, was the classification, clinical, wrested hard from a mammoth amount of clinical details laboriously sifted and pushed into a shape, which was workable and capable of being understood by any who sincerely worked with offenders at all levels. At first reading I found it remarkably original, which indeed it was, a sheer piece of genius. Nothing like this was to be found in the literature on the subject ever, and even now, with computer accessibility, it is still unique. Miss Graham struggled with the written work with care, and in doing so was an important contributor. This was all part of her office management, as she worked at the bibliography material and the finished typed copies. Other than this she became for many a pivot in the group. Often she would entertain members to a well-cooked and usually exciting meal, and many Sunday mornings I would wend my way to her home for late breakfast and to talk the day down into the late afternoon. The topics were mixed—literature, travel, art, world affairs, the Department and more. She was a fountain of knowledge, but of the "no-nonsense type." This was not the only social outlet. Mrs. Cormier was kind enough to ask us to an evening at her home, and in its fashion apart from my own enjoyment it also fostered a team spirit. We were a family of families, and it was in no way detrimental to the scope and schedule of the work. There were times when the entire Department would go out "on the town." There was a fine meal at some chosen café, and then the ladies would leave at about 11:00 p.m. and the remaining male members would seek out haunts where often some of our subjects would be present plus, of course, a modicum of alcohol to gladden the heart if indeed by this time it needed to be so gladdened! Somehow, at work and play there were no specific rules. Time was never a burden, nor did it ever drag, as the concern and respect for the Department and its Director were sufficient cause.

A Part

My specific subject was to seek out a mainly younger group of offenders, such as those at the FTC [Federal Training Centre], and to study their cases and the person concerned, not omitting the family unit in line with the Cormier Classification. So bi-weekly and more often, I attended the establishment and made many contacts with all kinds of subjects. The results were eventually published, but it was the idea, I believe, of Professor Cormier to study eventually every younger offender to find perhaps a causal aetiology, but this did not materialize.

Professor Cormier was a world figure who was known to the best in the field, the likes of whom are sadly mostly not with us anymore. Professor Trevor Gibbons, Professor Howard Jones, and so many more—this national standing came to the fore for me when I attended the international conference of criminologists in

Madrid some years back. McGill Forensic Clinic was very much on the map of units internationally. There was a wide scope of topics related, which in its way was of help with my project on the young offender. After all, the environment that is incarceration is the total act of punitive values applied and it created an abnormal life environment with all that this could and did mean for the offender so placed. From my contacts and the work, I would like to have followed them as the years passed. My return to the U.K. was not good for this idea, but I did manage to keep in contact, mainly by letter, with either the subjects themselves or the other authoritative figures. Canadian visits were also of great use, and contact with a Mennonite community in the back-river area of North Montreal was vital. They gave help with quite a number of the younger offenders, after release, on their farms, and one of the seniors was for years a chaplain at the Penitentiary. On one occasion I attended a Mennonite home for a weekend and was present when one of my group got married in a small wood.

From information, albeit incomplete, several of the fifty taken as a sample have done really well, but a much larger group have died, four by their own hand, seven by accident, and one from natural causes. Over 85% were getting into serious criminal trouble well into their twenties. Strangely, I was wandering through the H.M. Prison some years ago when a voice called out my name. It was one of the known fifty. I was able to help him to return to Canada after his release and I heard that he had reoffended but had been chosen to make a broadcast from an official station in West Canada. It is a strange world and full of interest and work to be done.

Inside the Bars

Work by Professor Cormier also included his knowledgeable application to the true and effective meaning of incarceration for both staff and inmate alike. This resulted in the publication of the volume *The Watcher and the Watched*. Prior to this he had described several active syndromes such as "cell breakage," "gate fever," and worked hard to explain the meaning and relevance of depression as seen for the offender, both before, during and after the sentence. Prisonization was also a topic he wrote about in all its negative and prognostic aspects. He applied psychoanalytical skills and modified programmes for application, the behavioural aspects and meaning of autoplastic activity as against alloplastic, and then the development and transition of activity which was initially egosyntonic and later with abatement egodystonic, all within his concept of the reality of a delinquent career. Here I have known him to use to good effect the medical model as a means to explain some complex behavioural activity. Though at times his work could be read easily, its base was deep and complexly profound within the actual dynamic meaning. He wished to be able to communicate to all who did work to alleviate the pain so often part of the offender's life-style. The work was practical and painstakingly achieved, but its humane aspect so often shines through, almost with missionary zeal and personal dedication.

Professor Cormier was, in my opinion, a great and dedicated reformer, and as such he was not always popular. This is the true mark of an original and honest individual. He was beyond his time and was very forward-thinking in his originality and brilliance. The work he produced was revolutionary and if applied could manage pain in a big cosmic fashion. Apart from his sincere humanitarianism, his work could have been and still can be of benefit to political thinking, economics, and other disciplines, apart from its direct application to penal and legal criminological areas.

The Department

The Department was the base where a great deal happened and where things happened that can still be of benefit for the future. I can remember the time when I was in his car returning from the Penitentiary to the Department during the mid-day period. He would be so keen to explain a point to me that many a red traffic light was breached!

Here are some further particulars:

1. As director, Professor Cormier was a giant in his field. He had an open attitude to the research to which he was totally dedicated. His humanistic vision and kindly authority were an encouragement to all who had the benefit of working for and with him. He was the operative key factor.

2. His team was as one, but as individuals their work was always given genuine consideration. As people, they mattered.

3. The ethos of the department was one of working amicability. The interpersonal quality bonded the members together.

4. Knowledge was greatly appreciated and keenly encouraged.

5. Though the resources were limited, the scope of the work was wide and ever-open for expansion and further clinical involvement.

6. The work could have absorbed other disciplines easily, with considerable benefit to large groups in society. The ambit of the basic discipline will not go away, and as yet it has hardly been touched officially.

This is but a small glimpse into Professor Cormier's Department—the office with the curved window on busy Pine Avenue West in Central Montreal. Its Director, Bruno Cormier, was a giant in his field, and perhaps one of the most brilliant intellects to have worked at McGill in recent times. There is evidence that in his day he was by no means fully appreciated; perhaps only those who actually worked with him were convinced of his greatness. His material output has not had the impact it deserves—criminology is not a part of the pop culture—but it is far-reaching and wide in its scope. Maybe the idea of marketing was lacking, but not the work itself. Even today his work needs to be spread out for greater appreciation.

Reginald A.H. Washbrook, *T.D., B.A., M.B., Ch.B. (St. Andrews), F.R.C. Psych. (U.K.), D.P.M. (London); Sessional Forensic Psychiatrist, Home Office, Prisons Department, London, England; Student in Theology, Westminster College, Oxford.*

Author of papers on mentally ill prisoners, alcohol and crime, neurosis and offending NFA inmates, drug addicts in custody, etc. Author of three volumes of poetry and one novel. Student of Advanced Criminology, Institute of Criminology, University of Cambridge.

Paul J. Williams

He was a pioneer in the truest sense of the word.
This clinic could not be compared to any other.

Grey was predominant! The sky was overcast on this March morning of 1964 as I wheeled up Montée St. François alongside the ominous fortress wall. I noticed that the guard tower was manned and realized that the inmates would be trudging across the yard from the bleakness of their cells to the boredom of their workshop. I then knew I would be a few minutes late for a meeting; little did I realize that this meeting would be different, one that would be brief but crucial to my career. It was to unleash a chain of events and experiences for me in this fascinating field which, on the surface, reveals few tangible rewards.

My mood complemented the circumstances. I was completing my second year as staff psychologist at St. Vincent de Paul Penitentiary. This was the "motherhouse" of the federal penitentiary system in the Quebec region. Although the inmate population was now reduced from some twelve to eight hundred, the result of a major riot two years previous, the workload remained excessive and the milieu oppressive. My personal contact with the inmates was good. I spent an inordinate amount of time working with the men locked up in Segregation and this was appreciated by inmate and penitentiary officials alike. My relationship with the guards had improved greatly over the past year, as they gradually realized that my working "with the inmates" did not mean working against them. In fact, the cathartic effect of the regular interviews with the inmates was reflected in an abatement of their verbal hostility towards the guards. The guards sensed this and would now refer inmates to me on their own initiative.

Despite this, the overall atmosphere of the workplace was depressing. I enjoyed working with the inmates and believed I was learning something about this phenomenon labelled "delinquency." On the other hand, I felt increasingly stymied with respect to practical solutions. After all, these were the years when brutality was officially sanctioned. The lash was a punishment still meted out by the Court and carried out by the penitentiary authorities; the strap was used as a means of "correcting" unacceptable institutional behaviour and believed to be a deterrent; the "diet" of bread and water was in vogue for those placed in the "hole," euphemistically referred to as Dissociation. All of the above coercive measures were carried out with procedural pomp, under the authorized stamp of approval. Apart from the numerous stabbings and beatings within the inmate population, my brief two years had been witness to two major incidents: the riot of 1962, which destroyed many cells, most of the workshops and resulted in the death of an inmate; and the hostage-taking in 1963, which terminated with the death of an inmate and a guard. Tension ran high; stress was the order of the day!

As I parked my car this morning, however, my spirits were uplifted by the thought of my upcoming meeting with the psychiatrist. We had met on occasion to discuss the handling and treatment of specific inmates. I frequently felt as though I were working in a vacuum, so these conferences with him were particularly invigorating. He knew I was seeing the men in Segregation on a regular basis and had expressed to me a particular interest in what he termed "the extreme deprivation of liberty." Sometime later we were to prepare a paper on this subject. Although our meetings were brief, as he usually seemed preoccupied and in a hurry, I always learned something from the encounters.

Bruno Cormier was a living paradox. He seemed to engender ambivalent feelings in those he met. He was "hated" by those inmates who became the target of his direct confrontation, yet respected by these same men who sensed his genuine concern for their self-defeating plight; he was a source of enmity to the institutional authorities because of his obstinate refusal to participate in, or even condone, the demeaning practices of the time while, at the same time, was regularly consulted by these very people with respect to institutional change; he was a thorn in the side of those colleagues in the field whose pronouncements emanated solely from theoretical ponderings but remained a principal invitee to national and international conferences. Slight in physical stature, he was an intellectual giant with an iron will; truculent with co-workers, he was graceful in a social setting.

The meeting was of shorter duration than usual. As I passed the final barred gate that led into the penitentiary yard, Dr. Cormier was some twenty paces ahead. He turned and stood waiting for me. Without preamble, other than a salutatory nod, he offered me a position at the McGill Forensic Clinic. We were standing in the yard, the last inmate stragglers wandering their way towards their work assignment in the typical penitentiary shuffle, under the surveillance of armed guard towers and canopied by a foreboding sky. My immediate inner reaction was akin to the rush of some intravenous anti-depressant. The dismal surroundings dissolved and a diffuse sense of calm preceded the shakes. I was being liberated, perhaps paroled is more accurate. My consternation was immediately apparent by my verbal response, "Will I be allowed to grow a beard?"

It is a credit to Dr. Cormier's expertise in human behaviour, with its myriad responses to various stimuli, that he didn't take to his heels in realization of major mistake. In fact, he simply replied with a grin, "Of course, why not?" Although this curious exchange was lost to my memory shortly after, Dr. Cormier was there to remind me. He frequently brought it up in social encounters over the years as he good-naturedly kidded me. This somewhat inauspicious beginning to career change was quickly amended as I delved into the new challenge.

The McGill Forensic Clinic was created by Bruno Cormier. He was a pioneer in the truest sense of the word. This clinic could not be compared to any other. In some respects it was better than others; in other respects it had its deficiencies. In any case, it was "Bruno's Clinic." It staggered along after his retirement, only because he never really retired. Its demise was concurrent with his own. The Clinic meant different things to different people. As for myself, it afforded me the opportunity to work in collaboration with professionals from different disciplines while, at the same time, maintaining a direct link with the inmate population of the penitentiary. I quickly realized that what had been demoralizing me while working at the penitentiary was not the hopelessness of the institutional milieu as much as the fact that I worked alone and had no institutional colleagues with whom I could exchange.

I began at the penitentiary in April 1962. The riot took place in June of the same year and by September the other psychologists had left. The daily routine consisted in dealing with immediate, concrete problems, the bulk of the requests and referrals coming from the inmates themselves. Although I had the support of an intelligent warden, Michel Le Corre, I had little interchange at the clinical level. Some of the Classification Officers had limited clinical training but their workload was heavily weighted with filling out forms and writing reports. Compared to today's standards, they spent more time interviewing inmates in those days, but because of the sparseness of the institutional facilities their contact was mainly to deal with the everyday pragmatic matters.

It was not long after my beginning at the Clinic that I found myself back in the penitentiary. Dr. Cormier, himself, spent an average of a day and a half per week running the psychiatric service within the walls. He was well aware of the need to maintain a "hands-on" approach if one is to maintain some semblance of reality in the study and treatment of human behaviour. My return to the penitentiary was characterized by a certain sense of freedom. Although I now had control over my time allotments and workload, there was another factor that came into play which, I believe, made my work more productive. It was a matter of perception—how I was perceived by both the inmates and the penitentiary personnel. I was immediately aware that something almost tangible had changed.

As I mentioned before, I had a good rapport with the inmates but, as a member of the penitentiary staff, there always existed an unseen but felt barrier. The phenomenon of the "watchers and the watched" applied to everyone, to a greater or lesser degree. I was not someone from the "outside" and, as such, had one hurdle less to clear. Similarly, I was now seen in a different light by the penitentiary personnel. My clinical observations and subsequent recommendations were now considered more seriously. In reality, I was the same person with the same expertise and limits as before, but this new aura of professional respectability opened doors more easily. I took advantage of my novel status.

The fact that I was now a research assistant at the Forensic Clinic, rather than a staff psychologist with the Canadian Penitentiary Service, actually opened doors to other penitentiaries in the region. The Federal Training Centre was a correctional facility for first penitentiary offenders, under the age of twenty-five. Its basic philosophy was centred on trade training. One of my colleagues at the Clinic, Dr. Washbrook, was going to this institution as part of his weekly routine. He was working with these younger offenders on an individual basis and asked me if I would be interested in starting a group with him. I was delighted and saw this as an opportunity to expand my experience. We did so, amassing six inmates from sixteen to eighteen years of age and held weekly group therapy for some eighteen months.

Dr. Washbrook was an experienced therapist who had worked with the Home Office in England. His genuine concern for the inmates was obvious to all, and the inmate response made the work pleasurable and an immediate source of learning for me. We would prepare for the group on the drive from the Clinic to the

penitentiary and rehash each session on the return trip. Three of
the six inmates were not eligible for release on parole, as they had
not been sentenced under the Criminal Code but, rather, sentenced to the penitentiary as "incorrigible." One of the "incorrigi-
bles" was a sixteen-year-old who had "escaped" from Shawbridge
Boy's Farm on numerous occasions. As it turned out, his constant
running away was in search of his mother who was a dancer and
part-time prostitute. It was evident that this "incorrigible" young
man needed more than trade training. We attempted to fill in
some of the gaps. Although there is no certainty, we may have had
some measure of success. At least, I have not come across him in
the system, over the past thirty years.

One of the strong points of the Forensic Clinic was the variety
of disciplines represented by the staff. This helped the Clinic serve
as a bridge between the penitentiary and the community-at-large.
Raymond Boyer, for example, held a doctorate in chemistry but
because of a significant personal experience was competent in the
field of corrections. He had been contacted by a member of the
Mennonite community who expressed an interest in providing
help to offenders. A discussion was held among Boyer, Washbrook
and myself, and after appropriate contacts were completed,
arrangements were made for the placement of one of our group,
upon release from the Federal Training Centre, in the home of a
Mennonite family.

Réal was seventeen years of age when he was released. He had
been physically and sexually abused as a child, the product of a
multi-problem family. His early adolescent years were spent mainly under the juvenile jurisdiction and led directly to the penitentiary. He now manifested all the "earmarks" of a protracted criminal career. He had spent some two difficult years inside. His principal institutional difficulties focused on the hyperactivity of youth
in a basically repressive, authoritarian system. He spent much of
his time doing extra chores as punishment for his exuberance.
Needless to say, he was the most active, both physically and verbal-

ly, in the group. The purgative effect of the group process eventually had some beneficial effect on his institutional adjustment. On the
day of his release, I drove him from the penitentiary to his new
home. The family comprised parents and five children, all younger
than Réal. He stayed with them some five years and was given the
necessary support throughout all crises. He later married and maintained direct contact with his adopted family until his untimely, acci-
dental death some twenty years later. Credit goes to this exemplary
family within the Mennonite Community, and the Forensic Clinic
was proud to have played an intermediary role.

The Forensic Clinic was instrumental in the training and
preparation of psychiatric interns. The interns usually "signed on"
for a year or two. Not all completed their term, since clinical work
with delinquents is basically different from work with other types
of maladjustment. For example, motivation on the part of the subject is a rare commodity. Thus, the basic thrust of the "treatment"
issues emanated from a different starting point. It is not everyone's cup of tea. There was one particular incident, however, that
I believe cut short the forensic career of one intern. I was sitting in
the psychiatric unit of the St. Vincent de Paul Penitentiary one
morning, chatting with a psychiatric intern who had recently
arrived at the Forensic Clinic. As part of their training, Dr. Cormier
would have the interns come on a weekly or bi-monthly basis to
the penitentiary. This morning, shock treatment was to be administered to a few patients.

As the intern and I were talking, I looked up and saw an
inmate walking hurriedly towards me. His glazed eyes seemed to
be staring through me. As he got close I could hear him mumbling
about "the Devil" and suddenly his hands were around my throat.
This all happened so fast that the fear response had no time to
trigger off. I reacted by firmly gripping his wrists, removing his
hands from my throat while talking to him gently. The incident
was over in a matter of seconds and he was escorted back to his
cell. When I turned to the intern I saw a chalk mask. The colour
had drained from his face. We had a coffee, a few words, and I

never saw him again. I'm sure he has had a successful career ... in another field!

Apart from the mandatory clinical conferences every Friday afternoon, I saw little of Dr. Cormier in the Clinic. This was simply because most of my time was spent in one or another of the penitentiaries. I had begun group work with inmates at St. Vincent de Paul and this kept me in direct contact with a sizeable number on a regular basis. Dr. Cormier and I had regular mini-conferences within the penitentiary walls in an attempt to co-ordinate our work. One important point to stress, however, is the fact that he was always easily accessible in time of need even when preparing his professional papers.

I first met Johnny in Segregation while I was still working for the penitentiary. He had recently been transferred back from Kingston penitentiary, a recalcitrant individual deeply involved in the wheeling and dealing within the inmate population. This always entailed a basic power struggle and inevitably led to serious trouble. He had been transferred to Kingston, as a punitive/corrective measure, some years before and was now back "home." Obviously, displacing the problem did not solve it. It was not long before he was administered the strap for threatening guards while in Segregation. Immediately after this humiliating punishment, he bared his buttocks to me through the cell door so as to make it clear that not only his feelings were hurt. He was right!

Now, some years later, while working at the Clinic, I received a telephone call from Johnny asking me if I would visit him at home. I had had only minimal contact with him since his release. It was while conversing with him one morning over a cup of coffee that distinct signs of confusion, memory lapse, and a lack of motor co-ordination became increasingly obvious. He was conscious of the fact that "something was wrong." His wife was away at work, while he stayed home with their three-year-old son. I stayed over the noon hour when she returned and discussed the matter with the two of them. I continued the discussion alone with his wife as I gave her a lift back to work. I was now able to put together a more complete picture of what had been taking place.

I related the story to Dr. Cormier upon return to the Clinic and suggested that a neurological assessment would be of some benefit. He made all the arrangements immediately and, as it turned out, Johnny was suffering from a brain tumour. We followed him through his difficulties, the subsequent brain surgery and to his death the following year. Dr. Cormier provided individual treatment for his wife during this trying period. I believe this was an excellent example of the Clinic's co-ordinated services.

Many services were provided by the Forensic Clinic and many professional papers were published and presented at various local, national, and international conferences. The presentations were always underscored by descriptive clinical material, based on direct client service under the aegis of Dr. Cormier himself. As I said previously, the Clinic meant different things to different people. Each worker brought a certain expertise; each had an area of particular interest.

As for myself, the most significant happening was the Dannemora Project. I was involved from the outset and was instrumental in developing the daily program for the Therapeutic Community. It was due to Dr. Cormier's international status, however, that the project was able to get off the ground. The New York State Department of Corrections had space available and a surplus of correctional personnel due to a major reduction in patient population because of a change in the law. They approached Bruno Cormier through McGill University, plans were prepared, agreements signed, and the Diagnostic and Treatment Center was opened on October 3, 1966.

The overall project has been described elsewhere. Suffice it to say, that, from my point of view, it was and remains the most significant experience in my career, which has now spanned more than thirty-five years. The most important issue is the fact that it touched directly upon the effects of the deprivation of liberty, the principal means by which our society reacts to anti-social behaviour. Incarceration is a necessary evil. It is evil because of its deleterious effects which are rarely taken into account. It is necessary, however, when employed to neutralize dangerous and/or repetitive criminal behaviour. The important matter is the manner in which the incarceration process unfolds. Can the effects of the deprivation of liberty be diverted in a positive direction?

The clinical foundation of Therapeutic Community lies in milieu therapy. The milieu itself is structured in such a way that the pertinent social forces within the community form the basis of the social learning. Verbal and emotional expression are encouraged rather than suppressed and personal responsibility is increased. The role of each participant in the process, whether inmate or staff, is fundamentally modified. Although the milieu does not become a "democracy," the artificial barriers among professionals, inmates, and guards are significantly diminished. On the other hand, the piecemeal approach to treatment, predominant in traditional institutions, is characterized by programs, courses, and individual therapy, but is ultimately doomed to failure so long as the prevailing negative milieu of the total institution is not drastically altered. Despite this knowledge, any attempt to establish a total program based on these sound principles has met with official refusal since it delves into the underlying *raison d'être* of incarceration.

In retrospect, my personal experience with the Forensic Clinic, Dr. Cormier, and his associates was the linchpin of my learning and practice. The open exchange with professionals of varying disciplines, the direct and regular contact with offenders both during and after their incarceration, and the opportunity to participate directly in local, national, and international conferences was of invaluable worth. My appreciation extends to the memory of that pioneering spirit, Bruno Cormier.

Paul J. Williams, *M.A., Executive Director, John Howard Society of Quebec, since 1980. Past President, Canadian Criminal Justice Association.*

Psychologist, Canadian Penitentiary Service, 1962-1964; Research Assistant, McGill University Forensic Clinic, 1964-1969; Clinical Co-ordinator, New York State, Department of Corrections, 1966-1971; Psychologist, Correctional Service of Canada, 1971-1980; Commission québécoise des liberations conditionelles, 1979-1984.

Bruno M. Cormier. The young scholar. B.A., Collège Ste-Marie, Montréal, 1942.

Below:
Bruno M. Cormier. Drawing by Pierre Gauvreau, 1942. (Photo: Maurice Perron)

Bruno M. Cormier. Photo taken at the
home of Jean-Paul Riopelle, Otterburn
Park, Québec, 1948. (Photo: Maurice
Perron)

Opposite:
Bruno and Ruby Cormier.
London, England, 1953.

Exhibition at the home of Pierre Gauvreau,
1947. *Left to right:* Claude Gauvreau, Mme
Gauvreau, Pierre Gauvreau, Marcel Barbeau,
Madeleine Arbour, Paul-Émile Borduas,
Madeleine Lalonde, Bruno M. Cormier,
Jean-Paul Mousseau.
(Photo: Maurice Perron)

Opposite:
Bruno M. Cormier. Studio Portrait.
(Posen Photo, Montréal)

Bruno M. Cormier.
Studio photograph, c. 1975.

Bruno M. Cormier. Receiving the
Isaac Ray Award of the American
Psychiatric Association from Dr.
Naomi Goldstein in Toronto, 1977.

Reception celebrating the 40th
anniversary of the *Refus Global* at the
Cormier's home, Montréal, 1988.
Back row: Jeanne Renaud, Ulysse
Comtois, Marcel Barbeau, Jean-Paul
Mousseau, Sam Abramovitch, Thérèse
Leduc, Fernand Leduc, Maurice Perron.
Front row: Michèle Drouin, Madeleine
Arbour, Madeleine Ferron, Françoise
Sullivan, Bruno M. Cormier, Charles
Daudelin.
Photo: David Moore

APPENDIX

The McGill University Clinic in Forensic Psychiatry: A Short History

Alan Hustak

 It was one of those institutions that evolved rather than began.

In 1955 Dr. Bruno Cormier, a free-thinking psychiatrist on staff at the Allan Memorial Institute in Montreal, was assigned to work part-time observing inmates in the St. Vincent de Paul Penitentiary.

Dr. Cormier maintained an office in what had once been the riding stables at the sprawling Allan psychiatric hospital. To facilitate his prison studies, the office became an out-patient clinic for inmates who had been released but still required counselling. From this practical but modest arrangement the McGill Clinic in Forensic Psychiatry was born.

As Dr. Cormier himself once said, "The beginning of forensic psychiatry in Canada was rather an informal alliance between the federal Solicitor General and the Allan Memorial Institute." Dr. Cormier was drawn to prison culture from his student days. As a practising medical intern, he harboured the revolutionary notion—radical for the time—that psychiatry could be used as a tool for social engineering. The idea was consistent with the thinking of someone who signed *Refus global,* Quebec's 1948 declaration of intellectual independence that challenged and helped to change Maurice Duplessis' repressive, autocratic society.

In early 1955 the Deputy Commissioner of Penitentiaries approached Dr. Cormier regarding the possibility of setting up a psychiatric hospital within the penitentiary (St. Vincent de Paul Penitentiary). Dr. Cormier was enthusiastic about the idea. What he proposed was "not a full-time position, not a post within the prison, but a psychiatric service that will establish a close relationship between the penitentiary psychiatric services and those offered in the community by the Allan Memorial Institute—that is, services that would include not only psychiatry, but also all of the allied disciplines, such as Social Work." Having secured what he was looking for, Dr. Cormier went to work. From the beginning his objective was to develop a clinical criminology based on the personality and the psychopathology of the offender, a knowledge of his social background and family history, and an understanding of the prison milieu, rather than limiting it to types and severity of offences or on isolated case histories.

"Through this kind of medical-psychiatric-social approach, types of criminality can be isolated, traced from inception to outcome. From this we can arrive at a diagnosis and a prognosis, with the possibility of intervention. A many-faceted, longtitudinal research of this kind, with intensive case study, requires a large population and we have been fortunate in having St. Vincent de Paul Penitentiary as our field of operations." His questions and his concerns about the caging of human beings became the subject of his first paper, "The Meaning of Deprivation of Liberty." The paper explored how prison fosters paranoia as a way of surviving and other symptoms attributed to the anxiety and situational stress that develop in prison.

He was convinced that half the people in jail did not belong there, that most people behind bars were there because they are pathologically ill, not criminals. At the same time, he began to explore the notion of dysfunctional families as incubators of criminal behaviour. What he learned challenged stereotypical notions: dysfunctionally intact families produce a larger number of delinquents and more severe criminality than so-called broken or single-parent families.

Even as he began his ground-breaking research, Dr. Cormier continued to push for an accredited clinic that would combine sociology and psychiatry. In 1956 he approached his boss, the head of the Allan Memorial Institute, the redoubtable Dr. Ewen Cameron, with his ideas. His clinic, he argued, would monitor convicts on a reliable, systematic basis, and offer "contact with criminal offenders before sentence and with those liberated under treatment." Cameron, who was considered by many to be the Godfather of Canadian Psychiatric Studies, proved to be sympathetic. "Research facilities for the making of instruments of death are apparently unlimited," Cameron told him. "It would be a sad commentary on our times if we cannot provide space for men to work on the great problems of health and happiness." Dr. Cameron sought approval from Dr. Cyril James, Principal, Vice-Rector, and the Chancellor of McGill University. In a memo dated Oct. 31, 1956, Cameron informed Cormier: "I have discussed the establishment of the clinic with Dr. James and he is much in favour of it. He has made the suggestion, which I think should be carefully explored, that a third partner be involved in the operation of the clinic, namely the department of law."

Maxwell Cohen was the acting Dean of Law at the time, and he endorsed the proposal. On April 1, 1958, Dr. Cormier was awarded a $5,000 Dominion-Provincial Health Grant. The money enabled him to move his office out of an institutional setting at the Allan Memorial and open his clinic in a three-story Victorian brownstone at 509 Pine Ave., directly across the street from his house at number 506. (The telephone number was easy to remember: 392-5010.) Although the clinic was in a separate building a few blocks down the street from the Allan Memorial, it was considered an extension of the Institution.

Dr. Cormier became the director of a staff of six, including two psychiatrists, a psychologist, two social workers, and a secretary. They studied the relationship of prisoners and prison guards, looked into their mutual dependencies and started compiling data about human behaviour that judicial officials had previously ignored. Dr. Cormier soon employed a dozen people, both full- and part-time, on research grants to continue, and he struggled from year to year with uncertainty.

In 1959 the Parole Act was enacted, setting up the National Parole Board as an independent administrative body within the Justice Department. It was the first serious attempt to set up a control mechanism to write pre-sentence reports, supervise offenders, and rehabilitate people who had been in prison to reduce the high rate of recidivism. Prior to this, psychiatrists often testified in court, but with little visible impact on sentencing. The act required criminals to be evaluated on an individual, systematic basis—something that had never really been done before. In many cases, he discovered that "to treat offenders is the only way to study them. It is a very rewarding experience to observe how these so-called anti-social people, if offered help and a place to come when in need are able to use these facilities. Because of this experience we have established as part of our research a service of consultation and treatment."

The Philippe Pinel Institute for the criminally and violently insane opened an out-patient clinic in downtown Montreal in 1960. It was designed to treat out-patients with severe behaviour disorders, and psychiatrists there began to compile information that complemented the work Dr. Cormier was doing. It allowed him to examine some of the city's most notorious criminals and histories of households filled with abuse and violence.

One of the first patients was a nineteen-year-old sentenced to be hanged for the murder of a scrap-metal dealer. After the killer's sentence was later commuted, Dr. Cormier began to study young people who kill—at the time those twenty years and under—and after conducting twenty-two case studies over an eight-year period, he wrote "A longitudinal study of adolescent murderers" with Baila Markus (1981).

The experience put him at the forefront of the campaign to abolish capital punishment in Canada. "For many of these individuals, the homicidal act for which they had originally been sentenced to die has been one of a number of symptoms which signalled the development of mental illness," he wrote to the Minister of Justice, Guy Favreau, in 1964. "It was only because the commutation of the death penalty has become more common that we have been able to make such observations more frequently. We have to wonder how many others who were hanged might also have shown symptoms indicating the development of a mental illness.

"Although most people who have committed murder are not psychiatric cases, we can still find no plausible clinical reasons which could possibly justify the hanging of any individual. There can be no justifying the death penalty by attributing to it deterrent powers, by considering it as the proper fulfillment of justice or by viewing it as a way of protecting society. Such an attempt to justify the death penalty is only an intellectual position in order to try to maintain the law of capital punishment. In no way does it fit the reality of the lives of the individuals whom we have come to know over the years.

"Any law, which in its conception does not have as its focal point the individual, offender and victim alike, and the society in which they live, is an unjust law."

In 1968 he lauched one of his most ambitious studies, a look at three generations of an offender's family. It was exacting research involving brothers, sisters, parents, and grandparents of the accused and enabled

Dr. Cormier to evaluate the behaviour, pathological and otherwise, of relatives who might offer clues to the factors which contribute to or inhibit criminal behaviour. The study was financed by a grant from the Ministry.

Dr. Cormier opposed a Canada Council grant for a project to compare two schools of criminology, one in Berkeley, California, the other in Montreal, arguing that criminologists were both intrusive and arrogant. "Criminologists may yet discover what psychiatrists are discovering—that they might have oversold themselves. It took psychiatry a long time to realize this. At this stage, I would simply say that like other professionals, they might acquire a creative humility which is a necessity in human science."

Dr. Cormier hoped to expand his clinical work and open a Forensic Centre that would integrate social work, law, medicine, and psychiatry. "It would be desirable to have two or three students each year seeking Masters of Law degree specializing in the field of criminology. It is hoped they would get some appreciation of modern treatment techniques in connection with the offender," he wrote to the dean.

The purpose of the Forensic Centre, he stated would not only facilitate a close co-operation within the faculties of law, medicine, the Department of Sociology and the School of Social Work, but also make possible the fullest use of all relevant knowledge in the field of behaviour disorders:

"It would function for teaching, research and clinical work within these disciplines, in areas of common interest. It would avoid duplication and overlapping, permit the pooling of resources and thus make a maximum use of available teaching staff. It will also have as its function, to establish links with institutions in the community. It is not planned that the Forensic Centre become a Diploma granting body—the participating faculties, departments and schools, will retain their exclusive diploma-granting function, but the centre will serve as a means of enlarging and strengthening their basic training progams."

It was a heady time and Dr. Cormier's department became a dynamic forum for the exchange of knowledge and for the advancement of forensic psychiatry as a new profession. It was able to support itself, in part, by doing parole investigations and by acting as consultants to the Justice Department.

If studying criminal behaviour is a science, Dr. Cormier was able to demonstrate that understanding the psychiatric and neurological reasons for it is an art. The data sheets in the archives show the real extent of the clinic's contributions. Dr. Cormier produced papers that provided insight into the nature of incest and pedophilia, examined the so-called incorrigible offender who embarks on a life of crime before puberty, and studied latecomers to crime—those who get into trouble late in their lives. He applied the standards of clinical research to discover the relationship between criminality and personality and explored the relationship of environmental factors and genetics on criminal behaviour.

In 1966, Dr. Cormier helped to establish the diagnostic, treatment, and research centre at Clinton Prison in Dannemora, N.Y. By then, he was struggling to pay the bills at home. Research grants dried up and McGill University contributed $20,000 through the Principal's Special Fund to keep the work going. Shortly afterwards, the Donner Foundation awarded the clinic a $100,000 grant, which allowed its work to continue for another eight years. But it still depended on the generosity of others to survive, and Dr. Cormier wanted it put on a secure financial foundation.

The political climate was right for Dr. Cormier to expand his work. "As you are aware, we have had in mind for some years now the setting up of a forensic clinic," he wrote to the Dean of Law, Maxwell Cohen, "The nucleus of such a clinic is already in existence as part of our research program. The time has now come to establish a forensic clinic on a permanent basis, adequately staffed and equipped." Cohen was sympathetic, but left as dean in 1969, and Dr. Cormier lost an important ally in his struggle.

Dr. Cormier was appointed President of the American Society of Criminology in 1970, the first Canadian so honoured, and the following year was proposed as a candidate for the Royal Bank Centennial Award. In the submission to the Royal Bank, Dr. Cormier was described as "an uncommon combination of the clinician, the scientist and the humanist:

"In the daily practice of his specialty, the treatment of behavioural disorders, he displays an undeviating drive to study the etiology and the course of criminal processes, their effect upon the individual and on those around him and on the society that contains them. He is concerned with the practical aspects of penology which permit the rehabilitation of the offenders."

Dr. Cormier's grants ran out in 1974, and the Royal Victoria Hospital assumed responsibility for the clinic. Three years later, secretarial staff was cut, then the number of research assistants dropped. Ironically, the department was downsized the same year that Dr. Cormier received the prestigious Isaac Ray Award for his outstanding contributions in the field of corrections.

By the mid-1980s, the pendulum in Canada swung back to punitive rather than rehabilitative initiatives for criminal behaviour, and the government of the day was not about to appear soft on crime. Dr. Cormier's clinic had become so successful, other institutions now copied it. Dr. Cormier continued to believe his work was complementary not competitive in nature. He continued to fight for sufficient services for all offenders.

"People have the same right to psychiatric treatment in prison as they do in the community," he told a criminal justice conference in 1984. "It is preferable the service be associated with a university where psychiatry, psychology, and criminology are integrated, because universities must be accredited and accountable."

Argue as he might, political will needed to fulfill his dream was not there. Still, the clinic carried on, operating on a shoe-string, publishing and presenting papers at various congresses each year. "We were able to do this because the psychiatrists and other clinicians in this specific speciality were not dispersed all over the place," Dr. Cormier explained. "By all over the place, I mean they were not attached to many services, doing one *vacation* (rotation) here and another *vacation* somewhere else. They were able to use their geographical full-time in the most constructive way and were able to do their own research on their own time."

By 1986, Dr. Cormier's was the only full-time position left at the Forensic Clinic. He was sixty-seven years old and about to retire.

Those inclined to judge him by the record of his discussion papers overlook his greatest contribution as a teacher. By the time he retired, he was able to boast that 125 students, including residents in psychiatry, had done their field placement at his clinic, many had written their Master's theses, and two of them had obtained Ph.D.s in the field of clinical criminology. In addition, students from the law faculty often came to the clinic to learn for themselves what made the criminal mind tick. As well, the number of caseloads continued to grow. In 1983, 2,900 patients went through the clinic, in 1986, 3,330.

In spite of Dr. Cormier's achievements, the University felt his work had become redundant. Because of budget cuts, McGill could no longer afford to run a forensic clinic as a separate entity.

Dr. Cormier was succeeded by Dr. Renée Fugère. The university, however, continued to maintain the Pine Avenue building, and the Royal Victoria Hospital paid for a secretary and a full-time psychologist; so Dr. Fugère managed to continue the work of the clinic—offering clinical services, teaching students of various disciplines, presenting papers at conferences, and publishing papers. Following numerous discussions, the McGill Post Graduate Coordinator appointed a task force committee to study the possibility of adding a block on legal and ethical issues in psychiatry to the Diploma Course (mandatory teaching for students in psychiatry). Two staff members of the clinic were involved, as well as other members of the Department of Psychiatry. As a result of those discussions, a new block on forensic issues has been implemented allowing senior residents to learn about civil and criminal matters, ethics in psychiatry and quality assurance.

Still, Dr. Cormier was disillusioned and no doubt disappointed. "I find it difficult to believe that the only English university in this province that has a faculty of medicine with its numerous clinical and research services in the various teaching hospitals would not maintain its presence in the research services and clinical criminology when this field is in fact in the process of expansion in major universities throughout the country," Dr. Cormier complained in a letter to Dr. Brian Robertson, director of the Allan Memorial Institute on April 25, 1986.

Although Dr. Cormier was no longer head of the clinic, he continued to see patients and to do research for it until he died. He died in June, 1991. Once he was gone, the clinic was subsumed by various departments until it virtually disappeared. It closed officially on January 6, 1997.

Dr. Cormier has died, but Dr. Fugère continues to work in forensic psychiatry through her private office. His name lives on in the award that is presented each year by the Canadian Association of Psychiatry and the Law to those pioneers who have made great contributions to Canadian forensic psychiatry.

The memory of the McGill Clinic is still alive—many legal referral sources, two years after the clinic's closing, still remember and share their knowledge of their qualitative work with the new people in the system. The memory of Bruno Cormier and his staff is still highly respected in the academic community, since the extensive, creative and innovative published papers still testify to his wisdom.

Life is a cycle where everything has a beginning and an end. In these times of restructuring, other programmes have been favoured to the detriment of the McGill University Clinic in Forensic Psychiatry. Time will tell if that choice was a wise one.

Alan Hustak, *journalist and reporter for Montreal's* The Gazette. *Born in Saskatchewan, he came to Montreal in 1967. His byline has appeared in almost every paper in the country. He has been a member of the John Howard Society and is the author of several books, including one on capital punishment in Canada titled* They Were Hanged.

Curriculum Vitae

Bruno M. Cormier, M.D.

Education

1942   B.A., Collège Ste-Marie (Université de Montréal)
1948   M.D., Université de Montréal
1948-50   Postgraduate Study in Psychiatry,
          Allan Memorial Institute
1950-53   Diploma in Psychiatry, McGill University
1950-58   Training in Psychoanalysis, London Psychoanalytic
          Institute and Canadian Psychoanalytic Institute
1954   Certified in Psychiatry, College of Physicians and
          Surgeons, Province of Quebec

Positions in 1989

Professor Emeritus, Department of Psychiatry, McGill University

Senior Psychiatrist, Forensic Clinic of Royal Victoria Hospital

President, La Fondation Cité des Prairies

Former Positions

Director, McGill Clinic in Forensic Psychiatry (1955-87)
Member, Scientific Committee of the International Society of
Criminology
Director of Psychiatric Services, St. Vincent de Paul Penitentiary (1955-
70)
Principal Consultant, Clinton Diagnostic and Treatment Center,
Dannemora, N.Y. (New York State Department of Corrections, 1966-
72)
Professeur titulaire invité, Ecole de Criminologie, Université de
Montréal (1974-78)

Memberships
Canadian Medical Association
Canadian Psychiatric Association
Canadian Psychoanalytic Society
Quebec Psychiatric Association
American Psychiatric Association
Canadian Corrections Association
Quebec Society of Criminology (past president)
International Society of Criminology
American Society of Criminology (past president)
American Academy of Political and Social Science
American Academy of Psychiatry and the Law

Forensic Clinic Staff

*Names of members of the staff
of the McGill Clinic in Forensic Psychiatry appear here.
Excluded are the names of those members who have contributed
tributes to this volume. When known, years of engagement and information
on current whereabouts are included.
In some instances it has proven impossible to confirm
full names of staff members.*

C. Barriga (1965-66, 1968-70)
   –private practice
P. Boulanger (1969-72)
   –deceased
R. Boyer (1955-80)
   –deceased
J. Cvejic (1969-71)
   –Douglas Hospital
B. Devault (1966-)
A. Ferstman (1966-69)
S. Fraid (1974-75)
   –deceased
A. Galardo (1962-66)
   –deceased
K. Gore (1994-98)
   –Tracom Mental Health Centre
Z. Harris (1982-84)
   –McGill School of Social Work
Z. Herman (1968)
M. Kennedy (1955-70)
   –deceased
L. Keitner (1967-72)
   –deceased
P. Lagier (1969-71)
H. Linder (1969-74)
B. Malamud (1969-72)
G. Morf (1967-69)
J. Northrup (1971-74)

V. Peck (1980-81)
   –deceased
J. Princz (1969-72)
   –retired
J. Rich (1968-69)
J. Sangowicz (1962-72)
   –deceased
M. Sendbuehler (1960-61)
M. Sinuk (1969-70)
S. Simons (1965-69, 1976-82)
   –retired
M. St-Germain (1968-69)
A.L. Thiffault (1960-64)
   –Quebec Parole Board
M. Trottier (1957-62)
   –deceased
J. Van der Vaart (1968-70)
S. Watters (1968-70)
J. Zambrowsky (1969-75)
   –lawyer

Administrative Secretaries

Lorna Graham
   –retired
Louise d'Amour
   –deceased

218

McGill University Clinic in Forensic Psychiatry

Bibliography

Published Papers

Angliker, C.C.J. (1970). The therapeutic community–Whom are we treating? *International Annals of Criminology*, 9 (2), pp. 443-446.

Angliker, C.C.J. (1971). The therapeutic community–Whom are we treating? *Laval Médical*, 42, pp. 12-14.

Angliker, C.C.J. (1974). La Formation des gardes de prison. *La vie médicale au Canada français*, 3, pp. 602-604.

Angliker, C.C.J., Cormier, B.M., Boulanger, P. & Malamud, B. (1973). A therapeutic community for persistent offenders. *Canadian Psychiatric Association Journal*, 18 (4), pp. 289-295.

Barriga, C., Boulanger, P., Boyer, R., Cormier, B.M. & van der Vaart, J. M. (1971). Young adult offenders—Ages twenty to twenty-four. *Canadian Psychiatric Journal*, 16 (1), pp. 33-40.

Bogopolsky, Y. & Cormier, B.M. (1979). Economie relationnelle de chacun des membres dans une famille incestueuse. *Canadian Journal of Psychiatry*, 24, pp. 65-70.

Boyer, R. (1963). La peine capitale en nouvelle-France. *Cité Libre*, 55, pp. 13-20.

Boyer, R. (1963). La question: histoire de la torture à travers les âges. *Cité Libre*, 59, pp. 1-13.

Boyer, R. (1963). The question: Judicial torture in New France. *Canadian Journal of Corrections*, 5 (4), pp. 284-291.

Boyer, R. (1964). Le bourreau au Canada. *Canadian Psychiatric Association Journal*, 9, pp. 521-532.

Boyer, R. (1964, November). Magic and witchcraft in New France. (La Magie et la sorcellerie en Nouvelle-France). *Proceedings of the Fourth Research Conference on Delinquency and Criminology*, Montreal, pp. 439-456.

Boyer, R. (1966). Les crimes et les châtiments au Canada français du

XVIIe au XXe siècle. Montreal: Le Circle du Livre de France.

Boyer, R. (1972). Barreaux de fer—hommes de chair. Montreal: Editions du Jour.

Boyer, R, Cormier, B.M., & Grad, B. (1966). Statistics on Criminal Processes. *Canadian Journal of Corrections,* 8 (2), pp. 104-119.

Cooper, I. (1978). Decriminalization of Incest: New legal-clinical responses. In: Eekelaar, J.M., & Katz, S. (Eds.). *Family Violence: An International and Interdisciplinary Study.* Toronto: Butterworth, pp. 518-528.

Cooper, I. & Cormier, B.M. (1982). Inter-generational transmission of incest. *Canadian Journal of Psychiatry,* 27, pp. 231-235.

Cooper, I. & Cormier, B.M. (1990). Incest. In: Bluglass, R. (Ed.). *Principles and Practices of Forensic Psychiatry.* London: Churchill-Livingstone, pp. 749-765.

Cormier, B.M. (1957). The psychological effects of the deprivation of liberty on the offender. *Proceedings of the Canadian Congress of Corrections,* Montreal, pp. 137-149.

Cormier, B.M. (1959). Some rights, duties and responsibilities in penology and suggested changes. *Canadian Journal of Corrections,* 1 (4), pp. 70-79.

Cormier, B.M. (1959). The psychiatric hospital in a maximum security prison. *Canadian Journal of Corrections,* 1 (4), pp. 3-14.

Cormier, B.M. (1960). The Latecomer to Crime. *Preparatory Paper III, Fourth International Criminological Congress,* The Hague.

Cormier, B.M. (1961). Divergent views between law and psychiatry on problems of sentencing. *Proceedings of Third World Congress of Psychiatry,* Montreal, pp. 323-328.

Cormier, B.M. (1961). Psychodynamics of homicide committed in a marital relationship. *Proceedings of Third World Congress of Psychiatry,* Montreal.

Cormier, B.M. (1962, September). *Proceedings of the 12th International Course in Criminology, Jerusalem.* Vol. III, pp. 134-135.

Cormier, B.M. (1962). Divergent views between law and psychiatry on problems of sentencing. *Canadian Medical Association Journal,* 87, pp. 229-234.

Cormier, B.M. (1962). La liberté des autres. *Cité Libre,* 47, pp. 6-11.

Cormier, B.M. (1962). Psychodynamics of homicide committed in a marital relationship. *Corrective Psychiatry and Journal of Social Therapy,* 8 (4), pp. 187-194.

Cormier, B.M. (1962). The latecomer to crime—A psychiatric study.

Proceedings of the 12th International Course in Criminology, Jerusalem, Vol. III, pp. 381-392.

Cormier, B.M. (1962). The role of research in criminology. *Québec Corrections Society Bulletin,* 1 (3), pp. 9.

Cormier, B.M. (1964). Réflections sur les prisons communes. *Bulletin de la Société de Criminologie du Québec,* 3 (3), p. 32.

Cormier, B.M. (1964). The law, psychiatry and the rights of man in judicial procedures: The pre-trial ward. *Proceedings of the Fourth Research Conference on Delinquency and Criminology.* Montreal, pp. 61-75.

Cormier, B.M. (1965). Le Droit, la psychiatrie et les droits de l'homme dans les procédures judiciares: Les prévenus. *Thémis,* pp. 99-114.

Cormier, B.M. (1965). McGill Clinic in Forensic Psychiatry. *Federal Corrections,* 4 (2), pp. 13-16.

Cormier, B.M. (1965). Pour une politique criminelle. *Cité Libre,* 79, pp. 15-23.

Cormier, B.M. (1965). On the history of men and genocide. *Lecture Presented at the Fifth International Criminological Congress,* Montreal.

Cormier, B.M. (1966). A criminological classification of criminal processes. In: Slovenko, R. (Ed.).(1966). *Crime, Law and Corrections.* Springfield: Charles C. Thomas, pp. 165-190.

Cormier, B.M. (1966). On the history of men and genocide. *Canadian Medical Association Journal,* 94, pp. 276-291.

Cormier, B.M. (1966). Depression and persistent criminality. *Canadian Psychiatric Association Journal,* 11, Special Supplement, pp. s-208–s-220.

Cormier, B.M. (1968). Contribution to a panel: A new total approach to the persistent offender in New York State. *Proceedings of the Frederick A. Moran Institute in Delinquency and Crime,* St. Lawrence University, Canton, New York, pp. 26-38.

Cormier, B.M. (1968, October). Discussion in: Lord Taylor, (1968). The role of environment in psychopatholgy, psychosis and neurosis. *Excerpta Medica International Congress Series, No. 187.*

Cormier, B.M. (1968). Psychiatric research in our changing world. *Proceedings of an International Symposium,* Montreal.

Cormier, B.M. (1968, March). Therapeutic community in a prison setting. *Proceedings of a series sponsored jointly by the Allan Memorial Institute and the McGill University School of Social Work, Montreal,* pp. 45-66.

Cormier, B.M. (1969). De l'histoire des hommes et du génocide. *Annales Internationales de Criminologie,* 8 (2), pp. 247-279.

Cormier, B.M. (1970). *International Annals of Criminology,* 1 (2), pp. 363-376.

Cormier, B.M. (1970). Les états dépressifs et les actes délictueux. *Annales Internationales de Criminologie*, 9 (2), pp. 377-415.

Cormier, B.M. (1970). Passage aux actes délictueux et états dépressifs. *Acta Psychiatrica Belgica*, pp. 103-153.

Cormier, B.M. (1970). Therapeutic community in a prison setting. *Annales Internationales de Criminologie*, 9 (2), pp. 419-441.

Cormier, B.M. (1970). Violence—individual and collective aspects. *Criminology*, 9 (1), pp. 99-116.

Cormier, B.M. (1972). The dilemma of psychiatric diagnosis. In: Resnik, H.L.P. & Wolfgang, M.E. (Eds.). (1972). *Sexual Behaviors: Social, clinical and legal aspects.* Boston: Little, Brown & Company, Inc., pp. 41-61.

Cormier, B.M. (1973). Symposium 25—Psychiatry and Clinical Criminology. Psychiatry, Part II. In: de la Fuente, R. & Weisman, M. N. (Eds.). (1973). *Proceedings of the Vth World Congress of Psychiatry*, Mexico, 1971. Amsterdam: Excerpta Medica. New York: American Elsevier Publishing Company, Inc., pp. 1078-1080.

Cormier, B.M. (1973). The practice of psychiatry in the prison society. *Bulletin of the American Academy of Psychiatry and the Law*, 1 (2), pp. 156-171.

Cormier, B.M. (1975). Mass murder, multicide, and collective crime: The doers and the victims. *Victimology: A new focus*, Vol. IV. In: Drapkin, I. & Viano, E. (Eds.). (1975). *Violence and its Victims.* Lexington: Lexington Books.

Cormier, B.M. (Ed.). (1975). *The Watcher and the Watched.* Montreal: Tundra Books.

Cormier, B.M. (1978). Behaviour and justice in primitive and civilized societies: The inuit and ourselves. *Bulletin of the American Academy of Psychiatry and the Law*, 6 (2), pp. 214-225.

Cormier, B.M. (1981). Expertise on dangerosity—A multi-discplinary approach. *International Annals of Criminology, Expertise in Criminology*, 19 (1-2), pp. 167-184.

Cormier, B.M. & Angliker, C.C.J. (1973). A therapeutic community for persistent offenders. In: Sagarin, E. & MacNamara, D.E.J. (Eds.).(1973). *Corrections: Problems of Punishment and Rehabilitation.* New York: Praeger Publishers, pp. 96-105.

Cormier, B.M., Angliker, C.C.J., Boyer, R., Kennedy, M., & Mersereau, G. (1971). The psychodynamics of homicide committed in a specific relationship. *Canadian Journal of Criminology and Corrections*, 13 (1), pp. 1-8.

Cormier, B.M., Angliker, C.C.J., Boyer, R., Kennedy, M. & Mersereau, G. (1972). The psychodynamics of homicide committed in a semi-specific relationship. *Canadian Journal of Criminology and Corrections,* 14 (4), pp. 335-44.

Cormier, B.M., Angliker, C.C.J., Gagne, P.W. & Markus, B. (1978). Adolescents who kill members of the family. Chapter 31 in Eekelaar, J.M. & Katz, S. (Eds.).(1978). *Family Violence: An International and Inter-disciplinary study.*Toronto: Butterworths, pp. 466-478.

Cormier, B.M. & Boulanger, P. (1973). Life cycle and episodic recidivism. *Canadian Psychiatric Association Journal,* 18 (4), pp. 283-288.

Cormier, B.M. & Boyer, R. (1963). Retaliation and primitive justice. *Annales Internationales de Criminologie,* pp. 71-80.

Cormier, B.M., Boyer, R. Galardo, A.T., Kennedy, M., Obert, A., Sangowicz, J. M., Thiffault, A.L. & Washbrook, R.A. (1964). The persistent offender and his sentences—A problem for law and psychiatry. *Canadian Psychiatric Association Journal,* 9, pp. 462-480.

Cormier, B.M., Boyer, R., Morf, G., Kennedy, M., Boulanger, P., Barriga, C. & Cvejic, J. (1971). Behaviour and ageing: Offenders aged 40 and over. *Laval Médical,* 42, pp.16-21.

Cormier, B.M. & Cooper, I. (1980, May). Incest in contemporary society: Legal and clinical management. *The Proceedings of the CPRI 20th Anniversary Symposium on the Family, University of Western Ontario, London.*

Cormier, B.M., Fugère, R. & Thompson-Cooper, I. (1995). Pedophilic episodes in middle age and senescence: An intergenerational encounter. *Canadian Journal of Psychiatry,* 40, pp. 125-129.

Cormier, B.M., Galardo, A., Sangowicz, J.M., Kennedy, M. & Lecker, S. (1964, November). Criminal acting out as a part of a depressive state. *Proceedings of the Fourth Research Conference on Delinquency and Criminology, Montreal,* pp. 309-332.

Cormier, B.M., Galardo, A. Sangowicz, J.M., Kennedy, M., Washbrook, R.A. & Williams, P.J. (1964, November). Episodic Recidivism. *Proceedings of the Fourth Research Conference on Delinquency and Criminology, Montreal,* pp. 171-193.

Cormier, B.M., Keitner, L., Kennedy, M. (1967). The persistent offender and his family. *Proceedings of the Fifth Research Conference on Delinquency and Criminality,* pp. 21-37.

Cormier, B.M., Kennedy, M., Obert, A., Sangowicz, J.M., Sendbuehler, M.J. & Thiffault, A.L. (1961). Some psychological aspects of criminal partnership. *Canadian Journal of Corrections,* 3 (4), pp. 445-455.

Cormier, B.M., Kennedy, M., Obert, A., Sangowicz, J.M., Sendbuehler, M.J. & Thiffault, A.L. (1961). The black sheep. *Canadian Journal of Corrections*, 3 (4), pp. 456-462.

Cormier, B.M., Kennedy, M. & Sangowicz, J.M. (1962). Psychodynamics of father-daughter incest. *Proceedings of 12th International Course in Criminology, II, Jerusalem*, Part I, pp. 14-54.

Cormier, B.M., Kennedy, M. & Sangowicz, J.M. (1962). Psycho-dynamics of father-daughter incest. *Canadian Psychiatric Association Journal*, 7 (5), pp. 203-217.

Cormier, B.M., Kennedy, M. & Sangowicz, J.M. (1965). Sexual offenses, episodic recidivism and the psychopathological state. In: Slovenko, R.J. (Eds.).(1965). *Sexual Behaviour and the Law*. Springfield: Charles C. Thomas, pp. 707-741.

Cormier, B.M., Kennedy, M., Sangowicz, J.M., Boyer, R., Thiffault, A.L. & Obert, A. (1965). Criminal process and emotional growth. In: Cameron, D.E. (Eds.). (1965). *International Psychiatry Clinics* 2 (1), Boston: Little, Brown & Co., pp. 3-41.

Cormier, B.M., Kennedy, M., Sangowicz, J.M. & Trottier, M. (1959). Presentation of a basic classification for clinical work and research in criminology. *Canadian Journal of Corrections*, 1 (4), pp. 21-34.

Cormier, B.M., Kennedy, M., Sangowicz, J.M. & Trottier, M. (1959). The natural history of criminality and some tentativeness hypotheses on its abatement. *Canadian Journal of Corrections*, 1 (4), pp. 35-49.

Cormier, B.M., Kennedy, M., Sangowicz, J.M. & Trottier, M. (1961). Criminal acting out in cases of reactive depression. *Canadian Journal of Corrections*, 3 (1), pp. 38-50.

Cormier, B.M., Kennedy, M., Sangowicz, J.M. & Trottier, M. (1961). Family conflicts and criminal behaviour. *Canadian Journal of Corrections*, 3 (1), pp. 18-37.

Cormier, B.M., Kennedy, M., Sangowicz, J.M. & Trottier, M. (1961). Some psychological aspects of sentencing. *Canadian Journal of Corrections*, 3 (1), pp. 66-86.

Cormier, B.M., Kennedy, M., Sangowicz, J.M. & Trottier, M. (1961). The latecomer to crime. *Canadian Journal of Corrections*, 3 (1), pp. 2-17.

Cormier, B.M., Kennedy, M., Sangowicz, J.M. & Trottier, M. (1961). The problem of recidivism and treatment of the latecomer to crime. *Canadian Journal of Corrections*, 3 (1), pp. 51-65.

Cormier, B.M., Kennedy, M., Sendbuehler, J.M. (1967). Cell breakage and gate fever: A study of two syndromes found in deprivation of liberty. *British Journal of Criminology*, pp. 317-324.

Cormier, B.M., Kennedy, M., Thiffault, A.L., Sangowicz, J.M., Obert, A. &

Boyer, R. (1963). The persistent offender. *Canadian Journal of Corrections,* 5 (4), pp. 253-261.

Cormier, B.M., Kennedy, M., Thiffault, A.L., Sangowicz, J.M., Obert, A., Boyer, R. & Laskin, R. (Eds.). (1964). *Social Problems–A Canadian Profile.* New York: McGraw Hill Company, pp. 435-443.

Cormier, B.M. & Markus, B. (1980). A longitudinal study of adolescent murderers, *Bulletin of the American Academy of Psychiatry and the Law,* 8 (3), pp. 240-260.

Cormier, B.M., Morf, G. & Mersereau, G. (1969). Psychiatric services in penal institutions (Part I) *Laval Médical,* 40 (9), pp. 939-945.

Cormier, B.M., Obert, A., Kennedy, M., Sangowicz, J.M., Thiffault, A.L. & Boyer, R. (1965). The family and delinquency. *Cahiers de contributions à l'étude des sciences de l'homme, Montreal,* vol.6, pp. 83-118 (Centre de recherches en relations humaines).

Cormier, B.M. & Sendbeuhler, J.M. (1963). Gate Fever. *Excerpta Criminologica,* 3 (5), pp. 520-522.

Cormier, B.M. & Simons, S.P. (1969). Forensic Psychiatry: The problem of the dangerous sexual offender. *Canadian Psychiatric Association Journal,* 14 , pp. 329-334.

Cormier, B.M., Simons, S., Barriga, C., Mersereau, G. & Morf, G. (1971). Psychiatric services in penal institutions: Part II. A Detailed survey of patients on a given day. *Laval Médical,* 42 , pp. 22-28.

Cormier, B.M., Washbrook, R.A., Kennedy, M. & Obert, A. (1964, November). A study of fifty young penitentiary delinquents from Age 15 to 25. *Proceedings of the Fourth Research Conference on Delinquency and Criminology, Montreal,* pp. 77-113.

Cormier, B.M. & Williams, P.J. (1966). La privation excessive de la liberté. *Canadian Psychiatric Association Journal,* 11 (6), pp. 470-484.

Cormier, B.M. & Williams, P.J. (1970). The Watcher and the Watched. *International Annals of Criminology,* 9 (2), pp. 447-52.

Cormier, B.M. & Williams, P.J. (1971). The Watcher and the Watched. *Canadian Psychiatric Journal,* 16 (1), pp. 15-21.

Cormier, B.M. & Williams, P.J. (1971). The Watcher and the Watched. *Current Contents,* 3 (15).

Ferstman, A. & Williams, P.J. (1967). The training of personnel in a therapeutic community. *Proceedings of the Fifth Research Conference on Delinquency and Criminality, Montreal,* pp.161-168.

Fink, L. & Cormier, B.M. et al. (1968). The Clinton Project. *Canadian Journal of Corrections,* 10 (2), pp. 321-326.

Galardo, A.T. (1965). Psychosexual development in the antisocial character. *Interdisciplinary Problems in Criminology: Papers of the American Society of Criminology, 1964.* Columbus: Ohio State University, pp. 143-149.

Kennedy, M. (1959). Dynamics involved in family offenses appearing before the court. *Canadian Journal of Corrections,* 1 (4), pp. 50-55.

Kennedy, M. (1960). *Contributions to the Fourth International Criminological Congress, The Hague,* pp. 67-69, 303-305, 358-375.

Kennedy, M. (1960). Delinquent acting out and family conflicts. *Preparatory Paper I, Fourth International Criminological Congress, The Hague.*

Kennedy, M. (1962). New vistas in psychiatry and social work practice. *Canadian Mental Health Supplement,* 31, pp. 30-31.

Kennedy, M. (1962, March). The social worker and research. *Canadian Mental Health Supplement,* 31, pp. 30-33.

Kennedy, M., & Cormier, B.M. (1964). Father-daughter incest: Treatment of a family. *Interdisciplinary problems in criminology: Papers of the American Society of Criminology.* Columbus: Ohio State University, pp. 191-196.

Kennedy, M. & Cormier, B.M. (1967). Work history and work patterns of the persistent offender. *Proceedings of the Fifth Research Conference on Delinquency and Criminality, Montreal,* pp. 39-44.

Kennedy, M. & Cormier, B.M. (1969). Father-daughter incest—Treatment of the family. *Laval Médical,* 40 (9), pp. 946-950.

Kennedy, M. & Keitner, L. (1970). Action and Reaction. *The Social Worker,* 38 (1).

Linder, H. Zambrowsky, J. & Cormier, B.M. (1973) La cohésion pathologique dans les familles multi-délinquantes. *La vie medicale au Canada français, idem.,* pp. 593-7.

Poser, E.G., Sittman, D., Derby, W.N. & Williams, P.J. (1967). Psychological survey of the persistent offender. *Proceedings of the Fifth Research Conference on Delinquency and Criminality, Montreal,* pp. 11-19.

Simons, S.P. & Cormier, B.M. (1969). Delinquent acting out and ego structure. *Laval Médical,* 40 (9), pp. 933-935.

Thompson-Cooper, I., Fugère, R. & Cormier, B.M. (1993). The child abuse reporting laws: An ethical dilemma for professionals. *Canadian Journal of Psychiatry,* 38, pp. 557-562.

Trottier, M. (1959). La complicité criminelle. *Canadian Journal of Corrections,* 1 (4), pp. 56-61.

Unpublished Papers

1960

Thiffault, A.L. "A Contribution to the Problem of Intelligence in Criminality." Undated.

Cormier, B.M. "Psychiatry: Sexual Offenders and Offences." Undated [early-mid 1960].

Cormier, B.M. "Exhibitionism." Undated.

Cormier, B.M. & Boyer, R. "Latecomers: Section VII. Study of 106 Offenders with Present Age and Legal Onset of 35 and Over." Undated.

1962

Cormier, B.M. "What Kind of Prison Does Montreal Need?" (Bk. IIIc).

Obert, A. "Problem of Guilt in a Prison Community." November 1962.

1964

Cormier, B.M. "The Law, Psychiatry and the Rights of Man in Judicial Procedures: The Pre-Trial Ward." Presented at the Quebec Society of Criminology: Fourth Research Conference on Criminology and Delinquency, November 17, 1964.

Cormier, B.M. "Towards a Penal Philosophy: Thoughts on our Common Prisons and Recommendations and Suggestions for a Progressive Criminal Policy in the Province of Quebec." Presented at the Quebec Society of Criminology: Fourth Research Conference on Criminology and Delinquency, November 21, 1964.

1965

Cormier, B.M. "Report on Auto Theft." January 7, 1965.

1966

Kennedy, M. "Primitive Justice–Notes on the Eskimos." March 1, 1966.

Kennedy, M. "Primitive Justice–The Eskimo." March 7, 1966.

Kennedy, M. "Primitive Justice–The Indians." March 10, 1966.

Kennedy, M. "Rousseau." March 31, 1966.

1967

Cormier, B.M. "Sexual Deviates, Society and the Law." Presented at the Alex G. Brown Memorial Clinic, Fourth Annual Conference on Addictions and Sexual Deviation, Toronto, April 27-28, 1967.

Kennedy, M. & Cormier, B.M. "Post Liberation Anxiety." Presented at the XVIIth Annual Meeting of the Canadian Psychiatric Association, Quebec City, June 17, 1967.

Cormier, B.M. "Draft: A Report on Sexual Offenders." September 28, 1967.

Cormier, B.M. "Training of Personnel in Judicial and Correctional Processes." November 23, 1967.

Cormier, B.M. "Draft—Prison Milieu and the Institutionalized Staff." December 7, 1967.

Cormier, B.M., Simons, S. & Kubiak, Z. "Persistent Criminality and Chronic Psychosis." Presented at the 17th Annual Meeting of the Canadian Psychiatric Association, Quebec City, June 1967.

1968

Kennedy, M. & Cormier, B.M. "Fraudulent Offenders." November 14, 1968.

Herman, Z. "Preliminary Remarks on a Study of Fraudulent Behavior." October 10, 1968.

1969

Herman, Z. "The Fraudulent Offenders." March 24, 1969.

Cormier, B.M., Morf, G. & Kennedy, M. "The Middle-Aged Offender—A Psychiatric and Social Problem." Presented at the Annual Meeting of the Canadian Psychiatric Association, Toronto, June 12-14, 1969.

Cooper, I., Williams, P. & Cormier, B.M. "The Volunteer-Inmate Relationship." Presented at the 29th Annual General Meeting of the Canadian Psychiatric Association, Vancouver, September 26-29, 1969.

Cormier, B.M. "Proposals Concerning Experimental Treatment Centre (Therapeutic Community) for a Penal Institution in Canada." (Bk. IIId).

Cormier, B.M. "Types of Regression Determined by the Deprivation of Liberty and Their Implications for Rehabilitation." Undated [late 1960s].

1971

Cormier, B.M. "Psychiatry and Clinical Criminology." Presented at the Round Table on Clinical Concepts in the Treatment of Persistent Behavior Disorders, Vth World Congress of Psychiatry. Mexico. November 28-December 4, 1971.

1972

Cormier, B.M. & Angliker, C.C.J. (Eds.). "The Clinton Project: a Prison Therapeutic Community: Diagnostic and Treatment Center." (Dannemora, New York, 1972).

"Psychiatric Services in Penal Institutions." Edited by the Clinic in Forensic Psychiatry, McGill University, Montreal, 1972.

Zambrowsky, J. & Cormier, B.M. "The Psychologically Broken Home and Delinquency." Presented at the 22nd Annual Meeting of the Canadian Psychiatric Association, Vancouver, June 20-23, 1973.

1973

Cormier, B.M. "The Wall: A Study on the Psychology and Psychopathology of Penal Security." Vancouver Tape. July 5, 1973.

Angliker, C.C.J., Cormier, B.M. & Gagne, P. "Death of a Family Member – The Adolescent Who Kills." Presented at the 7th International Congress of Criminology, Belgrade, Yugoslavia, September 17-24, 1973.

1974

Angliker, C.C.J. "The Individual and Social Psychodynamics of a Case of Homicide." Presented at the 23rd Annual Meeting of the Canadian Psychiatric Association, Ottawa, October 1-5, 1974.

Cooper, I. & Cormier, B.M. "Homosexual Incest." Presented at the 24th Annual Meeting of the Canadian Psychiatric Association, Ottawa, October 1974.

Linder, H., & Cormier, B.M. "Sons and Daughters in the Multi-Delinquent Families." Presented at the Twenty-Third Annual Meeting of the Canadian Psychiatric Association, Ottawa, October 1-5, 1974.

1975

Fraid, S. & Cormier, B.M. "Provocation: Legal vs. Emotional Reality." Presented at the Silver Anniversary Meeting of the Canadian Psychiatric Association, Banff Springs, Alberta, September 24-27, 1975.

Linder, H., & Cormier, B.M. "The Problem of Psycho-Social Heredity in One Hundred Multi-Delinquent Families." (Bk. IVa).

1977
Cormier, B.M. "Proposal Re: NATO Advanced Study." Presented at the Institute on Terrorism, Montreal, July 1977.
Cooper, I. & Cormier, B.M. "Infanticide." Presented at the 27th Annual Meeting of the Canadian Psychiatric Association, Saskatoon, September 1977.
Cooper, I. "Generational Study of Affective Deprivation in a Family." Presented at the 27th Annual Meeting of the Canadian Psychiatric Association, Saskatoon, September 28-30, 1977.

1978
Bogopolsky, Y. & Cormier, B.M. "Le Démon de midi et ses aspects criminologiques." Presented at the 28th Annual Congress of the Canadian Psychiatric Association, Halifax, Nova Scotia, October 18-20, 1978.

1979
Cormier, B.M. "Transfert et contre-transfert face au délinquant et à ses agressions." Presented at the VII Journées Internationales de Criminologie Clinique Comparée, Auberge Hatfield, Quebec, June 5-7, 1979.
Simons, S. "Mourning and Melancholia and the Abatement Process in Persistent Delinquency." Presented at the 29th Annual General Meeting of the Canadian Psychiatric Association, Vancouver, September 26-28, 1979.
Cooper, I., Williams, P. & Cormier, B.M. "Psychodynamics of the Volunteer-Inmate Relationship." Presented at the 29th Annual Meeting of the Canadian Psychiatric Association, Vancouver, September 1979.
Cooper, I. & Cormier, B.M. "Incest in Contemporary Society." Presented at the International Congress of Urban Life and the Child, Montreal, October 1979.
Cormier, B.M. and Cooper, I. "A Cultural-Historic View of Incest." Presented at the American Society of Criminology Meeting, Philadelphia, November 1979.

1980

Cormier, B.M. "Intervention: Its Means and Limits." Presented at the 4th Canadian Conference on Applied Criminology: Social Control in a State of Crisis, Ottawa, March 12-14, 1980.

Cormier, B.M. & Cooper, I. "Incest in Contemporary Society: Legal and Clinical Management." Presented at the Proceedings of the CPRI 20th Anniversary Symposium on the Family, University of Western Ontario, London, Ontario, May 1980.

Bogopolsky, Y. & Cormier, B.M. "Délinquance et criminalité: pathologie de l'affect et du comportement à travers les cycles d'âges." Presented at the 30th Annual Meeting of the Canadian Psychiatric Association, Toronto, Ontario, October 1-3, 1980.

1981

Markus, B. "Etude de cas d'un adolescent meurtrier." Presented at the Congrès de L'Association des Psychiatres du Québec, Quebec City, June 18-19, 1981.

Simons, S. "Facteurs pré-génitaux dans la psychologie des pères incestueux." Presented at the Congrès de L'Association des Psychiatres du Québec, Quebec City, June 18-19, 1981.

Fugère, R. & Cormier, B.M. "Pronostic de récidive dans les cas de tentative de meurtre à l' intérieur d'une relation spécifique." Presented at the Congrès de L'Association des Psychiatres du Québec, Quebec City, June 18-19, 1981.

Boisvert, D. & Cormier, B.M. "Aspects longitudinaux de la relation entre la criminalité et la psychose." Presented at the Congrès de L'Association des Psychiatres du Québec, Quebec City, June 18-19, 1981.

Boisvert, D. & Cormier, B.M. "La Démographique de demain: une impasse ou une réalité nouvelle?" Presented at the Congrès de L'Association des Psychiatres du Québec, Quebec City, June 18-19, 1981.

Cooper, I. "Clinical and Legal Management of Incest." Presented at the Canadian Congress for the Prevention of Crime, Winnipeg, July 12-16, 1981.

Cooper, I., Farley, D. & Doucet, A. "Men Who Batter—A Clinical Portrait." Presented at the 31st Annual General Meeting of the Canadian Psychiatric Association, Winnipeg, September 23-25, 1981.

Cormier, B.M. & Fugère, R. "Homicidal Attempts in a Specific Relationship: Psychodynamics and Prognosis." Presented at the 31st

Annual General Meeting of the Canadian Psychiatric Association, Winnipeg, September 23-25, 1981.

Cormier, B.M. & Markus, B. "Psychopathology of an Adolescent Mass Murderer." Presented at the 12th Annual Meeting of the American Academy of Psychiatry and the Law, San Diego, October 15-18, 1981.

1982

Cooper, I., Van Huffel, P. & Cormier, B.M. "The Erotic Phone Call: A Case Study." Presented at the 32nd Annual Meeting of the Canadian Psychiatric Association, Montreal, March 29, 1982.

Barbance, M. "Fantasme et passage à l'acte en délinquance juvenile." Presented at the Congrès de L'Association des Psychiatres du Québec, Montebello, June 16-19, 1982.

Cooper, I. & Cormier, B.M. "Inceste frère-soeur: mythe et réalité." Presented at the Congrès de L'Association des Psychiatres du Québec, Montebello, June 16-19, 1982.

Cormier, B.M., Fugère, R. & Cooper, I. "Beau-père/belle-fille: inceste et pédophile." Presented at the Congrès de L'Association des Psychiatres du Québec, Montebello, June 16-19, 1982.

Simons, S. "Corps-Esprit: une nouvelle perspective." Presented at the Congrès de L'Association des Psychiatres du Québec, Montebello, June 16-19, 1982.

Fugère, R. "Exhibitionisme: phénomenologie de l'acte et psychodynamique." Presented at the Congrès de L'Association des Psychiatres du Québec, Montebello, June 16-19, 1982.

Bogopolsky, Y. & Cormier, B.M. "Au mi-temps de la vie, la délinquance." Presented at the Congrès de L'Association des Psychiatres du Québec, Montebello, June 16-19, 1982.

Cormier, B.M. & Cooper, I. "Sibling Incest: Mythology, Pathology and Reality." Presented at the 8th International Congress of Law and Psychiatry, Quebec City, June 18-22, 1982.

Cormier, B.M. "Classification of Homicidal Processes in a Clinical and Research Perspective." Presented at the 8th International Congress of Law and Psychiatry, Quebec City, June 18-22, 1982.

Cooper, I., Cormier, B.M. & Bogopolsky, Y. "Incest Daughters and Their Pregnancies." Presented at the 32nd Annual Meeting of the Canadian Psychiatry Association, Montreal, September 27, 1982.

Cormier, B.M. & Markus, B. "A Study of Some Cases of Parricide." Presented at the 32nd Annual Meeting of the Canadian Psychiatric

Association, Montreal, September 29- October 1, 1982.

Cormier, B.M. "The Psychoanalytic Dimension of Alienation." Presented at the 32nd Annual Meeting of the Canadian Psychiatric Association, Montreal, September 29- October 1, 1982.

Peck, V. & Cormier, B.M. "Disclosure of Incest." Presented at the 32nd Annual Meeting of the Canadian Psychiatric Association, Montreal, September 29- October 1, 1982.

Cormier, B.M., Cooper, I. & Fugère, R. "Paedophilia or Incest: Stepfather/Stepchild." Presented at the 32nd Annual Meeting of the Canadian Psychiatric Association, Montreal, September 29- October 1, 1982.

Fugère R., Bogopolsky, Y. & Cormier, B.M. "Retaliation as a Fear: A Feeling and a Symptom." Presented at the 32nd Annual Meeting of the Canadian Psychiatric Association, Montreal, September 29- October 1, 1982.

McGrail-Hagger, S. & Cooper, I. "Incest and Its Aftermath: A Follow-Up Study of Incest Daughters." Presented at the 32nd Annual Meeting of the Canadian Psychiatric Association, Montreal, September 29- October 1, 1982.

1983

Cooper, I. "The Creation of the 1908 Punishment of Incest Act: Implication for the Present." Presented at the IX International Congress on Law and Psychiatry, S. Margherita, Italy, June 19-22, 1983.

Cormier, B.M., Bogopolsky, Y. & Fugère, R. "Expérience en criminologie clinique: intégration de la médecine, de la psychiatrie et des sciences humaines." Presented at the 2e Congrès Mondial des Services Médicaux Pénitentiaires, Ottawa, August 28-31, 1983.

1984

Cooper, I. "Professional Response to Intrafamily Child Sexual Abuse: Abuse, Misuse or Help?" Presented at the International Conference on Child Abuse and Neglect, Montreal, September 1984.

1985

Cormier, B.M. "La Parricide: du mythe à la psychopathologie." Presented at the Psychoanalytic Society of Montreal, Montreal, April 11, 1985.

Cormier, B.M. "Victim Trauma." Presented at the 1985 Congress on Criminal Justice, Vancouver, July 7-11, 1985.

Cormier, B.M. "Violence Against Children." Presented at the 1985 Congress on Criminal Justice, Vancouver, July 7-11, 1985.

Cooper, I. & Cormier, B.M. "The New Incest Protocol: Professional Avoidance of an Ancient Taboo." Presented at the 35th Annual Meeting of the Canadian Psychiatric Association, Quebec City, September 1985.

Cormier, B.M. "Criminal Responsibility and Psychiatric Treatment of Mentally Sick Offenders." Presented at the Council of Europe, Seventh Criminological Colloquium, Strasbourg, November 25-27, 1985.

1986

Cormier, B.M., Fugère, R., Cooper I. & Mirabella, J. "Pathological Cohesion and Severe Family Dysfunctions: A Study of Three Syndromes." Presented at the 36th Annual Meeting of the Canadian Psychiatric Association, Vancouver, September 24-26, 1986.

Cormier B.M. "The Effects of Incestuous Relationships on Sexual Development." Presented at the First International Congress on Sexual Development and Functioning Across the Lifespan, Montreal, October 23-26, 1986.

1988

Cormier, B.M., Fugère, R. & Markus, B. "La Cohésion familiale pathologique." Colloque: La clientèle, l'intervenant, l'approche rééducative. Presented at the 25e Anniversaire du Centre d'Accueil la Fondation La Cité des Prairies, April 13-15, 1988.

Cormier, B.M. "La Violence intra-familiale: Des Adolescents auteurs, victimes et témoins d'actes délinquants perspective, histoire et critique d'un clinicien." Presented at the Congrès International. Lille, France, May 9-10, 1988.

Cormier, B.M., Fugère, R. & Thompson-Cooper, I. "The Abused Child as Victim and Witness: A Clinical Perspective." Presented at the International Society of Law and Psychiatry Annual Meeting, Montreal, June 15-18, 1988.

Cormier, B.M. & Fugère, R. "Expertise in Child Abuse for the Court." 1988.

1989

Fugère, R. & Markus, B. "Et si on parlait de meurtre: étude sur quatre adolescentes meurtrières." Presented at the Congrès des Psychiatres du Quebec, Montebello, May 23-27, 1989.

Undated

Boyer, R. "La Prison de Montréal en 1852 et en 1962."

Cormier, B.M. Untitled [on Victimology, 1970+].

Cormier, B.M. "Pathological Mourning as a Component of Murder." "Outline," "Conclusion," "Case History on Murder," "Murder and Mourning."

Obert, A. "Problem of Guilt in a Prison Community."

Sangowicz, J. "Applied Research in Criminology."